"Ted Glick's *Burglar for Peace* tells a story that very few people have heard, and they should. The activities of the Catholic Left during the Vietnam War played an important role in bringing that war to an end. Glick's inside history of that sector of the anti-war movement is history that needs to be learned widely. This is especially true today when we are facing Trump and a Republican Party that harkens back to the worst days of the Nixon Administration, which was taken on, very much to their credit, by the Catholic Left."
—Ed Asner (U.S. actor in numerous TV shows, plays, and movies since the 1950s, former president of the Screen Actors Guild)

"Ted Glick's story of his experiences taking risks to end the Vietnam War, his political trials, and his time in prison fifty years ago makes for compelling reading. Prison was a turning point in my life, and Glick's story reveals something similar. His story and the commitment that resonates throughout it are witness to a piece of the American soul all Americans share—we love democracy, we honor truth, we despise lies and dictatorship, and we call upon ourselves to dig deep into our hearts for that courage to take the first step outside of our comfort zone, then another step out the door, to greet the world open-armed, embracing all that is good about our humanity and lives and fighting with every ounce of faith we can summon up for our right to be happy and just and fair and to call each other, regardless of skin color, ethnicity, or religion, brothers and sisters!"
—Jimmy Santiago Baca, award-winning American poet and author of *A Place to Stand*

"This is a book from a movement veteran who has made history and helps us learn lessons on how we can make history that is more just, sustainable, and democratic. This is a book from the heart, to move our minds and hands to action."
—Heather Booth, chair of the Midwest Academy

"In *Burglar for Peace*, Ted Glick uses his remarkable personal story to capture a pivotal moment in the history of U.S. social movements. His journey embodies many of the values and practices we urgently need now: courage, humility, and an abiding faith that our different struggles can unite in common purpose."
—Naomi Klein, author of *No Is Not Enough* and *This Changes Everything*

"*Burglar for Peace* is a blessing, a hope, and a way of acknowledging the sacredness of those we encounter, why this journey is difficult, the hills we must climb, and the reasons we dedicate our lives to justice. What makes Ted such an important author and pivotal leader is his understanding that we need an environmental movement that includes everybody, and we must be willing to sacrifice everything for future generations."
—Rev. Lennox Yearwood Jr., president of the Hip Hop Caucus

Burglar for Peace

Lessons Learned in Catholic Left Resistance to the Vietnam War

Ted Glick

To my wife and soulmate Jane Califf,
whose love, support, and constructive criticism
continue to make me a better person.

Burglar for Peace: Lessons Learned in Catholic Left Resistance to the Vietnam War
© Ted Glick
This edition © 2020 PM Press

ISBN: 978-1-62963-786-0 (print)
ISBN: 978-1-62963-815-7 (ebook)
Library of Congress Control Number: 2019946103

Cover by John Yates / www.stealworks.com
Cover image © *Rochester Democratic and Chronicle*, September 7, 1970
Interior design by briandesign

10 9 8 7 6 5 4 3 2 1

PM Press
PO Box 23912
Oakland, CA 94623
www.pmpress.org

Printed in the USA

Contents

Introduction

Frida Berrigan

They say that those who do not know their history are doomed to repeat it. That was the line my history teacher drilled into me back in Baltimore. The random dates and facts we memorized didn't really add up to a strategy for shaping a new future, but the sentiment makes sense.

Reading the book that you are now holding in your hands, I thought: What if repeating history isn't something we are doomed to but something we are called to? What if we need to be repeating history? Not following the exact same recipe but moving in the same contours and with the same spirit of the Ultra Resistance Ted Glick makes vivid.

The period of U.S. history that radicalized Ted Glick is not so unlike our own moment: implacable, unaccountable leadership; costly, bloody war far from our shores; an insidious effort to create an internal enemy and menace—then hippies and communists, now immigrants and socialists.

This toxic soup and other people's stand against it woke up young Ted, who was in college with a vague notion of becoming a lawyer and jumpstarting a career in politics. Once awake, Ted set off on a new course.

This book is full of bold actions with big consequences and long prison sentences. Occasionally, you can hear his marvel and surprise at what his younger self felt and accomplished. In Ted's account of the Rochester trial of the East Coast Conspiracy to Save Lives, what struck me most is the hope that was embedded in the action. The group set out to destroy draft records—but also to touch other people, to move them, to challenge them, to change them. This is part of the strategy of nonviolent direct action—provocation and conversion not just of the powers that be (we should be so lucky) but of the uninvolved and the uninformed.

The actions weren't just directed at the general public or the mainstream media but toward a much more intimate audience—the jury, the judge, the prosecutors—and we can see this hope repeated in decades of nonviolent direct actions.

- draft card burning
- statue toppling
- tree sitting
- flag removing
- water protecting
- war tax resisting
- plowshares beating
- weapons dismantling
- pipeline cutting
- sanctuary offering
- wall dismantling
- refugee harboring
- valve turning

Nonviolent direct action, civil disobedience, divine obedience—whatever you want to call it—is a set of tactics designed to right the wrongs, remove the harm, protect the victim, raise the alarm. But those who engage in this Ultra Resistance want to do more than that. As one of Ted's codefendants said to the jury at the end of their celebrated East Coast Conspiracy to Save Lives trial, "Hope it makes a difference in your lives."

We hope our action makes a difference in your lives. In this case, it is not the draft card or the oil pipeline or the nuclear missile that is the ultimate object of the action—the action extends into the courtroom, into the public square, into the hearts and minds of everyone it touches, and into jail.

This classic set of tactics is harder today than it was when Ted Glick and his codefendants stood in front of an older, more Christian, more conservative jury of twelve war supporters in Rochester, New York, in November 1970. They were able to question police officers and FBI agents. Father Daniel Berrigan was allowed to hold forth from the witness box college lecture style for what must have been hours. And while they were all convicted, the activists moved individuals on the jury to think about the war critically. One juror told the newspaper, "Not one person on the jury wanted to send those kids to jail."

Ted and his friends did go to jail though. And handfuls of people continue to go to jail for similar actions today, fifty years later.

Today, because of the legal precedents that allow prosecutors to limit testimony to the facts of the case, speaking truth and motivation and intention and the ways in which the facts moved an activist to act can all be ruled inadmissible and irrelevant. But there are still windows and cracks that creative activists can wriggle through.

When five "valve turners" went to trial in Minnesota in 2018, they planned to mount a case of the necessity defense for actions that disrupted the five pipelines that carry Canadian tar sands crude oil into the United States. They faced ten years in jail if convicted. The necessity defense was denied in other cases like theirs, but their judge allowed it. The activists planned to present evidence that they trespassed to shut down the pipeline, because it represents a direct and immediate climate threat. They hoped to convince the jury that their actions were their best option to confront the peril.

But they did not get the chance. In October 2018, they were acquitted, not because the judge or jury decided their criminal actions were justified and necessary, but because the judge determined that the government had not presented enough evidence to convict them.

Emily Johnston, one of the five, said afterward:

> While I'm very glad that the court acknowledged that we did not damage the pipelines, I'm heartbroken that the jury didn't get to hear our expert witnesses and their profoundly important warnings about the climate crisis. We are fast losing our window of opportunity to save ourselves and much of the beauty of this world. We turned those valves to disrupt the business-as-usual that we know is leading to catastrophe, and to send a strong message that might focus attention to the problem. We will continue to do that in every peaceful way we can; the stakes are far too high for us not to.[1]

The stakes are too high to not act. To not continue to act. Is the history of Ultra Resistance repeating itself in the valve turning actions? Or maybe it is rhyming, syncing into a spiral of inspiration, planning, action, evaluation. . . inspiration, planning, action, evaluation. . .

There is plenty of inspiration for action. We do not have to look all that hard. "This is a dangerous time, but the danger is of our own making," says the *Bulletin of the Atomic Scientists*. Their Doomsday Clock is at two minutes to nuclear midnight. The authors continue, "Humankind has invented the implements of apocalypse; so can it invent the methods of controlling and eventually eliminating them."[2] The *Bulletin of the Atomic Scientists* has been keeping time on the nuclear apocalypse since 1947.

Tick tock. Tick tock. You can hear it, but you have to listen with intention below all the other noise. The Doomsday Clock is tick tocking away, but it is less of a claxon and more of a metronome. On April 4, 2018, seven peace activists entered the Kings Bay Naval Submarine Base in St. Mary's, Georgia. They heard the tick tock. They went to make real the prophet Isaiah's command to "beat swords into plowshares." The seven chose to act on the fiftieth anniversary of the assassination of Martin Luther King Jr., who devoted his life to addressing what he called the "triple evils of militarism, racism and materialism."[3] Carrying hammers and baby bottles of their own blood, the seven attempted to convert weapons of mass destruction. They hoped to call attention to the ways in which nuclear weapons kill every day, just by their mere existence and maintenance.

They were charged with three federal felonies and one misdemeanor for their actions.

One of the seven is my mother, Elizabeth McAlister, who turned eighty in November 2019. She and two others—Father Steve Kelly and Mark Colville—remained in county jail for more than a year after the action. The other four are out on bond, wearing ankle monitors, and required to check in with their minders at regular intervals. My mother felt very useful in jail—generous, empathetic, and calm in a place that encourages none of those qualities.

The Kings Bay Naval Station is home to at least six nuclear ballistic missile submarines, each carrying twenty Trident II D 5 MIRV thermonuclear weapons. Each of these individual Tridents contains four or more individual nuclear weapons ranging in destructive power from 100 kilotons to 475 kilotons, each many times more powerful than the 15 kiloton bomb that decimated Hiroshima in 1945. Tick tock.

The nuclear clock ticks fast, but the wheels of justice grind slow, in part, because the Kings Bay Plowshares tried to mount a creative legal defense. Wriggling open what they hoped was a window that would allow them to speak directly to a jury, as Ted and his friends did in the

East Coast Conspiracy. The Kings Bay Plowshares sought to portray their actions as protected under the freedom of religion, using the Religious Freedom Restoration Act. They sought to demonstrate their "deeply held religious beliefs" that nuclear weapons are a crime against humanity and show that their practice of their religion has been burdened by the government's response to their actions. The Religious Freedom Restoration Act, they asserted, requires the government to take claims of sincere religious exercise seriously.

Unfortunately, the judge in the case refused to allow them to present this defense, and, in October 2019, they were convicted. They face twenty-five years in prison when sentenced.

When the Kings Bay Plowshares are sentenced, they will be repeating history, rhyming with the spirit of Catonsville and Rochester and Milwaukee and Camden and all the other draft board raids, spiraling with the valve turners and the pipe cutters and water protectors. They will draw strength from all these activists. They will recall these and so many others who refused to be intimidated or cowed by the power of the court, their adamant commitment to speak the truth, their vigorous cross examinations, and their constant efforts to connect as humans with the jury members.

They will repeat history. They will discover that the past didn't go anywhere. It is still here. It is still alive. It still has stories worth hearing and lessons worth learning.

Preface

> I find myself going deeper and deeper into this fast; that is to say, feeling more and more like it will end up going the whole way. I feel committed at this point to going that route if it seems necessary and if the course of events does not change. Perhaps by our deaths we will be able do what the Germans in the 30s, who knew what was happening, did not bring themselves to do. What would have been the effect if 5, 6, or 7 Germans had allowed themselves to die in protest of the crimes and direction of Hitler before he consolidated his power? No one knows, just as we do not know what would happen here.
>
> —from the author's personal journal on day twenty-five of a water-only fast to stop the Vietnam War

It was the summer of 1972, and the Nixon Administration was escalating the war in Vietnam with a massive bombing campaign in North Vietnam, mining the harbors of Hanoi and Haiphong, talk of bombing dikes, which, if breached, could lead to massive flooding and loss of life, and there was even talk of the use of nuclear weapons.

Father Dan Berrigan convened a group of committed anti-war draft resisters in his New York City apartment to discuss what more we could do about this urgent situation. Dan had an idea: a fast unto death, an open-ended, weeks-long refusal to eat, consuming only water, with no set time for it to end.

I had been on a thirty-three-day liquid-only fast just the year before, with ten others, including Father Phil Berrigan, while in prison for destroying Selective Service draft files and trying to remove FBI files from a federal building in Rochester, New York. I had an idea of how hard a long-term, water-only fast would be, but I responded positively to the idea, and for the next few months I traveled the East Coast organizing for this action. I participated in it from beginning to end, which turned out to be forty days, and then I spent time recovering from those long, often difficult days of voluntary starvation.

This was one of the kinds of not usual actions that took place during the Vietnam War. It was that kind of time.

This book is about a movement within the broader peace movement, the Catholic Left, built on not usual, nonviolently disruptive, high-risk actions.

As I write this is the spring of 2020, Trump and the Trump Republicans control the White House and Senate, with the House of Representatives firmly in the hands of the Democrats—for now. The Democrats control the House because of the massive ongoing resistance to Trump and his party since the day that he was inaugurated.

The country and the world need a powerful movement in the United States for social, racial, gender, economic, environmental, and climate justice, for a government of, by, and for the people, and it is happening— the Bernie Sanders campaigns of 2016 and 2019–2020, the 2018 House election results, and the many acts of mass resistance since Trump's election being the most hopeful expressions.

So why am I writing this book at such a critical time?

The idea of doing so came to me in 2015, as I neared my planned retirement soon after my sixty-sixth birthday in early October. I knew I wanted to do more writing in my retirement, even as I continued my primary work as an activist and organizer addressing the climate crisis.

As I thought about what I wanted to write, I remembered the many times over the years that I have told people about my life as an antiwar burglar from 1969 to 1972, the political trials I was part of, and the eleven months I spent in prison as a result. Without exception, when I tell this story, people are fascinated and very interested in learning more. Most know very little about the Catholic Left, or Ultra Resistance, which began in earnest in Catonsville, Maryland, in May 1968, when nine people poured homemade napalm on Selective Service draft files. This was the sector of the Vietnam anti-war movement that I was a very active participant in during those three or so years.

I was struck by how uninformed people were about this history, even people who were long-time activists like me. I started to think that writing about my experiences would be a valuable contribution.

I believe that it is important to study history, that we can learn things that are useful in the present and that will be useful in the future by understanding what has come before. I believe that in general, but I also believe that there are specific things to learn from the Ultra Resistance that can be helpful to the movements of today.

For example, those of us who risked long prison terms by entering draft boards, corporate offices, and FBI offices between 1967 and 1972 did so primarily because of the immediacy and urgency of the Vietnam War. Today, there is another issue that, while different from a violent war, is also very immediate and urgent: the climate crisis. There is a real possibility that, absent urgent action to shift from fossil fuels to renewable energy sources, along with energy efficiency and conservation, the world will experience catastrophic climate change, disastrous weather impacts, and the unraveling of human societies. Yet with the exception of the "valve turners" protesting the importation of dirty tar sands oil, those spending months in tree sits, and similar radical actions along the routes of proposed oil and gas pipelines, there are very few actions taking place that are analogous to what priests, nuns, Catholic laypeople, people from other religious backgrounds, and people who weren't religious at all, all acting together, did about the Vietnam War almost half a century ago.

I hope that this book is useful to those already active who are considering what could be the most effective forms of action today and what kind of movement we need to undertake them, not just regarding the climate but on a wide range of issues.

I hope the book is also useful for individuals who are not activists but who are coming to understand that they need to take seriously the state of the world and their role in it.

I prepared to write this book by reading a number of relevant books and by looking at things I had written in the past: letters from prison, letters back and forth between my parents and me and my then wife and me, a daily journal during two long fasts in 1971 and 1972, and various articles that I've written. A fair amount of it has been very eye opening, windows into parts of my personal past that I'd forgotten about or that I wrote about back then in ways I wouldn't have expected.

When researching chapter two, the period of time in 1968–1969 when I underwent "my personal transformation," I discovered, looking back forty-eight years later, as an experienced and seasoned revolutionary, that my first direct action, my first hunger strike, and my first disruption of business as usual all happened in the spring of 1969, just before I left college to work full-time against the Vietnam War and for social justice at home. I had no recollection that this had happened; I didn't even remember my three-day hunger strike.

And then there's my daily journal during the forty-day water-only hunger strike against the war in the summer of 1972. Throughout it I wrote about my death and how I viewed the possibility of it.

I was struck by how a twenty-two-year-old Ted Glick was consciously prepared to risk his life for what he believed in. And it feels good that I had been.

I'm seventy now, and five years ago, in 2015, I took part in an eighteen-day water-only hunger strike in connection with my work in the climate movement. A dozen of us fasted every workday from 7:00 a.m. to 6:00 p.m. on the sidewalk in front of the Federal Energy Regulatory Commission (FERC), in Washington, DC. FERC is a regulatory agency captured by the fossil fuel industry that acts accordingly. In many respects this eighteen-day fast was harder than the forty-day fast forty-three years earlier, but I and the others persevered until the end.

I hope and pray that my writing of this book will be of value to others who read it, and that together we can all create a world based on justice, equal rights, a deep connection to the natural world, and active love.

CHAPTER ONE

The Draft Resistance Movement, 1965–1968

> He was living still a month later
> I was able to gain access to him
> I smelled the odor
> of burning flesh
> And I understood anew
> what I had seen in North Vietnam
> I felt that my senses
> had been invaded in a new way
> I now understood
> the power of death in the modern world
> I knew I must speak and act
> against death
> because this boy's death
> was being multiplied
> a thousandfold
> —Father Daniel Berrigan, "In the Land of Burning Children"[1]

Five U.S. citizens died as a result of self-immolation to protest the Vietnam War: Alice Herz, March 1965; Norman Morrison and Roger Allen LaPorte, November 1965; Florence Beaumont, October 1967; teenager Ronald Brazee, referenced in the poem above, March 1968. These actions were likely inspired by the June 1963 self-immolation of Buddhist monk Thich Quang Duc, in South Vietnam, as well as the self-immolations of several other monks who followed him. Quang Duc was protesting the repressive and violent regime of Ngo Dinh Diem, the U.S.-backed ruler of South Vietnam at that time.

For those not alive then, it might be hard to appreciate how intense, how dangerous, how terrible those times were, so terrible that they would drive men and women to suicide for humanitarian and political reasons.

This was the first televised war. I remember watching war news on TV as a teenager, seeing young men not much older than me crawling through the Vietnamese jungle, while bullets flew around them. I heard the daily body counts of hundreds of people dead, people our government told us were our enemy.

All of this death and destruction was being inflicted by the U.S. military upon the people of Vietnam, both South and North, to support successive repressive South Vietnamese governments in the name of "fighting communism." Supporters of the war literally said, in all seriousness, "If we don't stop them over there, they'll soon be coming over here."

There was no "South Vietnam" prior to 1955. It was essentially a creation of the U.S. government when it refused to sign the 1954 agreement ending the war between France and Vietnam. France, the colonial power in Vietnam and Indochina from the 1880s until 1954, was defeated after eight years of war by a Vietnamese independence movement, the Viet Minh.

The United States, a major supporter of France's efforts to maintain colonial control of Vietnam, stepped in more actively after France was forced to leave, creating and supporting a pro-U.S. government in the southern part of Vietnam and calling the territory that government controlled South Vietnam. They did so even though the agreement between the leaders of the Vietnamese independence movement and the French government that ended the war called for free elections throughout Vietnam to choose a national government.

It was the 1950s and early to mid-1960s, and fear of the spread of communism ran deep and wide within the U.S. body politic. It was the time of the Cold War. In Africa, Asia, and South and Central America, popular movements were overthrowing colonial and neocolonial governments, and communists and socialists were a part, sometimes a leading part, of those movements. The U.S., as the leader of the "Free World," was on the wrong side of history, attempting to suppress or co-opt those movements.

There was also the nuclear arms race between the U.S. and the Soviet Union and the threat of a world nuclear conflagration that would devastate all life-forms on the planet. At the time of the Vietnam War, this existential threat to all life on earth was a very real and present danger.

As Betty Medsger wrote in her book *The Burglary*:

> The Vietnam War touched the lives of more and more Americans in profound ways. Nearly everyone had family members, neighbors, or friends who had been called—or expected to be called—to serve in the military and be sent to Vietnam ready to kill or be killed. A sense of urgency about the war permeated the society. The country felt electric. It was a time when everything seemed to intensify—in the war, in the peace movement, among those who supported the war, among those who opposed it, and in actions against people who opposed it.[2]

A Mass Anti-War Movement Emerges

Significant organized resistance to the Vietnam War began after President Lyndon Johnson, reelected in 1964, running as an anti-war candidate against conservative Barry Goldwater, proceeded to escalate the war after taking office. There were close to twenty thousand U.S. troops in South Vietnam when he was reelected. In March 1965, he initiated Operation Rolling Thunder, an expanded bombing campaign against North Vietnam. By November of that year, there were 125 thousand U.S. soldiers in Vietnam. At its high point, in 1968, there were over half a million.

It didn't take long for a mass anti-war movement to emerge. On April 17, 1965, twenty thousand people rallied in Washington, DC, in an action organized primarily by Students for a Democratic Society (SDS) and Women's Strike for Peace (WSP). On November 27 of that year, thirty-five thousand people encircled the White House in another mass demonstration.

Without a Selective Service System that could draft young men into the armed forces against their will, the Vietnam War never could have escalated so quickly and massively, and anyone who was against the war knew that. In 1965, in Mississippi, the anti-war Student Nonviolent Coordinating Committee (SNCC) issued a leaflet calling on young black men to "not honor the draft here in Mississippi. Mothers should encourage their sons not to go."[3]

Five men burned their draft cards in late July 1965 at the Whitehall Street army induction center in Lower Manhattan, New York. A month later *Life* magazine published a photo of one of them, Christopher Kearns, doing so. This infuriated ardent pro-war Congresspeople, leading to the introduction of legislation making draft card burners liable to a fine of ten thousand dollars and five years in jail. Arch segre-gationist Strom Thurmond was a prime sponsor of this effort. The new law passed through Congress quickly and went into effect on August 30, 1965.

The first person to publicly burn his draft card in defiance of this legislation was New Yorker David Miller of the Catholic Worker move-ment. Father Phil Berrigan, a leader of the peace movement, described it this way:

> On October 15, 1965, a young man stood in front of the Armed Forces Induction Center in downtown Manhattan. He was wearing a suit and tie, his hair was neatly combed, and when he lighted his draft card and held it aloft, passersby were stunned. David Miller had been one of Dan [Berrigan]'s students at Le Moyne College. Now he was the first American to publicly burn his draft card [since it was outlawed], an act of resistance for which he received a three-year prison sentence.[4]

Here is how David Miller later wrote about his action, undertaken before a crowd of about five hundred people:

> The expectant crowd fell hush in front of me. The hecklers across the street ceased their ranting and watched silently. I said the first thing that came to my mind. "I am not going to give my prepared speech. I am going to let this action speak for itself. I know that you people across the street really know what is happening in Vietnam. I am opposed to the draft and the war in Vietnam."
>
> I pulled my draft classification card from my suit coat pocket along with a book of matches brought especially for the occasion since I did not smoke. I lit a match, then another. They blew out in the late afternoon breeze. As I struggled with the matches, a young man with a May 2nd Movement button on his jacket held up a cigarette lighter. It worked just fine.
>
> The draft card burned as I raised it aloft between the thumb and index finger of my left hand. A roar of approval from the rally crowd greeted the enflamed card.[5]

Bruce Dancis, a leader of the peace movement at Cornell University, has eloquently described what thousands of young men were thinking during that time:

My draft card was (figuratively) burning a hole in my pocket, and I couldn't stand remaining complicit with the system that was so integral to perpetuating a war I abhorred. I was also concerned that the momentum of the antiwar movement had stalled. I felt people needed to take stronger, riskier actions both to keep the pressure on the Johnson administration and to increase the seriousness of the movement itself. I hoped my own action would, in a small way, help build a larger and more committed antiwar movement. I was willing to act alone, but hoped that others would be joining me in the not-too-distant future. That's when I decided to destroy my draft card and cut my ties to the Selective Service System.[6]

The most prominent draft resister was heavyweight boxing champion Muhammad Ali. After over a year of hassling with his local draft board over a conscientious objector application that was finally rejected, he refused induction on April 28, 1967, in Houston, Texas. This led to the revocation of his boxing license and a criminal indictment. Ultimately, Ali won on appeal, after initially being convicted.

Ali's statement about why he took this course was very strong:

> Why should they ask me to put on a uniform and go 10,000 miles from home and drop bombs and bullets on Brown people in Vietnam while so-called Negro people in Louisville are treated like dogs and denied simple human rights?
>
> No I'm not going 10,000 miles from home to help murder and burn another poor nation simply to continue the domination of white slave masters of the darker people the world over. This is the day when such evils must come to an end.[7]

Draft Resistance Gets Better Organized

Local groups formed during this time to reach out to draft age young men to encourage them to resist the draft and the war, and national meetings were held to try to figure out how to magnify the impact of the developing movement. One important meeting, a national We Won't Go conference attended by five hundred people from dozens of groups, convened in Chicago in early December 1966. Those attending the conference "brought back to their organizations not only ideas and contacts but a sense of purpose and solidarity within a rapidly growing almost-movement."[8]

Major demonstrations against the war were held in New York and San Francisco on April 15, 1967, attended by as many as half a million people. On April 4, Dr. Martin Luther King Jr. delivered his first public, widely reported speech against the war in Riverside Church, in New York City. On May 10, more than 250 students at twenty-five medical schools announced their refusal to serve in the armed forces. By mid-summer, Marty Jezer, a leading activist, estimated that there were sixty We Won't Go groups.

One hundred and fifty young men publicly burned their draft cards on April 15, in New York City's Central Park. On the same day, at the big San Francisco anti-war demonstration, David Harris, a leading, nationally known draft resister, who eventually spent twenty months in federal prison, announced plans for a nationwide draft card turn-in on October 16. On that fall day, 1,200 young men publicly returned their draft cards. In Boston 5,000 people turned out for a rally in support. Thirty cities held local events.

The next nationally coordinated draft card turn-in took place on April 3, 1968, with one thousand publicly turning them in.

Here is how Harris described the work of the resistance at this time in a June 23, 2017, *New York Times* op-ed titled "I Picked Prison Over Fighting in Vietnam":

> At draft centers, we distributed leaflets encouraging inductees to turn around and go home. At embarkations, we urged troops to refuse to go before it was too late. We gave legal and logistical support to soldiers who resisted their orders. We destroyed draft records. We arranged religious sanctuary for deserters ready to make a public stand, surrounding them to impede their arrest. We smuggled other deserters into Canada. We even dug bomb craters in front of a city hall in Florida and posted signs saying that if you lived in Vietnam, that's what your front lawn would look like.
>
> Then we stood trial, one after another. Most of us were ordered to report for induction, then charged with disobeying that order, though there were soon so many violators that it was impossible to prosecute more than a fraction of us.
>
> I was among that fraction.[9]

David Harris was one of my heroes. I had met him and his then wife Joan Baez in February 1969, when I traveled to Washington for a national peace conference. I had made the decision by this time that I was going to leave school, turn in my draft card, and work full-time against the war. And so, on May 1, 1969, I publicly deposited my draft card in an envelope in the chapel at Grinnell College in Iowa, sealed it, and gave it to the college chaplain for him to send to my draft board. Three other people did the same, and 160 people signed a "complicity statement" in support. Two hundred and fifty people were present in the chapel for the turn-in ceremony.

This happened on a day that the resistance movement had designated for people to turn in draft cards around the country. Although these "national turn-in days" had lost some of their appeal as a tactic among leaders of the resistance, this coordinated call for such actions worked just fine in the spring of 1969 for those of us in small college town Iowa.

The Pentagon Action

As someone who did not join the anti-war movement until 1968, at the age of eighteen, if there is one major action that I regret missing, it was the hugely historic action at the Pentagon in Washington, DC, on October 21–22, 1967.

Coming just a few days after the first nationally organized draft card turn-in, it was significant in a number of ways. First, it stood out as the first massive demonstration at the Pentagon. One hundred thousand people took part in the rally at the Lincoln Memorial before demonstrators marched across the Lincoln Memorial Bridge to the Virginia side of the Potomac, where the Pentagon is located. Second, it was publicly organized as an action that would include nonviolent civil disobedience, and thousands responded to that call and took part. Third, that day and evening was the first time that anti-war demonstrators interacted with rank-and-file army troops in a prominent way. And, fourth, according to draft resister Bruce Dancis, hundreds of draft cards were publicly burned. This is how Dancis described the experience in compelling detail in his book *Resister*:

> To repel the demonstrators, the feds amassed a force of more than six thousand U.S. Army troops (with twenty thousand more soldiers on alert), two thousand National Guardsmen, two thousand Washington police, and a large number of U.S. marshals.

But the authorities, outnumbered by the demonstrators, were unwilling at this point to use the troops to keep us penned in the north parking lot. Their hastily constructed wire and wood fences were torn down or cut through by protesters, who quickly advanced toward the steps of the Pentagon.

As I approached the building, the scene was chaotic. Helicopters were flying noisily overhead, while army sharpshooters on the Pentagon roof looked down on the crowd below. Several dozen demonstrators, breaking away from the main group, found an unguarded side door to the Pentagon and actually got into the building before being clubbed and arrested.

Thousands of demonstrators were already milling around when I arrived, while others began to engage in a mass sit-in just a few yards from the building itself. The soldiers, many from the Eighty-Second Airborne Division, were standing side by side in a protective ring around the Pentagon. The soldiers stood stoically with their rifles and bayonets, inches away from demonstrators, trying to avoid eye contact with protesters who attempted to talk to them. Some demonstrators even placed flowers in the soldiers' rifle barrels.

As late afternoon passed into evening, our ranks started to thin. Some people had to get back to the buses that had brought them to Washington, while others were simply tired from the day's events or getting cold. But thousands of us remained. As darkness fell, protesters began singing songs—"We Shall Overcome" and the Beatles' "Yellow Submarine" were among the most popular.

Jerry Rubin and a few others tried to incite the crowd to physically battle the troops and marshals. But when Rubin began throwing lit pieces of wood at the marshals, he was quickly stopped by cooler heads.

Instead of fighting the troops, speakers with bullhorns began to address the soldiers directly: "Join us! Our fight is not with you." One of the most effective was Gary Rader, the army reservist who had burned his draft card on April 15. He talked about his experiences in the army, the history of the war in Vietnam, and his decision to turn against the war and join the antiwar movement. As he spoke, one could hear the officers in charge ordering their men to "hold your line."

Facing the troops, Greg Calvert of SDS tried to convince them that they had far more in common with their age group peers demonstrating at the Pentagon than with their superior officers. "You are our brothers. We want you to come home to us. You don't belong to them, the generals, who are going crazy up there in the top part of the Pentagon because we're talking to you."

According to several accounts, at least two soldiers dropped their rifles, took off their helmets, and attempted to walk into the crowd. They were quickly grabbed by their officers and taken away.

In the eerie darkness, demonstrators started to spontaneously burn draft cards. Within minutes, it appeared that several hundred cards had gone up in flames. Bonfires were started from leaflets and pieces of wood fencing.

The siege continued until after midnight, when the marshals began making arrests of demonstrators who were sitting down. Some of the protest leaders with bullhorns urged the crowd to begin leaving the area, claiming victory. Others, like me, decided to proceed with what I had expected to do all day—take part in a sit-in and get arrested.

I had become separated from my Cornell friends by this time, so I joined those sitting on the ground, locking arms with the people on both sides of me. As we sat, the troops were ordered to inch closer to us, their boots pushing and kicking our butts. One by one, marshals came from behind the soldiers to pick us off and take us away. Many people went limp and were clubbed for their passive resistance.

I was lucky. The marshal who arrested me was less violent than some of the others, and I received only a few pokes in the ribs from the baton as he dragged me toward a nearby van.

[After getting out of jail the next morning], I made my way back to the Pentagon, where demonstrators were still conducting a vigil and staging another sit-in outside the building. I arrived just in time to see the marshals arrest more than two hundred additional protesters.

Some demonstrators later described the nighttime scene outside the Pentagon as "terrifying." It's not that I was impervious to danger, but I never felt scared. Then again, I wasn't one of the protesters beaten by the marshals. I returned to Ithaca proud to have been among the nearly seven hundred demonstrators arrested—the largest number of people ever arrested at an anti-war demonstration [as of then].[10]

The second half of October 1967 saw a definitive escalation from protest to resistance for a sizeable percentage of the anti-war movement. And there was more to come. Just six days after the march on the Pentagon came the Baltimore 4.

The Ultra Resistance Is Launched

Father Phil Berrigan was the man who started the Catholic Left/Ultra Resistance movement, the network of hundreds of activists on the East Coast and in the Midwest who were responsible for the destruction of perhaps a million Selective Service draft files, among other things.

Father Berrigan, or Phil, was a Catholic priest of the Josephite Fathers order. He joined that order and became a priest in part because of his experiences as a soldier during World War II. Living in New Orleans from 1955 to 1962, he taught at an all-African American high school. He began to think about and write articles opposing segregation and the racist hierarchy in the South. By 1961, he was participating in actions against segregation organized by the Congress for Racial Equality (CORE), and his civil rights activism kept expanding as the movement did.

As U.S. involvement in Vietnam increased, so did Phil's involvement in the peace movement. He was a cofounder of the Catholic Peace Fellowship in 1964. When he moved to Baltimore to become priest of a local parish, he helped to found and actively led actions of the Baltimore Interfaith Peace Mission.

In his autobiography, he wrote of his 1967 participation in a

big conference called by the historian and writer Sidney Lens at the University of Chicago. I spent a lot of time listening to [people] talk about shutting down the Selective Service process.

They were really full of ideas. One bright fellow suggested that they put chains on the buses that were taking 1-A draftees into classification centers. Another said, "You know, those draft boards ought to be raided."

Returning to Baltimore, I thought a lot about draft boards. Eighteen-year-old males had a choice: register for the draft or go to jail. They weren't asked what they thought about the war, whether they believed in saturation bombing, if they approved of napalm, if they wanted to die in some faraway rice paddy for a people who didn't want them there.

What if draft boards didn't exist? What if the cards all got lost, or burned, or tossed into the sea? How would the government locate military-age males?

"Yes," I concluded, "raiding those draft boards makes a great deal of sense."[11]

And so, on October 27, 1967, Phil Berrigan, Tom Lewis, David Eberhardt, and Jim Mengel, the Baltimore 4, walked into the Customs House in downtown Baltimore. Inside this building was a complex of eighteen draft boards. Berrigan wrote of what happened:

> Three of us broke through this little gate and entered the draft board proper, yanking open draft files and pouring our blood over them. This lasted about a minute, because the secretaries were furious, grabbed us from behind, and locked their arms around our waists. We didn't resist or try to break loose. We sat down and waited to be arrested. Jim Mengel, having made a last-minute decision not to pour blood, handed out copies of the New Testament. The enraged clerks threw them back in his face.[12]

The four were charged with felonies carrying a maximum penalty of twenty-three years in prison, and they were found guilty at trial, in early April 1968. A sentencing date of May 24 was set, and the defendants were released on their own recognizance, pending appeal. Ultimately, Phil and Tom were sentenced to six years in prison, David to two, and Jim to probation and mandatory psychiatric counseling.

The die was cast. The ice had been broken. And, as with most births, it didn't turn out all clean and nice.

The action generated immediate controversy. Not surprisingly, the Baltimore Catholic Archdiocese repudiated it. Surprisingly, the anti-war *Catholic Worker* newspaper reported on it but pointedly did not endorse it.

The reaction among most of the Catholic radicals who knew Philip Berrigan was equally mixed. Upon hearing the news of the Baltimore Four action on the radio, Daniel Berrigan admitted that he was "very far" from his brother's understanding of things. James Forest, a prominent Catholic Peace Fellowship leader, notes: "It really didn't turn me on at the time. It didn't speak to me." In a long letter to Forest, Philip Berrigan resigned from the Catholic Peace Fellowship. For the first time, strains were beginning to appear in the Catholic Left.[13]

But others reacted positively, enough that in the spring of 1968 a group of nine people came together for another action in the Baltimore area on May 17, one week before the sentencing of the Baltimore 4: they would become known as the Catonsville 9.

CHAPTER TWO

My Personal Transformation

> The only type of true revolution which will come in this society
> will be as a result of a change from the bottom of society, not from
> the top. If I spend two more years in college, more people will
> continue to go along with things as they are, and more lives will be
> ruined by service in the armed forces. I must spend the two years
> helping get men out of the armed forces, changing minds and
> attitudes and organizing groups to combat what is wrong.
> —letter from the author to his mother, February 1969

In December 1969, I went to a weekend meeting in Baltimore attended
by about a dozen people. The purpose: to form a group willing to go into
draft boards and destroy draft files.

Less than two months after this meeting I took part in a press
conference in Washington, DC, with a number of those who had been
at the Baltimore meeting. We announced that we were the East Coast
Conspiracy to Save Lives, and that a few days earlier, February 6–7, 1970,
we had taken action at draft boards in Philadelphia, Pennsylvania, and
the offices of General Electric in Washington, DC. We thought we might
be arrested on the spot, but we weren't. However, repressive action
against what J. Edgar Hoover called the East Coast Conspiracy to Save
Lives did take place later that year.

I was twenty years old at the time. I was on a road that I've never left
since, and I'm seventy as I write this. But this life of organizing and activism for progressive revolutionary change was not the path I expected to
be taking when I went off to college in the fall of 1967. I didn't know then
exactly what I wanted to do with my life, but my general idea was that

I'd probably become a lawyer and then run for political office, rising as high as I was able to. I had no real interest in being a lawyer, but I knew that many people in Congress were lawyers, thus my decision.

Growing up, my family lived a very typical, white middle-class life. We moved to the town of Lancaster, Pennsylvania, when I was five years old and lived there for two years before moving to the nearby suburbs, where we stayed for the next ten years. I joined the local Cub Scout and then Boy Scout troops and, by the age of fourteen, "having satisfactorily completed the requirements," was "certified as an Eagle Scout." I was also awarded a God and Country medal.

My parents were very religious—my father had gone to a Church of the Brethren seminary, was an ordained minister, and was teaching religion at Franklin and Marshall College—and I was taken to our local church every Sunday. I was involved in the children's and then youth choirs and became an acolyte when I grew older. I was vice president of the church youth group one year.

In high school I played the trumpet in the band and orchestra. I ran cross country in the fall, primarily to get in shape for wrestling in the winter, my main athletic pursuit. I was a thoroughly and completely normal, white, middle-class American teenager.

There was one thing that happened when I was fourteen or fifteen that had an impact on me over time: my father took me to hear Martin Luther King Jr. speak when he came to Lancaster. Though I can't remember a single word he said, I know that I was glad to have been able to see and hear him in person.

The other person I heard speak back then who had an impact on me was Sanford Gottlieb, a national leader of the peace movement. I heard him speak at Cornell University at a national Church of the Brethren youth conference the summer before I left home for college in Iowa. I can still remember that at the beginning of his talk he asked something like, "How many people believe we are fighting in Vietnam because if we don't stop communism there, it's going to spread to the United States?" I was one of a very small number of people who raised my hand. Gottlieb then proceeded to explain the history of U.S. involvement in Vietnam, and by the end of his speech I was definitely beginning to see things differently.

However, for the next year, I did nothing to act upon those growing concerns regarding both the war and racism. I read and studied, particularly after I went off to Grinnell College in the fall of 1967, but I did nothing that remotely resembled action. Two of the books that had the most impact on me were *Vietnam Viewpoints*, by Margaret Hoffman,[1] and *The Autobiography of Malcolm X*.[2]

Sometime in March 1968, I was asked by a fellow student in my dorm, who was active in the peace movement, if I wanted to go to an anti-war march in Chicago. Another guy with me was also asked, and he immediately answered no, but I didn't answer. I couldn't; I was torn up inside. I wanted to go, but I was afraid of missing classes, of falling behind in my education. Perhaps more truthfully, I was afraid to take a first step, which I might have felt, even then, would lead me away from the relatively safe existence I had been leading up to that time.

After an hour of agonizing over the question, I decided not to go. But looking back, I can see that that experience was necessary for the later steps to occur.

Birth of an Activist

April 4, 1968, was the beginning of my life as an activist. I remember being at dinner that night in the student union, and someone came by to report that Martin Luther King Jr. had been shot. I was very shocked. I wasn't able to study after I returned to my room. Then a few hours later I heard that King had died. I remember walking around the campus, dazed, unsure, stricken.

Dr. King had come to Grinnell and spoken to a very big crowd in a gym that was filled to capacity just a few months before he was killed. I had heard him speak, and after he finished to loud applause, I went up to the front and waited to shake his hand.

When I returned to my room, I finally *did* something. I wrote up a short paragraph calling upon Congress to pass legislation to eliminate the conditions that Dr. King was protesting and trying to change. I pasted it up on the post office wall, and one day later, with 420 signatures, it was sent off to Speaker of the House John McCormack and Senate Majority Leader Hubert Humphrey. Though it was not much, I had finally acted.

In May, I went to Nebraska to work on Bobby Kennedy's presidential campaign. When the school year ended, I returned home and, in addition to a job on the maintenance crew at the college where my father worked, I volunteered for two hours every night in the local Kennedy campaign office.

Then came the California primary and June 5. I had worked at the campaign office that night and afterward had gone with a woman co-worker to a nearby bar for some drinks. When I dropped her off at her home about 11:00 p.m., Kennedy was running well ahead. I was in good spirits.

I believe I left my radio on that night after returning home, because I remember waking up about 6:30 a.m., hearing something about Kennedy being shot. I got up, went downstairs, turned on the TV, and heard the news—yes, Kennedy had been shot and killed.

The next week was a very difficult one. I felt as if everything of value had been taken from me, and, in a sense, that was true. I had made the mistake of placing virtually all my faith and hope in one man, and when that man was killed, with him went my faith, my hope, my life.

I learned to play the guitar that summer and sang strong, bitter protest songs. I got into listening to Bob Dylan in the phase of his life when his songs were most powerful politically. I especially remember "Masters of War."

I returned to college for my sophomore year after watching the police riot and the brutal beating of people who looked just like me during the Democratic Convention in Chicago on TV. I started going to meetings of the local Students for a Democratic Society (SDS) chapter, joined AWARE, a group to combat racism, and became chair of a Student Course Evaluation Committee, evaluating teachers. I put in more time doing this noncredit work than I did in any of my classes.

In the middle of November, Fred Ojile, a member of the Milwaukee 14, a group that had poured homemade napalm on many thousands of draft files two months earlier, came to speak at the college. For the first time, I heard of the draft resistance movement and was confronted with the fact that my continuing to carry a draft card was, in a very real way, inconsistent with my beliefs.

Fred talked about "channeling," a policy of the Selective Service System to use its deferments—being classified 2-S, a student deferment, or 2-D, for divinity students, or being given a deferment because you're working in a job considered essential—as a way to "channel" young people into the occupations that the government considered "in the national interest." I went away from his talk with much to think about.

I returned home for the Christmas holidays, and I was a different person to my family. My mother told me some months later that she had been worried by my behavior. I remember spending most of the time by myself—taking walks in the wintry weather, listening to music for hours on headphones, with a book about religions of the world in my hands. I was studying religions as an indirect attempt to come to grips with the direction my life was taking—or not taking.

On December 27, something happened. Here's how I described it several years later:

> I remember looking up from the book and thinking about God—who He is, what He is, what He means. Suddenly I was struck, like a blinding light, like Saul on the road to Damascus, by three words—God Is Love. The words were not an intellectual reality, they were a living reality, which is what made them so powerful and intense, which is to say that I felt full of the "God" that is "Love." I felt within me an indescribable excitement, an exhilarating wonder, as if I had discovered something which had never been known before. I literally ran upstairs, wrote hurriedly something along the lines of "God's meaning is to be filled with love," and stopped writing only when called to dinner.

Two weeks later, I returned to Grinnell for the second semester of my sophomore year. After going to three classes on the first day, I felt very down, wondering why I was there. That night I went to a black history discussion group meeting—I had joined it several months before—and came away with deep feelings about how entrenched racism was, how deeply change was needed. I walked back to my room sorely troubled. Eventually my thoughts turned to why I was at college. The thought came that I wanted to leave and go work in the inner city somewhere or in the peace movement or anywhere I could be making a real contribution to people, to social revolution, to a new world.

Immediately following those thoughts came the realization that if I did so I would lose my Selective Service System student deferment. I would probably be classified 1-A and be liable to be drafted into the army.

Rage—anger—frustration: these were the next to hit. I came to feel oppressed, deep in the gut. I was being channeled, forced to be where I did not want to be. I don't remember ever having been so angry before that point.

I went back to my dorm and wrote a letter to my parents telling them that I had decided to quit school immediately, turn in my draft card, and go to work full time in the resistance movement. I waited three days to be sure this was not a spur of the moment thing—it was not—and then mailed the letter.

Dialoguing with My Parents

To my surprise, this letter hit my parents pretty hard. They were not expecting it. In it I said:

> I have learned too much about the immorality and injustice of the system, I do not have to learn any more about its wrongs, I am not concerned with my personal physical life, I believe that my act of noncompliance will do more to change the minds of people and the policies of the government than any other actions, and as such I have decided to become a whole man, a free man, and a man of conviction and return my draft cards to the government as an act of refusal to go along with a system that kills minds, souls and bodies with tragic frequency.

When my parents got this letter, they responded by urging me to wait to leave college until the end of my sophomore year, not to leave right away, to be sure this is what I really wanted to do. I ended up agreeing to do so.

My mom wrote to me on February 13 putting forward all of her arguments as to why I should change my mind. Among them:

> My most persistent and troubling worry, Ted, is whether you are really doing this for the right reason. Are you sure you are not running away from something—a personal problem, college, society?
>
> Are you aware that four outstanding senators have introduced a bill to end the draft and Nixon administration officials have said this will happen? Why must you turn in your card in order to work for peace, justice, antipoverty, etc.? How does such an act assure you more success than hard-headed work?
>
> How at age 19, with only two years of college, can you under-take the awesome responsibility of influencing other boys in such decisions—and after only a few months thought on your part—especially when it is an act with far-reaching personal con-sequences for them? Are you well-trained and mature enough for such a burden of responsibility?

And have you thought that your proposed action might really be an evasion of responsibility? Might your greater responsibility be to develop as fast and thoroughly as possible your potential through finishing college so that you can really be a leader of men?

Well, dear son, these are my most troubling questions. I have had to ask them—please don't turn me off because I have. I believe they are important ones for you to answer for yourself.

I responded to my dear mom on February 17:

The first thing I want so say is this: no matter how many senators, whether it be four or forty, oppose the draft, that has very little to do with my decision. I have become convinced that the Resistance is right when they say that is not just politics that is bad, it is the whole society that is bad. The policemen who have no concern for human life, the members of the Selective Service board who send men against their will to do what any man with a heart would never do—kill and oppress, the attitude so prevalent in this society that you aren't a "someone" unless you're a vice-president of a business, a member of the social elite, or in a position where you can wield power over someone else. People have been brought up in this society with dual values—they are told to want peace and to love your neighbor but they are also forced to enter the armed forces, take orders from someone who enjoys the feeling of superiority, and to become a general no-one.

The only type of true revolution which will come in this society will be as a result of a change from the bottom of society, not from the top. If I spend two more years in college, more people will continue to go along with things as they are, and more lives will be ruined by service in the armed forces. I must spend the two years helping get men out of the armed forces, changing minds and attitudes and organizing groups to combat what is wrong.

I cannot do these things in college because my conscience plays a very big part. If I have a 2-S, if I am a part of the Selective Service System which I hate, if I do not reject what is wrong and join what is right, then I am not being true to myself.

I am running from nothing, rather, I am running at something at full speed and with the most force I can mount—this society and its attitudes and modes of thought. If I was running I would not remain in the USA or even at Grinnell for the next three months—I would go to Canada. But that, to me, is copping out, and I could never do that.

I can no longer remain in college, any college, because of the time I have to spend being a student, the fact that I am sheltered from the draft here while the black and the poor go to Vietnam. The miseducation I am now receiving from my classes grates on my person. Who said that college is for everyone, anyway?

If I lead a life not of putting off to later but of acting out of love now, then I will influence others around me to also use love now instead of putting things off 'til later. And it is this spreading of love through example, *backed up by action*, that is the important thing you must realize. How can I tell others to refuse the draft when I am part of the system that is making them draftable?

ML King said in 1967, "We must move past indecision to action," and things have gotten worse. I need to be true to myself, not a hypocrite. This I will not be.

My father responded on February 26:

I cannot forego one subjective comment, for you are inextricably bound to me in the most complex, probably, of human relationships—that of a father and a son. That comment is that sometime in the past week, in large part because of your letters but also some self-understanding made possible by conversations with Mom, I have arrived at the clear impression that at the very center of your being you are a whole man now in a sense that coterminously is poignant and wonderful. There are now no barriers to open, person-to-person communication.

We have accepted rationally the fact that your decision is just that—YOUR decision. If there are anxieties about what your decision may mean in the future, that is quite natural, and it is also ambiguous—at the same time that we hate to think of a free spirit like you being locked up in jail, we are very proud to have a son who is an exception!

And he wrote this on March 30 following a visit home for spring break:

It was wonderful to have you home, Ted. I felt we had a chance to discuss a number of questions. Certainly, the care and thought you have given to your decision came through clearly. You may very well be in the vanguard of a new and saving direction to American life. We pray so. Let us help when and how we can.

I am very lucky to have had the parents that I did.

Draft Resister

On May 1, 1969, I returned my draft card to my local draft board in Lancaster, Pennsylvania. It was sent to them by the college chaplain Rev. Dennis Haas, who publicly received my card and those of three others in the college chapel in front of 250 people.

In my letter of explanation to my draft board, I said:

> I was not ready, at eighteen, to decide what course I should follow in regards to the draft. I received a 2-S deferment since I was in college, but if I had not been fortunate enough to have been born with some degree of intelligence, to have been raised in a healthy environment, and/or to have been white and from a family that was well-off financially, I might not have had the opportunity to go to college. I would then have had to register 1-A, and I would not have had any idea why I had to do so, what I was getting into, or how profoundly this action could change my life, for the worse.
>
> As I read and thought, the more I became, first confused, then sad, then angry, and now moved to the point where I must take a stand against what I feel is ruining the lives of many young people in this country as well as the lives of millions of people in Third World nations.
>
> I make this protest against death, I make this affirmation of life, because I deeply believe United States actions have caused and are causing such a high degree of suffering and have destroyed so many lives that I must cry out against these actions by this break-age and noncompliance with the Selective Service System. I do so with a feeling of inward peace now that I am no longer tied to what I consider wrong.

This wasn't my only anti-war action in the last couple of months I was at Grinnell. I took part in my first hunger strike, a three day one, as part of a campaign to get the college to remove academic credit for participation in the U.S. military's Reserve Officer Training Corps (ROTC) program on campus. As I remember it, the Grinnell faculty voted in support of that demand, but the program continued for at least a couple more years before withering away.

I took my first direct action in mid-April, with others, when we brought down the U.S. flag flying over the center of the campus and sent it back up the pole upside down, an official signal of distress. This spontaneous action one beautiful spring day generated twenty-four hours of sometimes heated discussion about the war, a gathering of hundreds that night in the student union, lasting until 1:30 a.m., and organized outreach about the war the next day into the town of Grinnell.

My last act at Grinnell College, an act of disruption, took place on commencement day. The college administration had decided to give an honorary Doctor of Humane Letters degree to Curtis Tarr, who was stepping down as Lawrence College's president to take a job as Assistant Secretary of Manpower for the U.S. Air Force. He went on to become director of the Selective Service System.

A group of us decided to present Mr. Tarr with an honorary Doctor of Inhumane Letters degree. The day of graduation, we distributed two thousand leaflets with the short text of our degree. In the middle of the commencement program, as the honorary college degree was about to be presented to him, I jumped onto the stage and attempted to read the text of our degree over the microphone. Simultaneously ten seniors came up onto the stage and, after I had read our degree, one of them spoke, criticizing the school for its cooperation with the evils of this society.

And so I left Grinnell College, never again to return to college as a student.

Somehow a job had been lined up for me to spend eight weeks in the summer traveling through Ohio and Pennsylvania going to Church of the Brethren summer camps for young people as a peace counselor. But before that job began, I attended a national conference of the church in Louisville, Kentucky.

Draft Card Burning

A week or two before I left my parents' home in upstate New York for Louisville, I received another draft card from my draft board—a 1-A card, meaning I was liable to be inducted at any time. I decided that it would be a good action to burn it at the Louisville conference.

There was a peace grouping within the church, the Brethren Peace Fellowship (BPF), and when I arrived in Louisville I told them that I wanted to burn the card. To their credit, all of them, young people and older long-time members of the church, were positive about the idea. And so, one afternoon in late June 1969, I was brought up onto the stage in front of two thousand or more people by one of the BPF members, who gave over his speaking time to me.

I began by telling those listening what I was planning to do and invited anybody who wanted to support this action to come and stand with me up on stage. About sixty or seventy people did; at least one hundred, maybe two hundred, went the other way, walking out of the auditorium to register their opinion about what I was about to do.

After I did the deed, I walked off the stage. I wondered if a law enforcement official was going to come and arrest me, but that didn't happen, not then, not while I was in Louisville, and not after I left and did my peace counselor traveling for the rest of the summer.

However, sometime in August, a letter from Selective Service arrived in the mail for me. In it was a notice directing me to show up at my Lancaster, Pennsylvania, draft board at 6:00 a.m. on September 2 to get on a bus to be taken to an army induction center in Harrisburg.

My plan had been to move to Lancaster following my peace counselor summer. This notice sped up those plans. I worked to organize an anti-war demonstration at 6:00 a.m. in front of the draft board, and a hundred people showed up to support me. At a certain point, the hundred young men who were there to be inducted or to report for preinduction physicals were told to get onto the buses. I waited until that had happened, then walked up to the lead bus door, read a short statement and burned the induction notice. My statement said, in part:

> I refuse to be inducted into the U.S. Army in order to kill my Vietnamese brothers for to do so would violate both my conscience and the Nuremberg principles, which stated that an individual is

responsible for his actions in war time. I will not be a party to this death and violence, because I am concerned with life and the liberation of man from oppressive and inhumane conditions.

I was pleased to learn afterward that stories about this action went out over both AP and UPI.

For the next few months, I lived and worked in Lancaster, setting up the Lancaster Draft Information Center, printing up and distributing literature, speaking, organizing for demonstrations, attempting to get a high school student union going, writing—things a movement organizer often does. But as the days passed, as no one came to arrest me, as the war continued and the bombings increased, as President Richard Nixon watched a football game while a half million anti-war demonstrators marched outside the White House, separated from him by buses parked bumper to bumper, I came to feel I had to do more. I felt I had to demonstrate more forcefully my opposition to this war, my feeling about the urgency of stopping it.

So, in November, I traveled to Philadelphia to make contact with Sister Joann Malone, a nun who was part of a group, the DC 9, which had taken action in March 1969 inside the DC offices of Dow Chemical. Dow Chemical was the manufacturer of napalm, a horrible flammable jelly dropped on civilians and enemy combatants in Vietnam from planes and helicopters by the U.S. military. Joann connected me with a priest in Baltimore, who invited me to the retreat in Baltimore, Maryland, in early December, referred to at the beginning of this chapter.

I was joining the Ultra Resistance.

CHAPTER THREE

From Catonsville Onward

> The world expects that Christians will speak out loud and clear, so that never a doubt, never the slightest doubt, could arise in the heart of the simplest man.
>
> The world expects that Christians will get away from abstractions and confront the blood stained face which history has taken on today.
>
> The grouping we need is a grouping of people resolved to speak out clearly and to pay up personally.
>
> —Albert Camus[1]

The Baltimore 4 draft board action in October 1967 received some initial national coverage, but it didn't continue. It also elicited a mixed response among nonviolent and Catholic peace activists. And even during the trial of the four in early April 1968, it didn't receive much press coverage.

The trial did reveal, however, that the action had been effective as far as the disruption of the draft board, in part because there had been no duplicate files. This was encouraging to the defendants.

Prior to and after they were convicted on April 16, with a sentencing date set for May 24, Phil Berrigan and Tom Lewis worked intensively with George Mische, someone who had responded positively to the Baltimore action, beating the proverbial bushes to find people to do another action. By the first week of May, "nearly three hundred people had been invited to join the next action,"[2] and a group had come together to form the Catonsville 9.

Phil had badly wanted one particular person to take part: his brother Dan. To Phil, as he wrote many years after the action, "My brother was the most valuable, the most insightful, the wisest, and perhaps the strongest member of our group."[3]

Father Dan Berrigan was Phil's older brother. He joined the Jesuit order upon graduation from high school in 1939 and was ordained as a priest in 1952. He became an award-winning and prolific writer, winning the Lamont Prize for a book of poems in 1957. Over his lifetime, he wrote or coauthored fifty books. He was a professor of New Testament Studies at Lemoyne College in Syracuse in the late 1950s and early 1960s, and from 1966 to 1970 he was assistant director of the Cornell University United Religious Work organization in Ithaca, New York. He was eventually named the group's pastor.

After cofounding the Catholic Peace Fellowship with his brother in 1964, he cofounded Clergy and Laymen Concerned About Vietnam in 1965. Martin Luther King Jr. was a national cochair of the organization, which sponsored his famous 1967 anti-war speech in Riverside Church.

Here is how Dan described the all-night recruitment visit and discussion with his brother that spring of 1968:

> Philip came to campus for a quiet visit, overnight. He came with a proffer. Into our sublime, serene island [Cornell University], our El Dorado, came Philip. He is not to be thought of as a portent: nothing so pretentious. He was a friend, and he came bearing a gift.
>
> Such a gift as stops the heart short. He and others, he stated simply, were not content that the action at the Baltimore draft center should rest there, a flash in the pan, a gesture. For it was more than that, and government lenience or sternness in the coming trial must not steal the thunder of the peaceable.
>
> The action, in short, must be repeated elsewhere; and he, for one, and Tom Lewis, for another, were prepared to repeat it, in Catonsville, Md. Would I join them?
>
> The idea was less frightening than it would have been months before. I was freshly returned from Hanoi, where I had cowered under American bombings. That helped wonderfully to clear the mind.[4]

After thinking about it for another twenty-four hours, Dan was in for the action at Catonsville.

And so, on May 17, 1968, Fathers Phil and Dan Berrigan, Tom Lewis, George Mische, Mary Moylan, Tom Melville, Marjorie Bradford Melville,

David Darst, and John Hogan entered the Catonsville, Maryland, draft board in the suburbs of Baltimore, gathered up hundreds of Selective Service files, took them outside to the parking lot and set them on fire with homemade napalm. As the papers burned, they recited the Lord's Prayer and spoke about why they had taken this action. Eventually the police arrived, and they were arrested.

The level of public interest in and media attention to the October 5–9 trial in Catonsville was like night and day, compared to the Baltimore 4. Dan's involvement might have been part of the reason. Or maybe it was because of what had happened a few months before in the streets of Chicago before a national TV audience outside the Democratic Convention, where hundreds of peace and justice demonstrators were beaten, maced, and/or arrested by the Chicago police. Whatever the reasons, it was a very big event.

On the first morning of the trial, supporters of the defendants staged a large anti-war march of between 1,500 and 2,000 people. "In its account of the march the *Baltimore Sun* highlighted—with a notable trace of surprise—the 'relaxed and often joyous mood' of the march as it meandered down Howard Street."[5]

There was a full house for every day of the trial. "Every day they packed the courtroom—nuns, priests, ministers, rabbis, students. They came from all over the country, and all over the world, and they stood in line every morning, rain or shine."[6]

Surprisingly, Judge Roszel C. Thomsen allowed a great deal of testimony from the defendants about why they had poured homemade napalm on draft files.

> We spoke about our religious training, our ethical beliefs, the many roads that had led, inexorably, toward Catonsville and into this courtroom. We told the court that the institutions of this country, and we included the church that some of us had served with great devotion and love, had broken down. We argued that law serves the empire, not the people.[7]

During the trial Dan read a statement on behalf of the group of nine, part of which said:

> We say: killing is disorder, life and gentleness and community and unselfishness is the only order we recognize. For the sake of that

order, we risk our liberty, our good name. The time is past when good people can remain silent, when obedience can segregate them from public risk, when the poor can die without defense. We ask our fellow Christians to consider in their hearts a question which has tortured us, night and day, since the war began. How many must die before our voices are heard, how many must be tortured, dislocated, starved, maddened? How long must the world's resources be raped in the service of legalized murder? When, at what point, will you say no to this war? We have chosen to say, with the gift of our liberty, if necessary our lives: the violence stops here, the death stops here, the suppression of the truth stops here, this war stops here.[8]

The defendants were convicted by the jury on October 10. They received prison sentences of between two and three and a half years. After eighteen months, their appeals were exhausted and it was time to go to prison.

That time out on appeal was put to good use by the defendants and many of their supporters.

The Ultra Resistance Grows

Over the two-year period following the Catonsville action, there were at least a dozen more, mainly but not exclusively at draft boards. Michael Ferber and Staughton Lynd listed them in their excellent history, *The Resistance*:

The Boston Two (June 1968): Frank Femia and Suzi Williams, both about twenty, poured black paint on several hundred draft records.

The Milwaukee Fourteen (September 1968): Some ten thousand draft files were burned by this group of almost entirely Catholic men, including several priests.

The DC Nine (March 1969): A predominantly Catholic group, including former priests and nuns, destroyed files of the Dow Chemical Company in Washington, D.C.

The Pasadena Three (May 20, 1969): Three Resistance workers burned about five hundred draft records.

The Silver Spring (Maryland) Three (May 21, 1969): Three resisters mutilated several hundred draft files with black paint.

The Chicago Fifteen (May 25, 1969): About twenty thousand draft files were burned by this younger, largely non-Catholic group.

Women Against Daddy Warbucks (July 1969): Five women mutilated several thousand draft records and stole the "1" and "A" keys from the typewriter in a New York draft board office.

The New York Eight (August 1969): A group of four women and four men (three of them priests) staged two raids, destroying seventy-five thousand draft files in the Bronx and several thousand more in Queens.

The Akron (Ohio) Two (September 1969): A resister and a Navy veteran set fire to an office housing five draft boards, destroying or damaging about one hundred thousand draft records.

The Beaver Fifty-Five (October 1969): Not fifty-five but eight, and not from Beaver but the Midwest, they struck a set of draft boards in Indianapolis and the Dow Chemical Company in Midland, Michigan.

The Boston Eight (November 1969): Four draft boards were struck and about one hundred thousand files destroyed by this group of three women and five men, including several Catholic clergy.

The East Coast Conspiracy to Save Lives (February 1970): Eleven people, including four priests and two nuns, destroyed many thousands of draft files in three buildings in Philadelphia, and many files of the General Electric lobbying offices in Washington, D.C.[9]

The East Coast Conspiracy group is where I entered this particular entity, the Catholic Left, the Ultra Resistance, or just "the community." And a community it was—one I was overjoyed to have found. As I expressed in a letter to my parents in late January 1970, about a week before we took action:

Since the beginning of December, I have been involved in the organization of a similar group [as the Milwaukee 14], a group which is planning a similar action, which I will be a part of. I cannot tell you where or when right now, but it will be in the very near future, and I will be sure to phone you as soon as I can do so safely. Being involved in such a group has been a very joyous process. All the time I was in Lancaster [September to December

1969], in the back of my mind I knew I wanted to be in one of these actions, and finally the opportunity was presented. The action, and the community of people associated with and involved with it, fulfill very deep needs of mine. So rejoice, your son is doing what is right, both for himself and for humankind.

Of the eleven of us in this group, which formed at the weekend retreat in Baltimore in early December referred to earlier, four of us, Richard Bidwell, Peter Fordi, Phillip Linden, and Joe Wenderoth, were priests. Two, Sue Cordes and Sue Davis, were nuns. All except one of them were in their thirties; the exception, Phillip Linden, was in his late twenties and was African American. The rest of us, Nancy Assero, John Finnegan, Charlotte Lacey, Mike Panella, and me, were between the ages of eighteen and twenty-four.

I remember very little about that first retreat, but I remember it being presided over by Father Neil McLaughlin, who lived in Baltimore and had taken part in the New York 8 action. Neither Phil nor Dan Berrigan were there. We met in someone's house in downtown Baltimore, sat in a circle over the course of the weekend, as we talked with one another, and we all helped to clear and wash the dishes.

Preparing for Action

Soon afterward, I moved to Philadelphia to take part in the preparatory work for the upcoming action. For a month and a half, I lived in a house in inner city Philadelphia with about ten other people, some of whom did not "surface"—go public—as part of the East Coast Conspiracy 11, but who played very active and essential roles. Our collective work allowed a group of us to eventually enter a complex of several draft boards on Broad Street in North Philadelphia in the late afternoon of Friday, February 6, 1970. We entered the twelve-story office building, went up to the very top of stairs that we had identified as a good place to hide, and waited for many hours.

From my experience, this was the primary way that the Ultra Resistance was able to get into buildings housing draft boards, war corporation offices, and FBI offices. Sometimes, as was true in this case, we could find a place that seemed safe where everyone taking part in the action could hide. More often, one person would enter the building during the day, usually on a Friday, hide in a closet, at the top of stairs, or somewhere else, and then open a door to let others in at the prearranged time late at night. Sometimes we were able to bust through a poorly secured door or drill the lock.

But there was much more to it, which is what I spent a month and a half helping to prepare.

We spent weeks studying the office we were planning to enter, the building housing the office, and the surrounding neighborhood. Various people would go to the office or building with specific instructions of what to look for and take notes. At night we would send out teams of two, usually a man and a woman, to sit in cars at the time we planned to carry out the action, i.e., from midnight to 3:00 a.m.

One thing we did for this action was to observe the light patterns in the building. We knew there was a night watchman, so we watched to see if there were lights that went on or off on particular floors at particular times.

While sitting in the car, we would also observe how much pedestrian traffic there was on the streets surrounding the building, if and when police cars came by and whether there were any vehicles, like garbage trucks, that arrived at the back or side doors of the building, as well as anything else of note.

Once, John Finnegan and I were out casing the building, our assignment to observe the light patterns on one side of the building. Trying to find a good place to observe from, we ended up driving our car up a short ramp onto a loading dock platform of some company. It was after midnight, so no one was around. However, not long after we settled in, a police car came by, stopped, told us to drive the car down the ramp to the street, made us to get out of the car, and took our ID documents. We might have gotten a ticket for trespassing. Fortunately, they didn't take us to the police station for interrogation, so after they drove away we went to another location to finish our night's work.

One of the women I sometimes went out with to do casing was Terry McHugh, a beautiful young woman my age from Philadelphia. We hit it off, and within a week or two we had fallen in love. As our relationship deepened, we talked about getting married, but that didn't come to pass, primarily because my first priority and full-time occupation, to the degree it was economically possible, was the resistance movement and these actions, while Terry had a full-time job working with children in some way. I still think of Terry often; tragically, she was killed in a car accident in 1977.

The action at the North Philadelphia draft boards office was one of three being planned. Two others were being organized by others from the Catholic Left community, one in Northeast Philadelphia and the other downtown. I and most of the others in North Philadelphia knew very little about the two other planned actions, I assume because of security considerations on the part of those coordinating the overall action.

Two of those people were John Grady and Phil Berrigan. I don't know if there were others or, if so, who they might have been, and I really wasn't concerned with that at the time.

Following the Catonsville 9 action, John Peter Grady got involved with the defense committee. He was a friend of Dan Berrigan and a sociologist who lived in the Bronx and was part of the anti-war movement. I don't know how many actions John played a role in, but I would be very surprised if it was less than a half dozen. He was well-organized, good with details, very dedicated, and very sure of himself, with a boisterous laugh that filled a room when he let it go, and he was our day-to-day leader in North Philadelphia.

I met Phil sometime in January at the house we were working out of. I remember coming down the stairs, and there he was at the bottom, with a big, broad smile. I don't remember saying much to him or him staying very long, but I'll never forget his big smile.

Our East Coast Conspiracy group action was a two-day, two-city affair. The plan was to pull off coordinated actions on the same night at the three big draft board complexes in Philadelphia, then go down to the Washington, DC, office of General Electric, a major war profiteer. I learned while doing research for this book that Phil oversaw the casing of the building in DC, while simultaneously keeping track of how things were developing in Philadelphia.

We took action in DC on a weekend during the trial of the DC 9, who had disrupted the Dow Chemical office.

Writing Poetry While Waiting

As I sat up at the top of the stairs in the North Philadelphia office building on February 6 with a dozen others, I wrote three short poems:

3:40 p.m.
Outside a bird flies singly by,
One against a background of

ruffled, solid, sun-brightened clouds.
The traffic 12 floors down
stops and starts,
slows down, accelerates,
screeches, honks, spreads pollution.
Philadelphians are walking
from place to place,
many of them
between the ages of
18 and 26.
Inside we sit and sprawl upon
a dirty, unused (!) before now
(put to good use)
concrete platform, and
the top steps
leading to it.
Words are few,
thoughts are many,
time is slow,
and the paint
on the walls
is crumbling away.
The window to our left is open,
(below us doors open and close,
and we hear a voice)
the one to the right closed,
not capable of moving.
The door to the roof
is behind the poet, barely open—
we will wait for dark
before walking upon it.

The sun is coming down slowly,
casting window frame shadows
upon the wall a half flight down.

We wait for the time.

8:15 p.m.
Two lights flash,
all is well,
within and without.
Within we feel a desire to act in love,
without which we are not as full.
Two lights flash
and there is no emergency.
The only emergency
is the one
we are responding to,
responding to hopefully
and with faith
that the Bible upon which
this is being written
is right when it says,
"The meek shall inherit the earth."
"Lo, I am with you always. . ."

If He is anywhere in this land,
we hope that He is here,
in this stairwell,
out on the roof,
down on the third floor,
where we are carrying out
His will.

9:30 p.m.
All of the words,
the long hours of talk,
the soul-searching and pain,
the slow awakening to the need—
all are over.
All that remains
is for
six hours to pass.

About 3:00 a.m., we went down the stairs and broke into the draft board office. We had probably put thousands of files into duffel bags when we called out at a certain point from an office phone (cell phones didn't exist back then) and learned that two of our larger group had been discovered and arrested inside the draft board office downtown. We were told to split as quickly as possible, and we did so, leaving the duffel bags in the office, and were soon on the highway on our way down to DC.

(Three months later, I was part of a group of young people from Philadelphia calling themselves We the People that successfully reentered the same North Philadelphia draft board office, neutralizing the alarms that had been put on the back door, and removed all of the relevant draft files, loading them into a rented van. We took off for a farm about thirty miles west of Philadelphia, where, the next day, we had a big file-burning party and went swimming.)

The East Coast Conspiracy group arrived in DC and at the appointed hour went to the General Electric office building. As we walked up to a side door, someone opened it, let us in, and gave us a quick briefing about what floor the GE office was on and how we could get into it. I remember entering the office, where we looked through filing cabinets for incriminating documents. We left an hour or two later without really finding anything, feeling a little deflated.

These feelings were shared by nineteen-year-old Barbara Shapiro Dougherty, the person primarily responsible for us getting into the GE building. In an unpublished manuscript, she described the several days leading up to our arrival:

Casing the GE Office

It was February 1970. I was in Washington, DC. I was on 14th St. sitting in a "speakeasy." I was looking up at a building on the corner opposite. It was the GE building. Michael was there, and I believe also Phil Berrigan and John Grady. We were watching the lights in the GE building. Grady was saying there was a guard and a cleaning crew.

Plans were made to find out if you could hide in the building to determine the exact location of the right offices and how the action could be done. And somehow then it became my project.

The next day news was that Phil had gotten access using a kitchen fork to bypass the lock into the room housing the elevator machines on the top floor, but there was no place to hide there. Grady had cased the church next door. It butted up against the building, and if a window could be opened it could be used to get the people in and out of the building.

I spent the nite on the roof of the building across the street from the GE building and determined that there was a lot of nite time activity and a lot of police in that area all nite long. . .

I rode to the 14th floor, got off the elevator and tried to open the door to the Ladies Room. It was locked. Without any real consideration or hesitation, I went into the GE reception office and asked a secretary if I could use her key to the restroom. Her eyes reacted without suspicion; she simply handed me a full set of keys and smiled. The Ladies Room key easily fit the lock to the door. All the keys immediately disappeared into the large lower pockets of my bulky coat. I went back down the elevator and left the building. . .

I checked which locked doors my keys would open. First, I opened the door that said "Lounge." Couches, refrigerators—again no place to hide. The office of the receptionist, for which it turned out I also had a key, had only a desk and locked files, again no closets or real hiding areas. This office led into an executive suite, and the only closet there was a liquor cabinet. Suddenly, I heard footsteps and doors closing. My body lurched a foot in fright. I dropped down under the desk and stayed there shaking like a leaf for over an hour. Finally my courage returned and I went about my exploration. . .

The rest of the night I spent running up and down the back staircase putting tape on the door to each floor to try to determine the activities of the guard and the cleaning crew and the switch-board operators. . .

I dialed the number. The worst thing that could happen next was that a switchboard operator would answer. The operator would have to be in the room on the 15th floor and would probably know something was wrong even if I just hung up. The phone rang and a voice answered. I said this was Barb and I needed Phil. And there it was, I was talking to Phil, and he was saying that if it could be done at all it had to be tonight. That the Philadelphia draft boards had been a problem, that the people were scared, but ready to come if I said yes. I said, "What time?"...

When I called Phil again I tried to make my voice sound full of confidence. This was a good action, it moved the statements of resistance one more step. How good it would be if it succeeded. Two a.m. was the time that the group would come to the back door of the GE building, and we would let them in. SHALOM!...

I went about the task of opening locked doors of the GE offices on 3 floors. Many of the doors were hard to jimmy the lock open so I cut holes in the glass. The impact of my hammer would time and time again leave me dripping with sweat. I made holes in the glass that I covered with Valentine's Day cards. This was so that if the guard checked the floor he might not know of the treachery I had committed...

Two o'clock came and so did they, in the building and up the staircase to the executive suite. Nobody drank wine [that I had set out for them] or even poured it, but I got the feeling they appreciated the gesture. I told them about the open doors and where to look and then I went down the back staircase out of the building and hailed the first cab back to Silver Spring...

I remember that [the next day] news was that the East Coast Conspiracy had not been caught during the GE raid, but they had not really taken the time to uncover much or any of the material I had reported existing. Disappointing.

The day after our in and out of the GE building, we drove to the Maryland shore, to the Atlantic Ocean. We were feeling good that we had pulled off the GE action, even if we had not found any smoking guns of note in the file drawers we had looked through.

We were at a motel at the shore for two or three days. We enjoyed each other's company, as we walked along the beach, celebrated our semi-successful actions, and communicated with others back in DC who were setting up a press conference, where we would publicly reveal our identities and "take responsibility" for the weekend actions.

Post-Action and "Surfacing"

The Ultra Resistance action continuum went through different phases. At times, those taking part identified themselves, and at other times they didn't. From the Baltimore 4 in October 1967 to the Chicago 15 in May 1969, those who did the actions waited for the police and the press to arrive. But starting with the Women Against Daddy Warbucks action in New York, in July 1969, things were done differently. Participants would "surface" a day or several days after the action and claim responsibility.

My understanding is that an initial central reason for doing it this way was to have greater control over the message put out to the media. People expected that when they surfaced and took responsibility they would be arrested on the spot, but that only happened the first time, with the Women Against Daddy Warbucks action. When we took public responsibility at our press conference in DC, none of the FBI men present with the assembled press did anything. None of us were ever arrested and charged for these actions.

There are two main reasons for this government response. One was the involvement of Catholic priests and nuns. That made it hard to paint us as a bunch of crazed hippies, communists, or terrorists. In addition, there were political risks in prosecuting us that had to be balanced against their obvious desire to stop the growth and increasing effectiveness of our movement.

The other reason was that we had successfully carried out an action and gotten away without leaving much concrete evidence of who had taken part, and the government knew they would have a hard time getting a conviction. "Taking responsibility" was not the same thing as confessing while being questioned by police or the FBI or in court.

In the summer of 1970, a new tactic evolved. A week or so after successful coordinated actions at all three draft board offices in Delaware, a public surfacing took place in a park in Wilmington. When Sister Elizabeth McAlister called for the people who were taking responsibility to come up to the stage, one hundred or more people did so, and a statement signed by about two hundred people was released.

By March 1971 and the successful raid on the Media, Pennsylvania, FBI office, action participants were no longer taking public responsibility.

In addition to the abovementioned Delaware and Media actions, there were many others after the February 1970 East Coast Conspiracy action, among them:

- North Philadelphia, Pennsylvania, May 1970
- Providence, Rhode Island, June 1970

- Pontiac (Michigan) 4, July 1970
- Minnesota 8, July 1970
- Rochester, New York, September 1970
- Union City and Elizabeth, New Jersey, December 1970
- San Jose (California) 1, December 1970
- Evanston, Illinois, April 1971
- Trenton, New Jersey, May 1971
- New Haven, Connecticut, July 1971
- Camden, New Jersey, August 1971
- Buffalo, New York, August 1971
- Bridgeton (New Jersey) 5, August 1971
- New and Improved East Coast Conspiracy to Save Lives, upstate New York, October 1971
- Yonkers (New York) 1, January 1972
- Citizens Commission to Demilitarize Industry (York, Pennsylvania), AMF bomb-making plant, March 1972
- Great Lakes Conspiracy to Save Lives and Planetary Peoples Liberation Front (Midwest draft board), summer 1972
- York (Pennsylvania) 5, AMF plant, December 1972
- trucks damaged at Niagara Air Force Base, January 1973[10]

There almost certainly were more. As explained in *The Catonsville Nine*:

> In the first eight months of 1970 alone, the Selective Service System reported 271 separate "anti-draft occurrences" at draft boards across the country. Some of these incidents were relatively minor—sometimes rocks were thrown through windows— while others caused serious damage to draft offices and the files. Repairing this damage slowed down the work in many Selective Service facilities. Late in 1969 draft offices in New York City began closing every day at 2:00 p.m. so that clerks could recreate and reorganize files that had been damaged in three separate raids. And in Chicago, it took forty extra employees a total of four months to recreate all of the files that had been destroyed.[11]

Clearly, all of these actions had a concrete impact on the ability of the Selective Service System to provide young men for the military. But just as important was the political impact of these actions. What happened in Rochester, New York, in the fall of 1970 is one of the best examples, after Catonsville, of how the willingness of people to put themselves on the line can have a very real impact on the thinking and actions of other people and the general public.

CHAPTER FOUR

Taking on the FBI Too

> Over Labor Day weekend, the files and cross-reference system of local draft boards 73–76 and the U.S. Attorney were destroyed and the records of the FBI disrupted. We, the Flower City Conspiracy, claim public responsibility for these acts. We have acted because we feel it is essential for groups of individuals to commit themselves to changing our present society. We feel change will come through changed individuals acting together. We took our action of nonviolent disruption to challenge the illegitimate government of this country.
> —statement of the Flower City Conspiracy, September 1970

Over the 1970 Labor Day weekend, an action was taken inside the Rochester, New York, Federal Building. There was a new wrinkle to this one; in addition to the destruction of Selective Service files, the Flower City Conspiracy group also entered the offices of the FBI and the U.S. Attorney. This was the first time that these federal agencies had been targeted as part of one of our movement's nonviolent raids.

Less than three months later, on November 27, 1970, as the trial of the Flower City Conspiracy in Rochester was nearing an end, FBI Director J. Edgar Hoover startled a Senate Appropriations Committee public hearing in Washington, DC, by announcing that Philip and Daniel Berrigan were "principal leaders" of "an anarchist group" that was "planning to blow up underground electrical conduits and steam pipes" serving federal buildings in Washington, DC.[1] In addition, he said they were "concocting a scheme to kidnap a highly-placed government official. If successful, the plotters would demand an end to United States bombing operations in Southeast Asia and the release of all political prisoners as ransom."[2]

Six weeks later, after a hurried scramble by the Justice Department, six people were indicted in Harrisburg, Pennsylvania, on charges of plotting to kidnap presidential foreign policy advisor Henry Kissinger and blow up government heating tunnels. If convicted, they faced life in prison.

Is it possible that Hoover made his announcement when he did because the trial of eight people, including me, for breaking into an FBI office and attempting to remove files was nearing its end and about to go to the jury, which it did, on December 1, just four days after Hoover's testimony?

It's a theory, nothing more, but it seems plausible, given J. Edgar's well-known vindictiveness. Our group hadn't just destroyed draft files; we were the first group to ever break into an FBI office, and we had almost gotten away with several suitcases full of FBI files.

We know that a couple of weeks after the Rochester break-in Hoover had privately raised the Catholic Left issue with Republicans in Congress:

> On September 23, 1970, Scripps-Howard staff writer Dan Thomasson published a story about a forty-five minute White House briefing of Republican congressional leaders the day before by President Nixon, Attorney General Mitchell and FBI Director Hoover. At the meeting Hoover advised congressional leaders that a group calling itself the East Coast Conspiracy to Save Lives had plans to "bomb sewers and conduits in the District of Columbia and to kidnap political leaders in an attempt to win release of leftist colleagues now in prison and to obtain other political concessions."[3]

It is realistic to believe that Hoover was receiving regular reports on how the Rochester trial was going, and, if so, he had to know that we eight defendants were doing pretty well. Indeed, just one week before Hoover's public testimony in November, Father Dan Berrigan had testified at the trial. He had read the Sermon on the Mount on the witness stand, and it was a big news story.

Dan was fresh in Hoover's memory. He had successfully eluded the FBI for four months in 1970, from April to August, after going underground rather than reporting to serve a sentence for the Catonsville 9 draft board raid in 1968. Furthermore, Hoover may well have been exercised by the fact that Dan was allowed to read such a famous Bible passage at the trial of those SOB burglars who broke into his Rochester office.

How best to counter that image? With public charges of planned bombings and kidnapping.

There may be no truth to this theory, but what is true is that the action in Rochester led to unexpected consequences and developments over the coming months and years: a successful raid on an FBI office in Media, Pennsylvania, three months after the eight of us were sentenced; the release of the Media FBI documents to the press showing the extent of widespread FBI illegal surveillance and disruption of civil rights, human rights, the women's movement, and other peaceful groups; Hoover's death from a heart attack on May 2, 1972, less than a year and a half after his November 27, 1970, testimony; and U.S. Senate hearings on this issue in 1975, leading to the establishment of the Senate Select Committee on Intelligence and legislation that mandated a range of changes to how the FBI and other intelligence agencies were supposed to function.

Getting Connected with the Organizers

I don't remember exactly how I heard in the summer of 1970 that there was a group of people planning an action in Rochester, and that I was needed to help pull it off. Here is how Jerry Elmer wrote about it in his book *Felon for Peace*:

> Actually, Ted had not been part of the Rochester group planning the Action over the course of the summer; in fact the first time I ever met Ted was when I arrived in Rochester on the weekend of the Action there. Suzi [Williams] and DeCourcy [Squire], the two primary organizers of the action, had carefully not involved anyone from the Catholic Left in the advance planning, but they were pleased to make use of Ted's labors on the night of the Action.[4]

I had been part of two major actions that summer, prior to Rochester and after my participation in the May We the People action in North Philadelphia. One was the successful coordinated raid on all three draft board offices for the state of Delaware in mid-July. The other was a small role—standing by a back door watching for the FBI—during the public sermon Dan Berrigan gave on Sunday morning, August 2, 1970, at a Methodist church in the Germantown section of Philadelphia, while underground.

I remember meeting before the church service in a nearby house. Eqbal Ahmad, soon to be a codefendant of mine at Harrisburg, led a meeting to go over all the details. The main thing I remember was that one issue was deciding who would stay with the young children of the couple in whose house we were meeting; Eqbal volunteered for that essential job.

No FBI agents came during Dan's sermon. Toward the end of it, he put forward what "good men and women" could do about the terrible times they were living in:

> A Christian can confront the law of the land, that law which protects the warmakers even as it prosecutes the peacemakers. The Christians can refuse to pay taxes. They can aid and abet and harbor people like myself who are in legal jeopardy for resistance, along with AWOL's. They can work with GI's, on bases helping those young men to awaken to the truth of their condition and their society, in coffee houses or with hospitality in their own homes. They can organize within their professions and neighborhoods and churches, so that a solid wall of conscience confronts the deathmakers. They can make it increasingly difficult for local draft boards to function. There are a hundred nonviolent means of resistance up to now untried, or half-tried, or badly tried. But the peace will not be won without such serious and constant sacrificial and courageous actions on the part of large numbers of good men and women. The peace will not be won without the moral equivalent of the loss and suffering and separation that the war itself is exacting.[5]

One week later, Dan was arrested by the FBI on Block Island, in Rhode Island.

I remember arriving in Rochester for my first meeting with the team that had been putting the action together. It was good to see Paul Couming from Boston. Paul had connected with the Ultra Resistance a few months before I had as part of the Boston 8 action. We had gotten to know each other in Philadelphia when preparing for the East Coast Conspiracy action in February.

I think I knew only one person who was part of the group of eight who ended up going into the building on the night of September 5: Joan Nicholson, a Quaker peace activist from Philadelphia. At thirty-six, she was also the oldest member of our group.

The two leaders of the group were Suzi Williams and DeCourcy Squire, both then living in Rochester. DeCourcy's younger brother Ralph was a draft resister serving a three-year prison sentence. DeCourcy, twenty-one, already had a five-year history of activism with various civil rights, peace, and women's groups. She poignantly included this in her short bio on a mimeographed leaflet we produced about all of us and why we did the action: "I spent several months by myself, living on Cuttyhunk Island, Mass., just thinking, writing and watching the ocean. I hope someday that may be possible again."

Suzi, twenty-one, had poured black paint over draft files in Boston in 1968, leading to fifteen months in federal prison in Alderson, West Virginia. She was arrested twelve times for peace activism prior to the Rochester action.

Frank Callahan, twenty-one, was a full-time student at Saint Joseph's College in Philadelphia, a winner of a George Washington medal from the Freedom Foundation, and a former teacher in Guayaquil, Ecuador.

Wayne Bonekemper, twenty, worked locally with the Rochester Draft Resistance Project.

Jane Meyerding, twenty, was a Philadelphia Quaker and a student at Temple University.

Joe Gilchrist, twenty-two, had attended Cornell University in Ithaca and had just won an appeal in Oklahoma of a five-year sentence for refusing induction.

Our statement included this paragraph:

> Our action, while only a small part of what needs to be done, has not only made the draft inoperable in Rochester and slowed down the functioning of the local FBI and U.S. Attorney, but will, we hope, encourage others to acts of conscientious resistance. Fear is one of the strongest weapons the government has and one which the Selective Service, FBI and U.S. Attorney use constantly. Our action demonstrates that these agencies are not invincible, and by acting publicly, we affirm that we are willing to stand up against the fear they engender.

Concerns and Problems

I had no problem with going into the Selective Service and FBI offices. People in the peace movement, as well as other movements, particularly the Black Freedom movement, were having experiences with the FBI that made it crystal clear that they were a major part of the apparatus to suppress dissent and resistance and maintain the very unjust and violent status quo.

Journalist Betty Medsger wrote about it this way:

As Bill Davidon [Philadelphia-based peace activist and member of the Ultra Resistance] moved from peace group to peace group that year [1970], searching for more effective ways to escalate opposition to war, he repeatedly heard a very troubling rumor. People told him there were growing fears that there were FBI spies in their midst. Fear of informers was having a poisonous impact, he was told. Trust was fraying. The concerns were repeated to him again and again. Very reasonable people from a diverse range of peace organizations expressed them.[6]

However, I didn't see the group's plans to enter and disrupt the U.S. Attorney's office in the same way, but I had had no role in making that decision; it had been made before I arrived in town.

I understood the reasons for it. I agreed that the criminal justice system that U.S. Attorneys are so much a part of unjustly prosecutes and imprisons people of color and low-income people very disproportionate to their numbers in the population. But it was a new idea, and I felt that it would be best to focus on just Selective Service and the FBI. I considered whether I should say something, and I may well have raised questions about it, but, in the end, I agreed to be part of the action despite some reservations.

As it turned out, I ended up becoming a pretty essential part of the action. I was the one who entered the building on Friday afternoon, September 4, 1970, at about 4:00 p.m., and I ended up spending thirty-two hours inside it before I let everyone else in. I hid inside a tower reached by climbing over a ten-foot-high iron grate fence meant to keep people from going up the stairs to the tower. I took a Bible and a small amount of food with me.

I can picture the scene and feel what I felt as I walked across the street after being dropped off near the entrance to the very old brownstone federal building that Friday afternoon. I felt fear like I had never felt before. It was like an invisible wall that I had to walk through to make it up into that tower. Being alone certainly had something to do with the tremendous fear I felt. Knowing that our plans included not just the Selective Service office but those of the FBI and the U.S. Attorney as well might have been another contributor. And it could have been that I had some slight inkling that the government knew of our plans.

I remember talking to Boyd Douglas on a pay phone several days before the action. I don't remember why I called him; someone must have given me a message to do so. I remember him wishing me luck with the action. I had met Boyd Douglas in Lewisburg, Pennsylvania, earlier that summer as part of a visit with others from the Ultra Resistance to see if there were any people interested in joining our resistance community and taking part in an action. It is possible the Rochester action was specifically mentioned in those meetings, but I don't recall.

Boyd Douglas was a government informant. He was a Lewisburg inmate, in prison for forging and passing bad checks. He was on work release, leaving prison each workday to go to school at Bucknell University. He had befriended Phil Berrigan, who entrusted him with carrying clandestine letters to and from Sister Elizabeth McAlister that, it turned out, had a lot of information in them about the discussions and plans of the Ultra Resistance.

I don't think I consciously suspected Boyd as I went into the building. However, once I was ensconced in the extremely dusty tower—there had to be a half-inch or more of dust on the floor, and it was clear no one had been up there for years—I noticed something. As I waited for the midnight hour when I would go down to let people in, through the dirty tower window on one side of the building, I could see, about a half block away, during the day on a Saturday, what looked like an FBI car with people in it. I was far enough away that it was difficult to be sure, but I remember becoming suspicious when I realized the same car had been there for a long time, and I was pretty sure someone was in it.

Once or twice over the course of that Saturday, I walked down the stairs and climbed over the iron grate to use the bathroom and drink some water. I did so carefully, concerned that someone might be on the top floor in one of the offices and see or hear me, but the fact that it was a Saturday on Labor Day weekend worked in our favor—I never saw or heard anyone.

Inside the Building

Sometime around 11:30 p.m., I went downstairs and called out from a phone booth on the first floor to make contact with the rest of the group and the people who were going to be bringing them to the building. All was good on their end, and I had put my concerns about the suspicious car in the back of my mind. We had important work to do!

All went well with the group entry into the building. I waited by the main entrance, head down, and when I saw the cars pull up to the curb, the seven getting out and coming up the eight or ten stairs to the door, I opened the door. Whoever was supposed to be watching for us from the government side was definitely not watching during the thirty or so seconds when the cars pulled up, unloaded, and left.

For the next five hours, we went about our work. I worked in the Selective Service offices with DeCourcy and others, although I don't remember who. I never did any work in either the FBI or U.S. Attorney's offices, but I did check in with people there once or twice to see how things were going.

About 2:00 a.m., someone told me that they had seen or heard a policeman coming up to the doors we had entered to check them. We continued to monitor this and discovered there was a pattern—he would check every half hour.

Frank Callahan talked about his experiences inside the FBI office with Suzi in this way:

> We got into the Federal Building. In the draft board office a note was found which said that the Rochester FBI and the State Selective Service had been alerted to the possibility of a draft action by the "East Coast Conspiracy Group" over the Labor Day weekend and so extra security precautions were being taken. Here we are, inside the building, reading this! So there's the first flash of paranoia.... I looked out the window while I was breaking into an FBI man's desk . . . and there's a police car on the ground floor level, flashing a light. . . . I came very close to vomiting. Just a real rush of fear. You're so scared you're not even thinking about being scared. Scared is the definition of your entire universe. Nausea and adrenalin.

Not everyone was so shaken up. Suzanne Williams was a veteran of an earlier action. Callahan says, "I whispered, 'Hey, Suzi, come here!'" She comes over. She looks out the window, turns to me, smiles, and says, 'Well, looks like we're screwed'—and went back to the files, back to work."[7]

I went to all three offices to check in with people, and we decided by consensus that we would leave about 5:15 a.m., in between what we expected would be 5:00 a.m. and 5:30 a.m. police checks. I called our outside team to tell them the plan. At 5:15 a.m., we were in place, waiting for the cars to arrive. I remember that it was about 5:20 a.m., the cars had not yet arrived, and a policeman came to the door ten minutes early, at least as far as we were concerned. He rattled the locked doors, saw us, and yelled something like "What are you doing in there?" Minutes later a whole bunch of police came pouring into the building.

I had been sitting in the pay phone booth on the first floor right around the corner from the entrance/exit, waiting there in case our outside team needed to call us. The first thing I remember seeing is a plainclothes detective coming at me, possibly with a drawn gun, and making some comment about how dirty I looked, probably because of my thirty-two hours in a dust filled tower.

We were soon in the very old and very noisy Monroe County jail.

Time in Jail

We were pretty bummed out, that's for sure. I remember doing a lot of singing in my cell, and I'm not a very good singer, but I was doing it to try to lift my spirits and to remember why I was there, the very good reasons we had taken this risk. It was definitely an "I know why the caged bird sings" moment.

When I got my one phone call I called home to Philadelphia and my then fiancée Sarah Forth. I can still remember her voice trembling when I told her what had happened. Sarah came up to Rochester a couple of weeks later. She wrote about that experience in a letter to concerned friends and members of our resistance community:

> September 19 and 20 I spent in Rochester with members of the Conspiracy support group and the family and friends of some of the eight in jail. Suzi and DeCourcy are still fasting—it's been two weeks now. DeCourcy's mother was in Rochester last week to visit and reported her in good spirits. She's starting to have difficulty with the three flights of stairs between the women's section on the fourth floor and the visiting room on the first floor. DeCourcy has not signed the waiver that allows her mail to be read so she may not receive mail. Joan, Ted, Joe and Jane had visitors on Saturday.

They and Wayne, Frank and Suzi have gotten visits from clergy and lawyers, also. The jailers have started questioning the right of out of town clergy to visit. And it's difficult for visitors other than parents (such as sisters and fiancées) to see people. This is not true for other prisoners. Most seriously, the eight still have not been permitted to meet together to plan their defense. This is a difficult issue since they were charged separately and there is no charge of conspiracy to commit these "crimes."

I was kept in a solitary cell, nothing but an iron bed frame and mattress, a toilet, and a sink. Most days, we were able to go downstairs to a "community room," where I could talk with others, play cards, and generally hang out. I remember a radio being on pretty much all day when I was in my cell, with loud popular music that I actually enjoyed, by and large. I would write letters to people on the outside. Here is some of what I said in a letter to the Brethren Action Movement (BAM) on September 17. BAM was the group that had supported me in my draft card burning in front of two thousand Church of the Brethren conference attendees in Louisville in the summer of 1969:

> I am writing these words from a 5' × 8' jail cell in the Monroe County jail. I have been here for eleven days, ever since I and seven others were arrested inside the Federal Building in Rochester at 5:30 a.m., on Sunday, September 6. As we were led away by the police we left behind us thousands of draft files torn up, as well as the offices of the U.S. Attorney and the Federal Bureau of Investigation disrupted. Initially our bail was $100,000. It has since been lowered to $50,000 for five of us, $25,000 for one of us, and remains the same for two of us. Our trial—on six charges, carrying a maximum sentence of 38 years in prison—is scheduled for October 19 [later pushed back a month]. I invite all of you who hear these words before that time to attend and join in our celebration of life.

There was a high point to my time in the Rochester jail, a letter from my ninety-year-old grandfather, my father's father. His name was John Titus Glick. My full name is John Theodore Glick, and I don't think it was an accident that we were both John T. Glick's. I loved him very much.

Granddaddy was not a political man, but he took the teachings of Jesus Christ very seriously. In the couple of years previous to my arrest when I had spoken with him about what I was doing with my life, while visiting in Bridgewater, Virginia, he seemed to understand and be supportive.

He wrote to me on September 13:

> You and those with you have been in my thoughts and prayers many times since I heard of your being in prison. It has not affected me adversely for I know you are standing for what you believe is right. What you have said by action is: "Ye have not yet resisted unto blood striving against sin" (Hebrews 12:3). "Your courage reverberates" (Galations 6:9). I am happy because I believe you are truly sincere, so do not worry thinking you have caused Granddaddy to be unhappy. To have a Grandson standing against power for conscience's sake is reason for joy, not grief. With prayer and best wishes for you and those with you, Granddaddy Glick.

I ended up spending twenty-three days in that old jail before getting out on bail. Five of the others got out at the same time. Suzi and DeCourcy refused bail. They called for the establishment of a Rochester Bail Fund to help low-income people in jail who were too poor to afford it. They said in a statement:

> A person's ability to pay money determines if he will be free or in jail while awaiting trial, despite the presumption that he is innocent until proven guilty. Those who are in jail awaiting trial are guilty already—guilty of being poor. Because of this blatant economic discrimination, we will not bail out until all bailable prisoners have been released from Rochester jails.

Some people were bailed out as a result of this bail fund but not all. Suzi and DeCourcy were in jail until our trial, through our trial, and then afterward to serve their sentences. Each day they were brought to court and returned to jail in handcuffs and chains.

Press Coverage and Community Organizing

A lot happened during the twenty-three days I was in jail, beginning with the newspaper headlines and news coverage immediately afterward.

The local Rochester *Democrat and Chronicle* for Monday, September 7, had a huge front-page photo of the draft board office with cut up draft files covering every inch of the floor. The major headline read, "Draft Office Here Wrecked, 8 Nabbed in Federal Bldg."

An Associated Press story that went out nationally carried the headline, "8 Held in Raid on 3 Federal Offices." The first two sentences said: "Eight young persons broke into the Rochester Federal Building Sunday and ransacked the offices of the selective service system, the FBI and the assistant U.S. attorney. All eight, including four women and the son of a college president, were in the Monroe County jail today."[8]

One week later, on the day of our arraignment, a front-page story in the *Democrat and Chronicle* had an unusual headline: "Draft Board Defendants: Giggles and Defiance." There was a photo of the four women defendants, all of them looking to their right and smiling at something, their hands in front of them locked in handcuffs. It was a nice headline and photo. The story itself was very straightforward, listing the six felonies we were being charged with and the maximum penalties of thirty-eight years and a $34,000 fine.

AP and UPI also sent out stories about the arraignment, though without the photo and "giggles" headline.

Our supporters, in particular a wonderful human being named Carolyn Micklem, had been active during our imprisonment. Carolyn was the coordinator of the Friends of the Flower City Conspiracy, and she did a great job.

One of the positive things that happened was that soon after our arrest a local alternative newspaper, the *Journal*, took up our case in a major way, publishing thousands of copies of a newsprint supplement that carried our statement, information about the eight of us, information about the bail fund, and our photos. Special supplements of the *Journal* were published several times leading up to and after our trial that November.

My fiancée Sarah, in her letter of September 21, quoted from above, wrote about what had happened to that point in time and what might be happening. She reported that several individuals from the Catholic Left, including Father Paul Mayer, later to become one of my best friends, had spent time in Rochester helping to get the support work organized and had plans to continue that. An office and phone was being set up for the bail fund. "As of Sunday, $325 had been contributed. The attempt to bail others out of the county lockup is quite sincere and money is needed for that." As of early 1971, an article in another special issue of the *Journal* reported that $9,000 had been raised, and twenty-five people had been bailed out.

A festival of some kind was in the works for October 17–18. A support statement had been written to be circulated in Rochester. It suggested that other communities plan "rallies, support statements or whatever."

Speaking engagements and media interviews were set up for us around town. I remember speaking before about 150 people in the basement of a local church and feeling support and concern for us, as well as uncertainty from some about the tactics we had used. I also remember speaking on the local public television station and getting positive feedback afterward.

An article in my files of unknown authorship but unquestionable authenticity wrote about the impact on Rochester and what happened in response to our action:

> The impact of the Flower City Conspiracy goes well beyond the offices of repression and injustice, for members of a variety of community and religious groups are facing up more seriously to the crises of our times and organizing for action. The Central Presbyterian Church provided space for three weeks of public meetings, workshops, meals, a day care center, press conferences, and other organizing around the action and trial of the Flower City Conspiracy. The *Journal* put out special supplements. A Bail Fund was established. The executive committee of the Monroe County Liberal Party unanimously commended the eight men and women "in their efforts to save lives that would be lost through the involuntary servitude forced on them by the Selective Service System." Metro-Act, a community group, said "History may show these eight young Americans as America's present-day Boston tea-party patriots." The Rochester Association of Catholic Laymen said they were "grateful for the courage of this group in risking personal jeopardy to dramatize the failure of the community to speak out against the dehumanizing aspects of our society. We pledge ourselves to the task of eliminating the injustices to which their actions speak."

During the trial there were workshops and evening events at the Central Presbyterian Church, which was so very conveniently located across the street from the courthouse. The church's governing body, the "Session," had put out a statement explaining their approval of our extensive use of their church:

> Our Session (ruling board) has approved the use of our building by the Friends of the Flower City Conspiracy because we believe that the Christian Church must be concerned with dissenting voices which the society at large may not want to hear. We have taken this action in spite of the fact that no Elder of our church has expressed approval of the actions which took place at the Federal Building on the morning of September 6.
>
> Still, since we believe that the spirit of Jesus Christ is alive and at work in the world we do not doubt that His spirit can work when men of good conscience differ honestly with one another and express their differences in an atmosphere of mutual consideration and understanding. We hope that this will be the nature of the process in these days that you will be our guests.

And it was.

There were workshops on new family lifestyles, prisons, poetry, nonviolence, imperialism, and more. Every night brought "the joy of bread together with other nourishing food prepared by many people. Some gave many hours to buy and prepare the food. Almost everyone helped—serving the food or washing dishes or scrubbing the floors."[9]

There was "continuous child care" and "exciting moments when wise (and sometimes famous) men and women shared their perspectives with us. David Dellinger, William Kunstler, Barbara Deming, Marj Swan, Douglas Dowd, Bishop Daniel Corrigan of Rochester, and Bishop Antulio Parrilla-Bonnilla of Puerto Rico."[10] The evening that Kunstler spoke there was a threat made on his life, and people had to check their coats, hand bags, and packages in a room separate from where he was speaking. After he spoke, a participant in a draft board raid in June in Providence, Rhode Island, David Chawes, publicly surfaced from underground; he was not arrested. According to an account in a local newspaper, the Rochester *Democrat and Chronicle*, he said, "I feel I could not have picked a better time to surface." Bishop Corrigan read a sermon written by the Berrigan brothers, apparently smuggled out of Danbury prison, where they were serving time together for the Baltimore 4 action (Phil) and the Catonsville 9 action (Phil and Dan).

Trial of the Catonsville Nine, a play authored by Dan Berrigan, was performed by the Colgate Rochester Players, November 13–15, right before the first day of the trial, November 16. And forty students at St. John Fisher College fasted for the first week of the trial.

Trial Planning and Strategy

Sometime after our arraignment the group was able to meet with a local lawyer, Herman Walz, to begin planning our defense strategy. Suzi and DeCourcy were able to take part in those meetings, though I don't remember exactly how or where.

We knew we were facing thirty-eight years in prison. We fully expected that we would be convicted and end up with five- to ten-year sentences. After all, we had been caught in the building with all kinds of evidence—like suitcases full of stolen FBI files—and we had disrupted the U.S. Attorney's office. We were under no illusions that we were going to be found not guilty by the jury.

Nobody, including Herm, as we ended up calling him, thought we should try to somehow make a technical legal case. The best approach, we all agreed, with little if any debate, was to do our best to focus the trial on the reasons for the action, on the issue of "criminal intent" (or the lack thereof). If we could get through to the jury, even one or two of them, on the issues, particularly the issue of the war, maybe we could get a hung jury. Nobody expected an acquittal. And, in any case, what we were all about as individual human beings and as a group was to be outspoken and forthright about injustice and evil.

This led to an agreement that we would all defend ourselves, with one exception. We liked Herm; he was not like too many lawyers who can be egotistical and arrogant. We felt a sense of connection with him. And we thought it would be helpful to have him as, in essence, our on-the-spot advisor as the trial took place. So Joe Gilchrist ended up agreeing to have a lawyer.

My eyes fill with tears as I think about what happened in that Rochester courtroom between November 16 and December 3. Without question, it was one of the high points of my life.

CHAPTER FIVE

Changing Hearts and Minds in the Courtroom

> We go into this courtroom with mixed feelings. On the one hand,
> we hope that this public trial and the events occurring around it
> will lead to more Americans committing themselves to lives of
> serious, sustained, unarmed struggle against War, Racism and all
> forms of violence so evident in this society. On the other hand we
> must admit that we go into this courtroom somewhat skeptical
> about the possibilities of the real issues being dealt with during
> the trial. We hope that we are proven wrong in this belief, a belief
> that has developed due to the courtroom experience of other peace
> activists.
> —Flower City Conspiracy statement on the first day of the trial

Our trial began on November 16, 1970. Here's how the first day was
described in the November 17 issue of the local daily mass circulation
newspaper in Rochester, the *Democrat and Chronicle*:

> It could have been an informal gathering of eight young people
> sitting around two tables pushed together.
>
> They could have been in a college dormitory or a coffee shop,
> talking about the war, the draft, the poor.
>
> But it was the U.S. District Court room on the third floor of
> the Federal Building and the four men and four women were on
> trial yesterday, charged with ransacking draft files in three offices
> in the same building over the Labor Day weekend.
>
> The defendants appeared confident, their speeches seemed
> articulate and well-prepared. Their actions weren't disruptive...

The jurors [picked the day before] come from a cross section of occupations. All of them indicated they feel that the war in Vietnam is legal and moral. Ten of them said they believe in the Biblical commandment, "Thou shall not kill," and they all felt the drafting of men into the army was just.

The statement we had read the day before, as we went into the federal building, concluded in this way:

The fact is that it is we who are on trial today. We feel that if this were a court of justice, all charges against us would be dropped and the U.S. Government would be on trial for its destruction of millions of lives in Vietnam, Cambodia, Laos and Latin America; for its murders at Jackson State and Kent State; for its repression of the Black Panther Party; and for its ignoring or silencing the cries of the hungry and homeless in this country and in the world.

The trial turned out to be nothing less than a revelation. To our surprise, we were able to say almost all that we wished to, for several reasons: our decision to go the self-defense route; the extensive press coverage before trial and the community support we had built; and the resultant leniency of our judge, Harold Burke. The transcript of the trial reads like a group biography, with almost all of the major motivating forces in our short lives up to that point being present.

I have gone through that transcript and selected those areas that give the clearest account of our "intent" upon entering that federal building. Intent was a key issue throughout the trial. As is usual in cases of this kind, the prosecution insisted that the issue was the tearing up of pieces of paper, the breaking into desks, the attempted removal of files, the violation of the law. But as I stated at one point during a cross-examination of Joe Gilchrist by the assistant U.S. attorney prosecuting the case, Mike Wolford: "The issue is not who did what and where. The issue is human life and whether or not we are going to change ours in order to save our brothers and sisters who are dying under American bombs."

In another instance, DeCourcy Squire stated our case even more simply and movingly. She was questioning Richard Pfuntner, one of the policemen who entered the federal building to arrest us. DeCourcy's line of questioning went as follows:

DeCourcy: At the time that you entered did you notice the sign that said it [the federal building] was closed for the holidays?

Lt. Pfuntner: Yes, ma'am.

DeCourcy: Despite the fact that the building was closed for the holidays and that it was under the exclusive jurisdiction of the United States, did you feel it was your duty to enter this building because you felt a crime was being committed here?

Lt. Pfuntner: Yes, ma'am.

DeCourcy: So did I. That is why I entered the building.

Herm Walz: What did you say?

DeCourcy: Yes, that is why I entered the building too.

✳

Broadly speaking, we focused on three main categories throughout the trial: the war, FBI repression, and our political/philosophical/religious motivations for acting.

The War

Dan Berrigan

Dan Berrigan was brought to Rochester from Danbury Federal Correctional Institution, where he was serving time for the Catonsville 9 draft board raid. He had been subpoenaed by Joe Gilchrist, who had been advised by Dan at Cornell University in Ithaca, New York, when he was a student. Herm Walz, as Joe's lawyer, questioned Dan.

Herm Walz: As to what you told Joe concerning the four conditions which would make up a just war, would you tell me again, and a little more slowly and in greater detail, what those four conditions are?

Dan Berrigan: That there be a strict limitation of violence on the part of both sides in any given war, which is to say, that there be an agreement upon the protection of civilian life and an agreement upon weapons which are allowable and those which must be outlawed.

Herm Walz: Did you discuss that particular requirement with him in terms of the current situation?

Dan Berrigan: Yes, sir.

Herm Walz: What did you tell him?

Dan Berrigan: I suggested on the basis of personal experience in North Vietnam during the air war that this requirement was being brutally disregarded and violated by the United States because I have seen the type of weaponry which was aimed only at civilians and which had no effect and no possible meaning for the destruction of buildings or bridges or railroads or anything else. I told him, moreover, that I had seen the parts of bodies of civilians who had been struck by such weapons and whose bodies were preserved in alcohol. We called it "anti-personnel weaponry," I recall. It violates as clearly as one could think of this first requirement about justice in wartime.

Herm Walz: I wonder if you discussed with Joe about your experiences in Vietnam during the bombing raid which took place while you were there?

Dan Berrigan: Yes, I did.

Herm Walz: Can you remember anything of what you discussed with him, especially about the children? Did you mention to him that there were children involved in that?

Dan Berrigan: Yes.

Herm Walz: What were some of the things you told about that?

Dan Berrigan: I think I remember trying to convey especially the very weird feeling of being an American under your own bombs. Having come there on a mission of mercy on behalf of Americans, I expressed to him the ineradicable impression I had of innocents under fire, children in bomb shelters, children who had died in the air raids, the children's bodies which I had seen as a result of anti-personnel weaponry and the fact that from then on, the war came down to a very simple issue with me that I tried to share with him. That is to say, nothing in the world less than a human life is worth a human life, and since property all over the world is less than human life, we must all over the world defend human life, even at the price of property.

Herm Walz: Did you tell him about being with children at that time?

Dan Berrigan: I think I described to him the beauty and the calm of the children and the fact that one was feeding the other and that they seemed quite used to bombs—God help us.

Barbara Deming

The following is an exchange between Suzi Williams and Barbara Deming, a middle-aged woman who had been active in the civil rights, anti-war, and women's movements for many years, about Barbara's trip to Vietnam. In this testimony, she is speaking about conditions in South Vietnam in 1966.

Suzi Williams: Did you see any evidence of inflation or any other type of a bad economic situation?

Barbara Deming: Yes. Our own direct experience of it was limited since we didn't do much spending while we were there, but everyone we talked to spoke of the terrible state of the economy, that the American presence was absolutely destroying not only their people, their land, their culture, but gravely their economy. For instance, Vietnam used to be a country that exported rice and now it has to import it. That is just one example.

Suzi Williams: Did you see, along this line, evidences of poverty among the Vietnamese there?

Barbara Deming: It was very striking in Saigon that there were a certain number of very well-off people who were profiting from this war and then just in every direction you looked there were beggars and derelicts, children with hardly enough to wear, begging or crouching in the street. People were in obvious misery.

Suzi Williams: Did you see any children or old people or any other types of civilians who had wounds of any sort from weaponry used during the war?

Barbara Deming: Yes, I saw much more of that in my trip to North Vietnam where I visited hospitals. Some of the people in the hospitals would be people brought up from the south for treatment. It was there, for example, rather than the south, where napalm is used so much, and I saw two napalm victims and learned things I had never known about napalm. For example, when napalm falls on you, it literally melts your limbs together, so one of the people I saw there being treated, his arms had just been melted to his side. They had been able by an operation to separate his arms, but his fingers had melted together. They were beginning to separate his fingers. He could barely hold a pencil.

One thing I never realized about napalm is even if you survive it, and even if they can help you in those ways, there are terrible scars from it. Any time there is the slightest motion of air in the room, these scars will itch unbearably. I also saw a man who had been hurt by the chemical spraying that they do so much of, and which our government says, "It is just to take leaves off trees so the airmen can see what is going on." But this man was a doctor and he had been treating for months many people who had been gravely harmed by this spraying. Finally he had been hurt by it himself and brought north for treatment. He had been healed a lot, but he was still almost blind. His digestive system was completely disordered and it would be for the rest of his life.

Suzi Williams: Did you talk to any people there who had been victims of relocation because of the war?

Barbara Deming: I guess the people I talked to had been relocated into jails, a good number of them, but I'm not sure that any of them were among the thousands and thousands who had been moved from their homes. They did tell us, very definitely, that among the Buddhist people, where it's terribly important for you to live on the spot where your ancestors have lived, that merely the act of removing so many people from their homes was like a kind of death to these people. In a way, that would not be too bad on Americans who are quite used to moving their homes.

Suzi Williams: Did you see any schools after they had been bombed?

Barbara Deming: Yes, everywhere we went among the buildings bombed were schools, hospitals, Catholic churches. It was on Christmas day that I stood in a bombed Catholic church, Buddhist pagodas, and workers' homes. In fact, on the way to and from the larger towns we visited there would be simple little villages where once they had thatched roofs where now the whole village would be destroyed. We visited one, a Catholic village that had been utterly destroyed and now had been rebuilt, but every time a house had been bombed—clearly a nonmilitary objective—just a war of terror.

Tony Avirgan

Tony Avirgan was a draft resistance organizer who, in his own words, was "working with the Philadelphia Resistance in organizing opposition to the war." Two months prior to his testimony at our trial, he had spent a month in Indochina. Below are questions I asked him about that trip.

Ted Glick: Were there any unique American weapons that were in evidence when you were there?

Tony Avirgan: We saw quite a few examples of all sorts of anti-personnel weapons, but particularly when we were at a farm in Wa Bin Province, which was a province that was bombed heavily this last weekend. We came to a building on the farm where there was the casing of a very large bomb hanging on a chain and the woman there explained to us that this had formerly been a delay bomb. When American bombs dropped on the farm, most of them would go off on impact, but quite a few were timed to go off an hour or two hours later. They would bury themselves in the mud or rubble that other bombs caused. When people came back out of the shelters to clear away the rubble, these bombs would go off, injuring the people, and therefore it was necessary to have someone stay outside during the air raids and watch where these bombs dropped, and mark on the chart, so they could be disarmed. This one had been disarmed. The guts had been taken out and they used it for a bell to call people to work.

Ted Glick: Did you give any gifts to the people in North Vietnam?

Tony Avirgan: Yes, we brought several things from the United States to give to them. The main gift that we gave them was a large stack of records that had been taken from Selective Service offices in the United States.

Ted Glick: What was their reaction to this?

Tony Avirgan: They were quite moved by it. They told us that it was one of the most precious things they had received, and they would treat it as something that was given to them of real honor. They were emotionally moved that there were Americans who would take such risks, that there were Americans who would disrupt their own lives and take great chances in the United States for the people in Vietnam. Some of the people in the room were moved to tears.

Ted Glick: You said you also visited South Vietnam, is that right?

Tony Avirgan: That's right.

Ted Glick: Where were you mainly, what areas of South Vietnam did you visit?

Tony Avirgan: We spent most of our time in South Vietnam in Saigon.

Ted Glick: What were conditions like in Saigon?

Tony Avirgan: The parts of Saigon that we saw at first were conditions people have probably seen pictures of here, with beggars all over the streets, prostitutes, several prostitutes on every block, bars, honky-tonk night clubs and places like that. On our last night in Saigon the students that were with us asked us if we really had seen Saigon and we said, "yes," and they said, "come with us and we will show you the real Saigon."

They took us to an area just two blocks away from all the bright lights on the streets that Americans usually go on. We came to another entire city that was still within Saigon, but looked like something that I have never imagined would be possible. The only thing that I have ever seen that was close were pictures of Calcutta. There were thousands and thousands of people as far as we could see, as far as we could walk in an entire night, living in the streets, living in mud with no homes. Entire families were laying there, and if they were lucky, they had a grass mat or a little straw mat, and if they weren't so lucky, they just had newspaper to lay on, but most people had nothing. They lived in that way. There was a stench that was overwhelming in the entire area. There were dead rats all over the place. It was something that I will never be able to forget and something that I never imagined would have been possible.

Ted Glick: Did you talk to any Vietnamese about why Saigon was in such a condition?

Tony Avirgan: Yes. We spoke to quite a few of the people. We spent a whole evening walking around speaking to people and at first when we approached they would jump up and be quite hostile. Then the students that we were with explained that we were Americans who were interested in peace. The people were quite interested in speaking to us. They explained that they were refugees from the countryside and that the American planes had been coming with more and more frequency and dropping bombs and defoliants in all of the countryside. They told us that last year at this time 70% of the people in South Vietnam lived in the countryside and 30% lived in the cities, but now, because of the defoliation and bombing, that had gone to 50–50 in just one year. Millions and millions of people had swarmed into Saigon to escape the bombing and defoliation and a few other large cities as well. When they got to Saigon, there were no jobs. There was no industry, and the only jobs that were available were working in some way for the Americans. They were unwilling to do this so that they were there to starve. They got their food by going through garbage cans or going to the market place after it closed and picking up scraps, but basically, they were starving. They explained, and we saw, that the situation was one of real emergency. Quite literally people were dying every day, not only from the bombing in the countryside but right there from starvation and disease in the cities.

We noted when we left to go to Japan that if you had been in Saigon you couldn't enter Japan unless you had been inoculated against black plague because that was a very serious problem in Saigon. We felt it was a much more urgent situation than people realized in the United States. Thousands of people are dying every day.

Ted Glick: One final question. From your conversation with various different groups of Vietnamese in South Vietnam, were you told by any of these groups how the Thieu-Ky government was maintained in power?

Tony Avirgan: Yes. Everyone that we spoke to explained that the Thieu-Ky government was made up of a very tiny clique of millionaires and military people and that the only way that they were able to maintain power was through the presence of the United States military and United States weapons, and that if these were removed, other people would be able to form their own government in a very short period of time. But the only way that Thieu-Ky could maintain any power at all was through the United States military presence there.

FBI Repression

During the trial we were able to question FBI agents on the stand, but we had a very hard time getting them to say anything about what the FBI did. Here are examples of the kind of evasive nonresponses we got from all of them.

FBI Agent Maurice Anthony

Suzi Williams: How come you have to have your desks locked?

FBI Agent Maurice Anthony: A security measure.

Suzi Williams: What do you do that you requires that your desk be so secure?

FBI Agent Maurice Anthony: General business.

Suzi Williams: Well, that is pretty vague.

FBI Agent Maurice Anthony: So is the question.

Suzi Williams: Give me an example, then, please, of things that you do that require these desks to be so secure that you could no longer use them now that they can't be locked.

FBI Agent Maurice Anthony: Departmental Order 3464 does not allow me to comment on investigative procedures.

The Court: What do you have in the desk? Everything can't be confidential.

FBI Agent Maurice Anthony: I would lock up a pencil if I had a lock to secure my desk.

The Court: Is that why you secure a desk, to secure the pencils from being stolen?

A: We secure the desks to prevent entry by any unauthorized person.

The Court: You must have something in the desk that you want to keep locked. I'm sure it isn't pencils.

FBI Agent Maurice Anthony: My desk contains miscellaneous supplies, papers, black papers, forms, things you usually conduct my work with.

Suzi Williams: You know you can keep papers and forms as well as pencils in an unlocked desk. We didn't take any pencils or blank forms that I remember.

FBI Agent Maurice Anthony: I choose to lock my desk no matter what it contains.

Suzi Williams: Then this is just a matter of personal preference. It isn't being something that you have to do, so you really could use those desks?

FBI Agent Maurice Anthony: Not in the condition that they are, no.

Suzi Williams: Why not? You really haven't told me.

FBI Agent Maurice Anthony: Because I choose to lock my desk.

Suzi Williams: Do you keep guns in your desks?

FBI Agent Maurice Anthony: I do not.

Suzi Williams: Do you know if any of the other agents do or not?

FBI Agent Maurice Anthony: It is possible. I don't know.

Suzi Williams: They do?

FBI Agent Maurice Anthony: (No response)

Suzi Williams: Do they keep handcuffs in desks?

FBI Agent Maurice Anthony: It is possible.

Suzi Williams: Do they keep manuals in their desks, such as manuals on how to develop a racial informer?

FBI Agent Maurice Anthony: I do not know.

DeCourcy Squire: When was the last time you were in your office before the Sunday of September 6?

FBI Agent Maurice Anthony: The Friday before.

DeCourcy Squire: And this time everything was in the files, papers and manuals were on the shelves, and other things were in the drawers?

FBI Agent Maurice Anthony: It was normal operations. I didn't make specific notations.

DeCourcy Squire: Your electronic eavesdropping equipment was still in place?

FBI Agent Maurice Anthony: I have no electronic eavesdropping equipment.

DeCourcy Squire: The FBI office.

FBI Agent Maurice Anthony: I do not know about the office, about electronic eavesdropping equipment.

DeCourcy Squire: Maybe I don't remember, but you work here in Rochester in the office in this building?

FBI Agent Maurice Anthony: Yes, I do.

DeCourcy Squire: That is what I thought. Your listed informers were still in the files where they are usually kept?

FBI Agent Maurice Anthony: I cannot comment on any investigative procedures.

FBI Agent Paul Joensen

> Suzi Williams: How long have you worked for the FBI?
>
> FBI Agent Paul Joensen: Nineteen years.
>
> Suzi Williams: Are you aware of the sections of the Constitution which guarantee freedom of association and freedom from illegal search and seizure and the right to property?
>
> FBI Agent Paul Joensen: I am aware of these provisions.
>
> Suzi Williams: You don't feel that wiretapping and taking down people's license plate numbers when they attend a meeting where there is a controversial speaker violate those rights?
>
> FBI Agent Paul Joensen: I have no knowledge of taking down any license plates, so I can't comment on that. I also have no knowledge concerning the use of illegal wiretaps.
>
> Suzi Williams: You ought to find out what goes on in your own office, really.

Our Motivations for Acting

In the testimony excerpts below, the various political, philosophical, and religious motives behind our actions are examined, beginning again with Dan Berrigan's testimony in relation to Joe Gilchrist.

Dan Berrigan

> Herm Walz: Will you tell me the way in which you advised Joe as to his duties regarding a Christian response in the light of the things that you did?
>
> Dan Berrigan: In the case of Joe Gilchrist, my urging was that he ponder and meditate and read the New Testament if he so wished, because there I had discovered light for my own life, and that he remain a free man, a free agent from that time forward, understanding that human life was the first value in the world and that property was very secondary to it. Under such a teaching, I suggested he might find it implied by Christ's words that it was less heinous, less criminal to burn papers than children.
>
> Herm Walz: You mentioned the term, "free man." Did you discuss that with him in the context of the advice that you just told us about?
>
> Dan Berrigan: Yes, I did, and I thought that the first sign of a free man, as I suggested to him, was that he found himself unable to

live with the enslavement, with the deaths of others, and that he would have to continue seeking that sign in the world in his life.

Herm Walz: I'm sorry. I didn't understand what you said at the very end of your answer.

Dan Berrigan: I suggested to Joe that the first sign of a free man was a man's inability to live with the enslavement or death of others.

Herm Walz: Did Joe talk with you about a Christian citizen's obligation in the face of what his conscience told him was an immoral law?

Dan Berrigan: This naturally came up in the light of the war. I don't think it could have been avoided, and I recall vividly an exchange that we had, on just this point, that is to say, that there might conceivably be a just modern war. I would even go so far as to debate the possibility of it, but the evidence against that in the case of Vietnam was so overwhelming that a thinking person could not but take clear options in opposing it, and since he was presumably a thinking person, an adult person, the options would grow clearer every day.

Herm Walz: Were there other discussions besides simply Vietnam in relation to your counseling Joe regarding the Christian's obligation in the face of an immoral law?

Dan Berrigan: Yes, there was, because the issue of law here in a sense was larger than the issue of the war but certainly included it. That led us to a discussion of the general attitude, the attitude of a man in any culture, any civilization, any country, to the law of the land, and to the conflicts that might arise, and certainly in times of war has always arisen, between conscience and the law, as would affect the young person, especially, through the draft. We pondered and discussed that point. You see, beginning with Christ himself, and certainly throughout the history of the West, there have been in every time, every civilization, men who have had to say "No" to civil law in the name of the law of God. I dared to share with him my belief that such a time had arisen for us, and not by way of pushing his conscience into a corner but by way of helping enlighten it.

Herm Walz: Concerning the question as to the morality of the Selective Service law, would you tell us what you discussed with him?

Dan Berrigan: I told him as nearly as I can recall now that I thought that the question of citizenship came to rest upon the individual example in this form: Could one be a good citizen and still obey the draft law? I suggested that that was a question that he must wrestle with, night and day. Since he was at least as well read as I, with the details, statistics on bombings, civilian deaths, the soldier deaths, the defoliation attendant upon the war, I could in good conscience leave the details of his decision to him, which I believe was my obligation. So in that case, I was merely trying to suggest to him that he would stand or fall as a human being and as a citizen today and for the future exactly in proportion as he faced the draft question.

Herm Walz: Did Joe question you about a Christian's responsibility for the acts of his government?

Dan Berrigan: Yes, sir.

Herm Walz: And will you tell us what you told Joe about that kind of responsibility?

Dan Berrigan: I suggested to him that a government of the people and by the people and for the people could not act against the people and still retain its legitimacy; that this was the basis of Christian-Social Theory of being a citizen in the State and "rendering to Caesar what was due him." I suggested that he investigate very seriously that point in our history in which government for, of and by the people had turned against the people and no longer was listening, so that a war could be waged in our name against our consciences. At that point what is the good man to do who is something more than a citizen?

Herm Walz: Did Joe ask you about a Christian's response to the principles laid down at Nuremberg concerning personal responsibility.

Dan Berrigan: Yes, sir.

Herm Walz: Would you tell us what you told Joe about that?

Dan Berrigan: Very briefly, I suggested that he read the evidence himself, that is, the evidence introduced by American jurists at Nuremberg. We agreed that after we had studied these initiatives together, it was overwhelming, too, that the United States had taken a very serious, a very responsible part in formulating those principles which resulted in the imprisonment and execution of German war leaders. We were also forced to conclude that this American zeal for conscience and international law was coming home to roost, and since Vietnam, we found our word returning on the winds against us, that is to say, we would now, before the world, be the defendants in cases of atrocities, violation of the lands, destruction of culture, actions which many sober jurists have not hesitated to call "genocide."

Herm Walz: Did he discuss with you instances which he saw as being government conduct of doubtful legality?

Dan Berrigan: Yes, sir.

Herm Walz: And what were those instances which you discussed?

Dan Berrigan: Well, they were instances which are open to anybody who reads American history from the first days, the Boston Tea Party, the Abolitionists of the 19th Century, the resisters of any war in which America has fought, especially the Mexican war, and, in general, those wars that got extremely cruel and extremely dubious towards the end of the last century.

Herm Walz: Did you discuss with him the difference between violence against the person and violence against paper?

Dan Berrigan: Yes, sir.

Herm Walz : What did you tell him about that distinction?

Dan Berrigan: I suggested that property was meant to be a tool of human life rather than replacing it and that it would be a terrible moment for us as individuals or for family people or for believers or for anyone if suddenly we found the tool was turning on us, was turning lethal, and that such property should exist as would serve human life. I remember asking him if he thought it would have been legitimate in Germany in the Thirties to burn down a German concentration camp.

Ted Glick: Could you talk about the things you talked about with Joe in regard to the responsibilities of the American citizen who believes in the beliefs embodied in the Declaration of Independence, such as life, liberty and the pursuit of happiness?

Dan Berrigan: I will try to summarize it as well as I can. It seemed to me at the time we were both struck by the idea that our own documents, like the Constitution and the Declaration of Independence, were extraordinarily important for us and they should be read and pondered, because they contained the language of people who were really laying their lives out for change, for human betterment. They expressed an ideal that we have never totally abandoned, and even though we have been very slow and unwilling to grant life, liberty and the pursuit of happiness to all of our people, we still have hopes. We still have good people. We still have our own lives to deal with, and that it would be very good for a young American today to read those documents, think them through in the light of what the country and himself were enduring and inflicting.

Ted Glick: Did you explain to Joe about your feelings as to your responsibilities as an American citizen as it related to your action at Catonsville?

Dan Berrigan: Yes.

Ted Glick: What did you say to Joe?

Dan Berrigan: Men have gone to jail, men have endured confiscation of property, exile, and even death itself, because they would not agree that America was best served if her property were put above the welfare of people.

Joe Gilchrist

Ted Glick: I show you Defendants' Exhibit 1, and this is St. Mark, Chapter 11, verses 15 through 17, where it says: "And they came to Jerusalem." Would you read this passage?

Joe Gilchrist: Verses 15 through 17?

Ted Glick: Right. Do you think that this passage had anything to do with your consideration that your action was a Christian one?

Joe Gilchrist : I believe the passage is quite explicit in pointing out by the man Christ in Biblical times that property was second to human life and human values, yes.

Ted Glick: Would you read this to the jury, please?

Joe Gilchrist: All right. (Reading): "And they came to Jerusalem, and Jesus went into the temple, and began to cast out them that sold and bought in the temple, and overthrew the tables of the money changers and the seats of them that sold doves; And would not suffer that any man should carry any vessel through the temple. And he taught, saying unto them, 'Is it not written, My house shall be called of all nations the house of prayer? But ye have made it a den of thieves.'"

Ted Glick: In your study throughout high school and throughout college, did you consider that the United States was a Christian nation?

Joe Gilchrist: Oh yes, most certainly.

Ted Glick: Did you consider that the Declaration of Independence had embodied in it Christian principles?

Joe Gilchrist: Yes.

Ted Glick: Would you read that part of it that led you to believe in the United States being a Christian nation?

Joe Gilchrist: I would say it wasn't just parts of it, although some parts are more important than others, but the whole document.

Ted Glick: Would you read whatever it is, then, that you think important?

Joe Gilchrist: "When in the course of human events, it becomes necessary for one people to dissolve the political bonds which have connected them with another, and to assume among the powers of the earth, the separate and equal station to which the Laws of Nature and of Nature's God entitled them, a decent respect to the opinions of mankind requires that they should declare the causes which impel them to the separation.

"We hold these truths to be self-evident, that all men are created equal, that they are endowed by their Creator with certain unalienable rights, that among these are life, liberty and the pursuit of happiness. That to secure these rights, governments are instituted among men, deriving their just powers from the consent of the governed. That whenever any form of government becomes destructive of these ends, it is the right of the people to alter or abolish it and to institute a new government, laying its foundation on such principles and organizing its powers in such form as to them shall seem most likely to effect their safety and happiness.

"Prudence, indeed, will dictate that governments long established should not be changed for light and transient causes; and accordingly all experience hath shown, that mankind are more

disposed to suffer, while evils are sufferable, than to right themselves by abolishing the forms to which they are accustomed. But
when a long train of abuses and usurpations pursuing invariably
the same object, evinces a design to reduce them under absolute
Despotism, it is their right, it is their duty to throw off such government, and to provide new guards for their future security. Such
has been the patient sufferance of these colonies; and such is now
the necessity which constrains them to alter their former systems
of government. The history of the present King of Great Britain is
a history of repeated injuries and usurpations, all having in direct
object the establishment of an absolute tyranny over these states."
Ted Glick: Do you consider what you just read as at all applicable
to today's situation in this country?
Joe Gilchrist: Yes, I do. I'm hopeful, however, that the government
is not going to be so unresponsive to the crying need for change,
not only in foreign but in domestic policy, that it would neces-
sitate actions quite so bold as those delineated in the Declaration
of Independence. I would rather like to think that society will be
responsive enough to the needs of life and death of people that
through nonviolent action of protest, civil disobedience, traditional forms of protest, marching, picketing and so on, that society
might be able to change. I still have that hope. You know, it fades
as we go on. I had that hope two years ago, and things have only
gotten worse since my first act of civil disobedience.
Ted Glick: Going back to this passage from the Bible, St. Mark,
Chapter 11, verses 15 through 17, do you now consider the activities
of your government to be Christian activities in regard to their
drafting of men to fight a war in Vietnam?
Joe Gilchrist: No, I do not.
Ted Glick: Would you therefore feel some kinship to the action of
Jesus in regards to your action of destroying draft files?
Joe Gilchrist: That is a pretty hard question. I think to take it a
little further, it is interesting to note that when Christ was brought
before Pilate, before his Crucifixion, the charges he was facing
were that he had sworn to tear down the Temple with his bare
hands, brick by brick, in three days. There were laws protecting
this property, and eventually that is what they got him for... There

were laws also protecting the money-changers in the Temple. Christ disregarded those laws and found it more important to get them out of the Temple and preserve the Temple as a house of prayer. Perhaps in the same vein, then, what I am interested in or what I am trying to do is to bring America back to those principles of Americanism that we were founded upon, life, liberty and the pursuit of happiness, and to try to help lead America away from the death machine that the military-industrial complex, including the Selective Service System, has become. Part of this, I think, will necessarily involve some individuals putting themselves in jeopardy and doing such acts as overturning the tables of the money changers or ripping up draft files. These are serious times and serious questions, and we can't approach them lightly and can't use old answers.

Joe Daoust

Frank Callahan: Have we ever discussed in respect to property destruction and in terms of civil disobedience the act that Father Berrigan was the first to commit, the act of the destruction of draft files?[1]

Joe Daoust: Yes. After it happened, partly because he is Jesuit and that [Saint Joseph's] is a Jesuit college, it was a rather common topic around campus. As I recall, we talked about it then in terms of a symbolic act, of people who felt a compulsion to act as Dan Berrigan did and have to choose a method that is both nonviolent and forceful. Since they have a dream that has to come true, they have to be forceful. Since that dream includes people, they have to be nonviolent, and I can remember contrasting that with other actions that were going on, with people supposedly involved in violent revolution or with people who merely called themselves pacifists and thereafter withdrew from trying to change society. We contrasted those two things: the person who wants revolution and will go to any means to get it, and the person who wants nonviolence and is willing to give up on his quest to change society in order to avoid confrontation. We talked specifically about the morality of the destruction of property, of Selective Service files.

Some of the examples we cited, for instance, were the Czechoslovakian invasion, when the Czechoslovakians broke the laws that were imposed upon them because they were not serving them. The plot to kill Hitler—I remember bringing that up with you—people who not only broke laws but resorted to violence in order to avert a very great evil; the French Revolution and the American Revolution, when we overthrew a whole system of laws because they were no longer serving adequately the needs of the people they were meant to serve. In this context, as I recall, the discussion came around to why not only a priest or someone who is involved in organized religion but really anybody who calls himself Christian may at times have to break laws or destroy property in order to do the things that both law and property are meant to serve in the first place.

We talked in terms of your own responsibility, people who were beginning to feel your way, about how as long as this was merely a worry in the back of our minds, or we just said we were upset by the fact that it was going on, we were worse than the people who didn't even let themselves be worried about it. I can remember at that time there was a story that broke which we talked about, about a practice going on in Vietnam whereby some of the Army people were cutting off the ears of dead Oriental human beings and stringing them up outside of their tents in order to win a battalion prize. We talked about the fact that the man who had organized this kind of contest had recently been appointed head of ROTC to train future officers at another college in the Philadelphia area. I remember talking about how we felt that this was not really morally as wrong as what we were doing, as long as we merely remained in the area of talk, because these people probably believed in what they were doing. The real crime was the fact that most of us could go on watching television, going out on dates, eating meals, piling up credits in college while people were being killed in our name, and we did not agree with that killing. But the real crime, as we talked about it that night, was our lack of responsibility since we didn't agree with what was going on and we were doing nothing about it.

I remember we had a Liturgy that night, the central theme of which was the Good Samaritan message, and we remarked on the facts in the Good Samaritan parable. It wasn't the robbers who beat up the Samaritan who got condemned. It was the Priest and the Levite who neglected him and simply passed him by. Christ quite often pitied people who out of passion or ignorance or rage or even just out of sheer evilness of their will chose to victimize other human beings, but that the people who he really couldn't stand were those who simply ignored what was going on when they saw victimization.

Cross examination of Suzi Williams by Prosecutor Mike Wolford

Mike Wolford: Miss Williams, I think you testified that your readings of Gandhi had a great deal of effect upon you, is that correct?

Suzi Williams: Yes, that it was possible to become involved in trying to change things without harming persons.

Mike Wolford: In particular, Gandhi's philosophy regarding civil disobedience, isn't that correct?

Suzi Williams: I picked that up more from Henry David Thoreau, the American writer. I read his essay in high school.

Mike Wolford: Now correct me if I am wrong, Miss Williams, but under, say, the classical theory, the traditional theory of civil disobedience, when a person violates a particular law, feeling that law unconstitutional or illegal, he expected to be punished for that, isn't that correct?

Suzi Williams: That is the classic civil disobedience theory, I don't adhere to it in that respect.

Mike Wolford: Well, for instance, Martin Luther King, did he adhere to this particular classical theory?

Suzi Williams: Yes, as far as I can tell, except I don't feel he was at all nonviolent when he was calling for cops to protect him.

Mike Wolford: Why don't you explain to us then where you differ from that particular theory of civil disobedience?

Suzi Williams: I guess I take after the Christian theory more than the Gandhian theory, in that I don't feel people have a right to judge each other. Therefore I'm not interested in the concept of punishment and judgement to begin with, and therefore I am not at all willing to take the consequences for breaking laws.

Mike Wolford: You don't feel people have the right to judge you, although you do feel you have a right to violate a particular law, isn't that correct?

Suzi Williams: Yes, so does anyone else.

Mike Wolford: So does anyone else have the right to violate laws but they shouldn't expect to be punished for that violation?

Suzi Williams: I would rather have people worry about whether or not they were violating people, and not whether or not they were violating laws. There are a lot of nasty things people do to each other that are perfectly legal.

Mike Wolford: Do you think people should worry more about people? Should they worry at all about property or things, or should they just disregard property and things as though they don't exist and they have no right to be protected?

Suzi Williams: I think people should worry a great deal less about property than what they do. I think a great many people in a country as ours have a great deal more than they need, although I would not want to take it away from them by force, but I would try to persuade them that they didn't need to go through life hauling a wheelbarrow.

Mike Wolford: You say they should worry less, but they should be somewhat worried about property, shouldn't they?

Suzi Williams: I suppose, but not. . .

Mike Wolford: Not obsessed with it?

Suzi Williams: I don't think they should hold property to be over people. I think they should be concerned about property where it serves human beings.

Mike Wolford: And when these conflicts occur, then property rights lose their right to exist, is that correct?

Suzi Williams: Yes, when the property is used as a tool for human destruction, I don't believe that property has a continued right to existence.

Mike Wolford: Who is to make that determination whether there is this conflict, or whether this particular piece of property doesn't have the right to exist?

Suzi Williams: We all have to decide for ourselves, I think.

Mike Wolford: Despite the fact that there are sanctions put on the destruction of this property and the fact that we have a representative government that has passed laws protecting these property rights?

Suzi Williams: The government doesn't represent me.

Mike Wolford: They don't represent your views, is that correct?

Suzi Williams: They don't represent my views or my situation. I feel a lot of them got into power because they had more money than the other people, or because they were ready to play ball with the various influential groups in this country such as the military and the industries.

Testimony of Frank Callahan (the Last Defense Witness)

That summer [1968] I went to Ecuador with the Institute of Latin American Studies at St. Joseph's. I worked there for about three months as a teacher at the Collegio Nacionale, Dayoto Arosomana Gomez. Ecuadorian schools have long names, and I taught there for about three months. I was teaching English. This was a prefabricated school with about four classrooms built over a swamp. The city of Guayaquil has a population of about 650,000 people. Well over half of them live in the swamp which surrounds the city, and the city began getting larger. People were drifting in from the countryside because they can't make a living there, and some came to the city to find work. Overnight they will throw up a house. That is exactly what it is, a few roads built through the swamp, this watery part, and it is a dirty, unhealthy place to live. It is not so inspiring to get up every morning and look up at the sky and see the vultures going overhead.

At any rate, I was teaching classes, three, four classes a day in English, and also a couple of sports classes, and the English classes were interesting. I would have about 125 to 150 students in a room which would be perhaps two or three times the size of the jury box, and only a half of the students would have books.

Most of their mothers were prostituting themselves to make a living for the family. These kids, when they weren't in school, would spend ten, twelve hours a day selling Chiclets or shining shoes, and I was teaching them English. They were dying and I was teaching them English and I didn't have the capacity to teach them anything else.

While we were down in Ecuador, the seven of us doing this kind of work got a chance to tour the Standard Fruit Company operation.

Ecuador is the largest exporter of bananas. Its economy is largely agricultural. If they didn't have the banana product the country would die.

At any rate, the Standard Fruit Company handles all the business for Ecuador, all the banana business. We went down there and looked at the operation one day when they were loading the banana boats. As it turns out, the highest paid laborers in the entire country of Ecuador are the guys who carry the bananas from the banana boats, up a ramp like that (indicating), very steeply slanted. They carry eighty pounds of bananas at a time. They work 18 hours a day, six days a week, and they make fifty dollars a month. They are the highest paid laborers in Ecuador at slave labor. And it was interesting to watch this.

It was also interesting to discover that the largest portion of the foreign aid that our government gives to Ecuador is military: that the foreign aid program in connection with Latin America wraps up with what is called the military-industrial complex. They weren't helping to change the conditions which kept these people so desperate for work and so desperate for means to stay alive that they would be willing to do that kind of slave labor for fifty bucks a month.

It was a frustrating three months, because there was absolutely nothing I could do down there to help. I tutored two or three people of about 25, who wanted to be bilingual secretaries so they could make more money. That was probably the only concrete accomplishment out of the whole summer.

We have so much potential that can be used to strengthen life. That 98.6 billion dollars that we are spending for defense could be swallowed up in one year in medical research alone, but we are not doing it and the Selective Service isn't the whole problem, just as Vietnam isn't the whole problem. They are symptoms of something much larger. If it hadn't been Vietnam, it would have been somewhere else, maybe Ecuador, where largely a strongly parallel situation exists. We have got to deal with these problems before they happen, and we can't afford to deal with them again with guns.

The Case Goes to the Jury

So ended our nearly nine days of testimony. All that remained was for us and the prosecutor to sum up, the judge to charge the jury, and the jury to decide.

In the summations, the key point continued to be the question of intent, of what our motivations were for acting. The prosecutor tried to define the issues in a narrowly legalistic way. We insisted that our intent was not to commit a crime but to save lives, not to vandalize but to speak out, not to avoid responsibility but to accept it.

The case went to the jury at 2:00 p.m., Tuesday, December 1. By dinnertime, a verdict had not been returned, rumors of a hung jury were floating in the air, and I remember working hard at not allowing my hopes and dreams to run too far afield. A hung jury in an open and shut case where not only Selective Service but, for the first time, the FBI and U.S. Attorney's offices were hit? Impossible. Yet our movement is rooted in faith in people and, despite the totally white, pro-war nature of our jury, we could not help but think, "Perhaps this time, a miracle."

It was not to be. At 9:00 p.m., we were called into the courtroom to receive the jury verdict. When asked for their decision the foreman, a welder felt by us to be the least sympathetic of the twelve, spoke the words "guilty with a recommendation of leniency" forty-eight times, six felonies apiece for each of the eight of us. Within minutes we were surrounded by federal marshals, soon to be whisked off to begin an imprisonment of, depending upon the individual, anywhere from nine to fourteen more months. But before the metal bars closed behind us, with several of the jurors and many of the spectators crying, this exchange occurred in the courtroom:

> The Court: I order that all defendants found guilty, that is, all of the defendants in this case, be immediately committed to custody. I fix sentence to be imposed a day after tomorrow, Thursday, December 3, at ten o'clock in the morning.
> Mr. Walz: Your honor, may the jury be polled?
> The Court: Poll the jury.

The Clerk: Ladies and gentlemen of the jury, if your verdict is as the Court has recorded it, kindly answer "yes" if your name is called (Whereupon, the jury was polled, and all jurors answered affirmatively that that was their verdict.)

The Court: The Marshal understands that all the defendants are to be taken into custody immediately?

Marshal King: Yes, Your Honor.

The Court: This jury is excused until December 3, at ten o'clock in the morning.

Defendant Glick: We wish you would come to the sentencing so you can hear what we say at sentencing, please. I would like that.

The Court: I don't understand what you said.

Glick: I am talking to the jury.

Defendant Nicholson: Also, I would like them to come to our sentencing.

Defendant Glick: We really wish you would.

Defendant Williams: And thanks for listening.

Defendant Nicholson: I hope it makes a difference in your lives.

"Hope it makes a difference in your lives." That was our real intent throughout the trial—to help to transform people with the information we presented and the passion and force we personified. As we learned later we were quite successful in that regard, as in the case of the jury, the main focus of our work.

Despite the fact that they had convicted us, they had done so only when, after being hung nine to three in favor of conviction, the judge's positive response to the question, "Can we recommend leniency?" unhung them. (I later won an appeal on this point after spending eleven months of an eighteen-month sentence behind bars. My conviction was overturned by an appeals court, because the judge had secretly conveyed a note with that positive response to the jury's question. There is not supposed to be any secret communication between judge and jury once deliberation begins. And the appeals court judge who wrote the decision overturning my conviction, Judge Irving Kaufman, wrote that this secret communication had a substantive impact in that it unlocked a hung jury.)

In a newspaper story in the *Democrat and Chronicle* on December 3, the jurors were quoted making these comments:

Charles White, a Xerox employee, reported that it was the note from Judge Burke that changed his vote to guilty. He said the note led him to believe that "the sentence would fall in balance with the crime. If we felt the sentence would be long," he said, "there would still be a hung jury."

The jury foreman, Joseph Palazzo, stated, "I hope the judge is lenient on them. I had to say 'with recommendation of leniency' 48 times, and I said it to get the message across. I hope none of them gets more than a year." He went on to say, "They were at the wrong place at the wrong time. There were better ways of making their point, but they're young and Quaker and have beliefs that are far different from anyone else you could imagine."

"What got me," he continued, "is the pictures they showed of bombed hospitals. If the U.S. goes out to bomb a hospital there must be military activity there because the U.S. just doesn't go around bombing hospitals."

The newspaper went on to say:

"Criminal intent was the hang-up," said Mrs. Donna E. Tricamo.... "The recommendation for leniency helped," she said, "because not one person on the jury wanted to send these kids to jail."

Another juror, Mrs. Susan L. Winegard . . . said several of the jurors hoped to find the defendants not guilty on at least one count. Mrs. Tricamo said several of the jurors kept raising the issue of the war in Vietnam which wasn't one of the issues that Judge Burke charged the jury to consider.

The nature of the war in Vietnam was a primary issue of the defense during the trial. Each of the jurors when selected said that he or she believed the war in Vietnam is moral and legal.

Mrs. Winegard said that, while the jurors thought the defendants were sincere in their beliefs, there was nothing they could do because the defendants did break the law. She said that once Judge Burke said the jury could recommend leniency, it decided to do so unanimously.

White said he thought even five years is an excessive sentence for the crime committed. He said he hoped the jury's recommendation would convince Judge Burke to give a light sentence.

Several jurors said they were tremendously affected by the trial and the defendants and had changed some of their views. "I have very mixed emotions about the war as a result of the trial," said Mrs. Tricamo. "I don't look at these kids as criminals—they must really believe in what they did. I think we all learned something from these kids," Mrs. Winegard said.

"I agree with what the kids said," said another juror, Mrs. Anna Proia, a Delco employee. . . . "I feel sick about them going to jail," she said.

White said that when he first heard about the invasion of the federal building, he thought of them as criminals and "hippie punks."

White said he came to realize during the trial that the defendants were "honest and their beliefs are fantastic whether you agree or disagree. My opinion of the war has changed," he said. "I have become more of an opponent."

Alessi, one of several jurors who were in tears when the verdict was read, said, "my life has been very changed."

Beginning what turned out to be ten more months in prison, these revelations were, to say the least, a very big deal. As it turned out, I would soon find that those lessons learned about how people can change, those things gained from the Rochester experience, were of major importance to me behind bars, were sustainers and rocks on which to stand in times of trouble and despair. Rochester had been and still is one of the most profound periods of my entire life. But I had a new experience, a new reality to cope with: prison.

CHAPTER SIX

Prison

> I was not raped in prison. I didn't get into any fights. I suffered no
> physical abuse at the hands of fellow inmates or prison guards. But
> I had to disguise my fear during my stay in county jail and for the
> first few months of my time in federal prison. Although it would
> not be accurate to describe this fear as terror, I experienced a form
> of largely unabated tension. I was wound up tight, while trying to
> look cool, unafraid, and impervious to the danger around me. I
> learned to always be aware of my surroundings and avoided being
> isolated in any section of a jail or prison. I was prepared to fight if
> I had no other choice.
> —Bruce Dancis, in *Resister*[1]

Bruce Dancis's words above describing his time in federal prison in
Ashland, Kentucky, are words I can echo. I met fellow draft resister
Dancis in Ashland right after I arrived there in December 1970, just a
day or two before he left at the end of his twenty months behind bars.
His description of that time in his book *Resister* is a very good read.

Bruce spent all of his prison time in Ashland, but I didn't. I spent
time in three federal prisons—Ashland, Danbury, Connecticut, and
Springfield, Missouri. I also spent over a month in the Rochester
(Monroe Country) jail after I was arrested and again after I was convicted,
as well as a week in the Harrisburg, Pennsylvania (Dauphin County) jail
after my arraignment in May 1971 as one of the Harrisburg 8 defendants.
And I had overnight stays in county jails in Bloomsburg, Pennsylvania,
Pittsburgh, Pennsylvania, Buffalo, New York, and Indianapolis, Indiana,
as I was transported by U.S. Marshals from place to place.

I will never forget one of my early experiences a few days after arriving at Ashland. I had been put into a dormitory, where I lived for several months before getting an individual room in another building. There were about fifty single beds on one side of the building and fifty on the other side, with bathrooms and a common room with a TV in between. Next to each bed was a three-foot by two-foot metal locker with a combination lock to store personal items.

After I moved in, I spoke to the guy next to me on one side. He asked why I was there, and I told him. He told me he was in for stealing a check from an envelope while he was working at a post office. He also told me, after I had explained the Rochester action and my opposition to the war in Vietnam, that he was a Vietnam veteran and that he had killed "seventy-three gooks" while there. He didn't say it in an aggressive, macho way. It was more like a combination of a matter-of-fact boast and a confession.

I don't remember that we talked much after that conversation, but there wasn't any hostility or tension between us either.

Another person with a bed near mine whom I did talk with often was Red, a Vietnam veteran and a young black man from inner city Detroit. He was in for drug dealing. He was very expressive and talkative, but not in an obnoxious way. He seemed impressed by the action I was in prison for, and he liked talking with me.

In a letter to my then wife Sarah a couple of months into my prison term, I told her about a long conversation I had had with Red. I explained that he was a vet from a poor section of Detroit

> who's had to struggle all his life. He talked about the conflict within him between his "animal" feelings—his violent impulses and his hurting of people—versus the desire to help people and the resulting conflict that seems to be raging within him. He talked a lot about "Nam," very explicit stuff, like shooting people's arms off. He talked about his liking people, about his hard times as a kid. He really opened up.

The vast majority of the people I met in all of the prisons I spent time in were from low-income and working-class backgrounds. A disproportionate number were black and brown, with the exception of Ashland, where most of the inmates were white when I was there. Many of the Ashland inmates were from Appalachia, and many were in prison for stealing a car or "borrowing" it for a joyride. For these transgressions, they were usually given a zip-six sentence, meaning that they could end up in prison for as long as six years, depending upon how well they adjusted—or came across as having adjusted.

Interactions with People of Color

The closeness to so many people of color was a new thing for me, and the experiences I had interacting with them were important to my personal development as a person with an anti-racist consciousness.

On my way from the Rochester county jail to Ashland, I spent an overnight in the county jail in Buffalo, New York. While there I met a man, Sam Washington, who had an amazing story. He was in his thirties and had spent somewhere in the neighborhood of fifteen years in prison up to that point. He had escaped from prison at least two, maybe three, times. He had made himself into a jailhouse lawyer. My recollection is that the crimes he had committed were burglaries, at least that's what he told me.

Sam spent a lot of time with me that evening in the Buffalo county jail. He was very interested in what I had done and why. We remained in contact by mail afterward and years later my father wrote to his parole board in support of his release. Sometime in the late 1970s, when I was living and working in New York City, I met him one more time after he got out of prison and came to visit.

Sam and Red were among the first black men that I spent time talking to and interacting with who helped me realize that "there but for fortune go I," that I was born with privileges and should never forget that. More importantly, I should do all I could to challenge all forms of privilege, discrimination, and oppression.

I remember another time when I was lying in my bed in Ashland reading, and a few black men were talking about getting visits from their girlfriends. One of them began to talk about how hard the visits would be, because sexual attraction could not be acted upon. Another one said something like, "Well, that's not me. I'm looking forward to just being able to talk with her, to interact on a human level with someone I love." I wouldn't say I was surprised by this, but it affirmed my belief in the basic humanity of all people, no matter what their culture or race.

What Was It Like at Ashland?

When I was there it was a youth prison; my guess is that the oldest inmates were in their mid-twenties.

I had a job as a tutor in the prison library. There were four other prisoners who were also tutors. Three of them had been part of the Chicago 15 draft board action in August 1969, Bill Durkin, Ed Gargan, and Bill Sweeney. The other tutor was an African American man, Will was his first name, who was in for refusing induction into the army. The group of us got along well and spent many hours hanging out together, waiting for someone to come into the library in need of help. My recollection is that I couldn't have spent more than two hours each day actually being a tutor.

All prisoners wore the same kind of clothes, basic khaki pants and shirts, with army surplus coats when it was cold.

There was a not too big gym, where I played basketball, and an outdoor yard, where I could take circular walks, lift weights, and watch the sunset and the surrounding hills. There was even a very basic miniature golf course outside and a ceramics room, where I made a few things and sent them out to family members and close friends.

There were no walls encircling Ashland, but there was a fifteen-foot-high chain link fence topped with barbed wire and razor wire and guards with guns in towers. I remember people talking every once in a while about how you could escape by throwing blankets over the razor wire, but there were no escape attempts when I was there.

Every Saturday night we'd be treated to a movie in the gym. Some of them were okay, but most were pretty boring or not the kind of movies I like. I remember sometimes seeing fellow inmates getting high sniffing glue or paint fumes from plastic bottles they had smuggled in and pulled out during the movie when the lights were off.

The food wasn't the greatest. I once wrote to Sarah about breakfast:

> The day began with my going to breakfast and having a bowl of Post Toasties. I know why I usually skip breakfasts—they're terrible. The scrambled eggs are like a rubber slab, the bacon is cold and hard, and the other food is tasteless—bland is the word, I believe.

As I remember it, I could write and receive as many letters as I wanted, though I could only write to a particular list of people, maybe ten or twelve. Visiting was pretty liberal; visitors could stay all day, and though I think there was a visitors list, I remember that there was a way for those not on the list to visit.

Daily Life

Here's how I described my day at Ashland on the first day of spring, March 21, 1971, a Saturday:

> Got up about 10:30—I slept through from 12:00 a.m. till then— went to the gym for a little bit, then to lunch. Afterwards I wrote to Aunt Beth and my family, then went to ceramics where I made another cup for the Raines [John and Bonnie Raines, good friends from Philadelphia]—only one to go now—and left mom's pitcher to be fired. I went on the yard, did 18 chin-ups, ran and came back to the dorm. I sat outside for 15 minutes or so, just listening to the birds, feeling the winds, hearing the prison sounds, being aware of being imprisoned. Then I went to dinner, played some golf and did 21 chin-ups, then came back and am writing you. Soon I'll be going to a movie. I'll come back, finish writing you, and then spend the rest of the night either writing more letters or reading.

Many days in prison were difficult, both spiritually and emotionally. In early March I wrote to Sarah:

> The fact is that I'm oppressed here, I'm controlled, I'm alienated due to the work I do (or perhaps that I'm not doing) and as a result I'm what?—not feeling my manhood. . .? In other words, due to the control over my life that other people exercise (today at noon I went for a walk over lunch hour on the field and was yelled at to get off, for what reason I don't know), I do not feel pride in myself, I question my personhood, my worth as a think- ing human being. There is little I can give to you from in here, dear Sarah, at least little which I can see as actually helping you to grow and become more loving and a better person. I can't be with you to hold you and talk with you and care for you when you're down. I can't discuss various things that are going on, except once a month when you visit and incompletely in these letters. In short, I cannot express my manhood by being gentle and loving at the same time that it is difficult to express it by independent, free action.

Violence in Prison

What about violence in prison? Although I never personally experienced it, it came close once, and I heard of and saw it.

When I was in the Rochester jail waiting to be sent to Ashland, I was in the "hangout room" downstairs one day. The room was crowded. Lunch was served, and, somehow, while sitting around a table eating with maybe twenty others, I accidently flicked something, maybe a spoon, into someone else's food, scattering some of it. The guy glared at me, and I apologized in as cool a profuse way as I could. Other Flower City Conspiracy defendants—I remember Joe Gilchrist in particular—spoke up in my support, Joe saying something like, "He's got a problem, but we're working on him," attempting to cut through the tension.

A few minutes later I got up from my seat, taking my food with me. As I walked near the person who I had accidentally offended, he jerked around and brought his arm down hard on my food so it spread all over the floor. I didn't say anything. I cleaned it up as best I could, and nothing more came of it.

While at Ashland I twice heard of men being raped. One was a fellow draft resister who had experienced this while being held at Leavenworth Penitentiary on his way to Ashland. I learned about it from a draft resister brother who had been with him there. The other time was when I was hanging out one evening with a group of men in my dormitory whom I was starting to develop a nice friendship with. At one point, one of them told us that he had heard that someone he knew had been raped just a few days earlier.

When I was transferred to Danbury, I once saw someone lying on the pavement in the yard apparently unconscious with a pool of blood under his head. He did recover. And my white, tall, strong, macho bunk-mate, who I got along with okay, once told me after I noticed cuts on his face about being beaten by "Puerto Ricans." My educated guess was that he had provoked them in some way.

Neither Ashland nor Danbury were like some other prisons, particularly maximum security penitentiaries, where violence is much more frequent. But it was always close to the surface, always a possibility, always something to be aware of.

Then there was the time in the Rochester jail when all of us were kept awake all night by some guy who literally seemed to be going crazy—making noises, jabbering, going on and on in an unintelligible way, banging the wall. He was finally transferred out, to a hospital, I hope, as the sun rose after a whole night of ranting. Not an enjoyable experience.

As the days passed in prison, I tried to follow through on what I had written to Sarah about my "three responsibilities":

> to keep my body, mind and spirit alive, well and growing, through reading, writing, thinking and praying; to communicate to you and others on the outside the reality and the myth of prison and thus help you (and myself) overcome our natural fear, at the same time that I will communicate from this viewpoint my ideas on prison as it relates to the community of resistance to offer what help I can; and to talk with the fellow prisoners and guards and to organize as much as is possible, to provide some hope and some community to those in here. If I can continue in those tasks during my imprisonment, it will have been a valuable experience.

Toward those ends, I organized two "independent study" correspondence courses while in Ashland. One was a "Creative Writing" class with one of my uncles, Wendell Glick, who was an English professor at the University of Minnesota. The other was titled "Contemporary Religious Trends," with John Raines, a professor at Temple, a personal friend, and, I learned a few years ago, a participant with his wife Bonnie in the successful raid on the Media, Pennsylvania, FBI office three months after I was convicted in Rochester.

In early April, I was moved out of the building housing a hundred men in two rooms into a much nicer situation, a building with individual small rooms. They were concrete cinder block rooms with a bed and identical three-foot by two-foot lockers, but I was alone in the room. That made my reading and writing for the two correspondence courses and my letter writing much easier.

Indicted on My Mom's Birthday

But my new and improved living situation was disrupted on April 30, my mother's fifty-first birthday, when I was indicted as one of the Harrisburg 8, charged with "conspiracy," a nonexistent conspiracy whose ultimate aim, so the indictment said, was to kidnap Henry Kissinger and blow up heating tunnels under Washington, DC, government buildings.

This was a "superseding indictment," a replacement for one that had been hurriedly issued by the Justice Department in mid-January. That indictment charged six people from the Catholic Left community with much more serious "conspiracy to kidnap" charges that could have put people away for life, or worse, were they convicted.

I was surprised that I was indicted. I had in no way been involved in even discussions about kidnapping anyone or bombing anything. Indeed, I had joined the Ultra Resistance because of its commitment to nonviolence

Of course, I fully understood that the Nixon Administration that was in power at that time was a repressive government, known for illegal wiretapping, inflammatory rhetoric, criminal prosecutions of peace and justice activists, and outright physical attacks, including killings, against Black Panther Party members. I had followed the Chicago 8 trial a year and a half before, a clear case of government repression against antiwar and Black Freedom activists, following the police riots during the Democratic National Convention in 1968.

I was brought into the supposed conspiracy, because the government, in its indictment, had said the plan of the alleged coconspirators was to engage in draft board raids in Philadelphia, Delaware, and Rochester as a lead-up to the kidnapping and bombing plot. I had been involved in all three of those draft board raids, and the government had evidence of my involvement for at least two of those (Rochester and Philadelphia) and the word of their informer Boyd Douglas for Delaware.

Within a couple of days of learning this news, my thoughts started turning to what I should do about this new situation. One thing that I decided to do was to file an appeal of my Rochester conviction so I could get out of prison and help to organize and prepare for the Harrisburg trial. I already knew that I had a good legal argument because of the notes secretly passed between the jury and the judge. Following our conviction, Herm Walz, our lawyer, had told us this was a viable basis for an appeal, but none of us were interested. We were feeling okay about our year to year-and-a-half sentences and didn't want to risk being reindicted and retried if we won on appeal.

Fortunately, I had six months to file an appeal after being convicted, and there was still one month to go. Bill Cunningham, a lawyer at the Center for Constitutional Rights, filed that appeal, as well as a motion for my release on bond until the appeal was heard. In late September, that motion was granted, and I was released, and the following year, in early July 1972, the U.S. Court of Appeals in New York City overturned my Rochester convictions, as I mentioned at the end of chapter five.

The other thing which I decided to do was to try to get myself transferred to Danbury Federal Correctional Institution. My codefendant Phil Berrigan and the unindicted coconspirator Dan Berrigan were there, and, if I were transferred, I would be much closer geographically to the other defendants as well.

I ended up spending about three more weeks at Ashland. I remember being brought up to the warden's office on the day I was indicted. He asked if I would like to be put into protective custody. He professed to be concerned that when word got out of what had happened, I would be subject to harassment by some of the other prisoners who, he thought, would see me in a different light. I told him no, I didn't want a change in my living situation, and, indeed, not only had I had no problems, I had had a lot of good discussions with others about how messed up a government that would do this was, given that I was completely innocent of the charges.

On May 24, I was picked up by two U.S. Marshals to be driven to Harrisburg for a May 25 arraignment. Somehow, while sitting chained in the back seat traveling through rural West Virginia, I got into a discussion with them about the war and why I had taken action against it. At one point, one of them said something like, "You know, it's too bad we can't just take you out into that field [that we were driving by] and shoot you." That brought a quick end to my attempts to educate these two marshals.

They dropped me off for the night at the Allegheny County Jail, in Pittsburgh. I'll never forget that experience. I remember being led through the prison to my cell by a trusty, a prisoner given special privileges in return for good behavior. It was a very old prison, dark, noisy, and intimidating, with what seemed like an awful lot of cells stacked in rows on top of one another. The trusty asked me if I wanted some food, and I ended up eventually getting some cold mashed potatoes up in the cell he led me to. It was just the basics: a metal frame, a thin mattress, an army blanket, a toilet, and a sink.

I had a hard time sleeping, primarily, I think, because I knew that the next day I was going to be seeing a lot of people I hadn't seen in many months, and I wondered how the arraignment was going to go. But it was also because of my overnight accommodations. I remember pacing back and forth in that six-foot by eight-foot cell for hours, first one way, then the other, figuring out all the ways you could pace in a small cell as a way to pass the time and, finally, feeling drawn to lie down and sleep.

The next morning, I was awakened very early so that the Marshals could get me to the arraignment on time, which they did.

Here's how I wrote about the experience in a letter to Sarah several days later, while in the Harrisburg county jail waiting to be taken to Danbury:

> Seeing all of you, being with you, the rightness of being with you, with others, talking with Phil, all of it was the first really intense experience in six months—like another world. It was difficult to sort it all out. Tuesday night I lay awake trying to go over each event that occurred in those five hours at the Federal Building— being welcomed by [former girlfriend] Terry as I was walked up the steps by the Marshals, seeing you and my parents, being with you as I changed clothes and shaved—felt very good and natural— being with the people before court, seeing Mark and Lindsley and Bonnie [Raines], Barry, Paul [Couming], everyone in the court- room, the arraignment, exchanging glances with you, the minutes together afterwards, saying goodbye to Liz [McAlister]—her long hug—saying goodbye to you, my dearest, the sadness afterwards— being brought here, being filmed by TV cameramen—it was over- whelming, to say the least.

In the middle of all of that was a very uneventful, mundane court- room arraignment.

One week later, I was uneventfully taken to Danbury.

Danbury Federal Correctional Institution

The physical set-up at Danbury was different than Ashland. The yel- lowish, two-story buildings formed a kind of rectangle, within which was a baseball field taking up most of the yard, bleachers, a circular side- walk around the yard, and handball and paddleball courts off to the side. Facing the yard were lots of dormitories, most of them full, with eighty or more people in bunk beds, with the standard-issue metal lockers. Some inmates had individual cells in at least two of the buildings, and it was noticeable that most of them were white and in for white collar crime, organized crime, or other similar things, while a majority of the prisoners were Black and Latino.

Facing the yard was the dining room and a building housing the commissary, a library, administrative offices, and conference rooms. There was also an area past the yard rectangle toward the back of the prison where a factory of some kind "employed" prisoners. Prisoners working there literally made pennies an hour. My vague recollection is that they might have made especially thick and long gloves to be worn by people in the military who were loading artillery shells into long guns.

I was assigned to a construction crew. Similar to my tutoring job at Ashland, there was very little work for us to do. I probably averaged about one hour of actual work a day; I remember the guard who was our boss telling us often by late morning that we should take off and go do something else.

The letters policy was similar to Ashland, but visiting was more restrictive. You were strip-searched when going to and coming from a visit, allegedly for drugs. That wasn't much fun, and it was degrading not just for the inmate but for the guard performing the inspection. We also had a time limit, probably because there were lots of visitors and limited space.

However, and it is a big "however," Danbury for me was very, very different than Ashland, because of the presence of Phil and Dan Berrigan. And by that I don't just mean that I was able to spend lots of "quality time" with them, though there was certainly a good bit of that.

The difference was that every weekday evening, Monday, Tuesday, Wednesday, and Thursday, I was in a political discussion group. Mondays and Wednesdays were a kind of "great books" group in a room in the library that Phil and Dan organized and ran. They got books from the outside for the fifteen or twenty of us who took part. The one book I remember reading and discussing there that had a definite impact on me was the pro-feminist, *Sisterhood is Powerful*.[2]

On Tuesdays and Thursdays, I met with Phil, Jon Bach, and Mitch Snyder. I could be forgetting someone. This was a group Phil organized of people who he considered to be the most dedicated and who had the most potential to carry on the struggle for peace and justice as a lifetime commitment. There were no books for this group, which met around a dining room table after dinner.

These regular evening discussions carried over to our days, and a very definite community of resistance was built. Those of us in this community spent time together out on the yard during the day, continuing to talk about the issues discussed in the evenings. We developed friendships and had each other's back. I remember Jon Bach once commenting to me about something I had said to one to the inmates serving me food. I angrily commented after getting what seemed to me to be a definitely smaller portion in the dinner line than the guy in front of me. Jon told me he didn't think it was a good idea for me to have said that. He felt it could generate inter-inmate tensions that weren't worth it, and he was right.

There was nothing resembling this kind of community of resistance at Ashland.

In late July, after their first parole hearing, Phil and Dan Berrigan heard that they had been turned down and probably would have to serve out the rest of their sentences. For Dan, that would be as much as another two years, for Phil, about four.

That evening, Phil came to the small group in the dining room with an idea. He expressed his concern that if Dan was forced to serve out his full sentence, he might not survive prison. His health had deteriorated while in Danbury. Phil also saw this parole denial as an opportunity to take action even from inside prison against the war.

Taking Action Inside Prison

We discussed all of this, came up with a plan, and moved to implement it. The first thing we decided was that we couldn't just call for Dan to be released from prison. His and Phil's treatment by the parole board was not much different than what other prisoners experienced, and we needed to address that. In addition, we thought that, as prisoners and as a way of showing solidarity and raising the issue of the war, we wanted to address the issue of the abhorrent "tiger cages" in South Vietnam, used by the government the U.S. was supporting.

We came up with three sets of demands:

- that there be a fair and reasonable review of the Berrigans' parole turndowns, with the intention being to force Dan's release and a shortened amount of time until Phil came before the parole board again;
- that, in the case of the parole board and its methods, all prisoners hear back from the board within two weeks of his/her meeting with a parole examiner (sometimes it took as long

as two months), that all prisoners be able to see all material in his/her file when he/she was interviewed for parole, and that all prisoners be given a reason if turned down;

- that the "tiger cages" on Con Son Island in South Vietnam, a very brutal form of imprisonment, be dismantled. A *New York Times* article on March 3, 1973, described them as: "small concrete trenches with bars on top in which five to seven prisoners were cramped in a space about five feet wide, six feet long and six feet deep."[3] Torture was common.

We were able to get personal commitments to take part in a long-term hunger strike in support of these demands from eleven men. We decided that we would begin on August 6, Hiroshima Day, by passing out leaflets calling for a work stoppage. The leaflets were run off clandestinely on a mimeograph machine inside the library by a sympathetic prisoner who worked there. We would call for the work stoppage to start on the following Monday, August 9, Nagasaki Day.

We decided that, tactically, the best way to do it was to have two groups. One, which I was part of, would distribute the leaflets first thing Friday morning, August 6, as people were waiting outside their dorms for the 8:00 a.m. call to report for work. The other six would spend the next three days talking up the planned work stoppage.

On the morning of August 6, we acted. I don't think I was distributing leaflets for more than a minute or two before I was busted, and it was similar with the other four. We were put into what were called "Intensive Training Units," a euphemism if there ever was one for solitary confinement or the hole. But everyone in the prison soon learned what was up. For the next three days, we didn't eat and waited anxiously for Monday morning to arrive. I wrote a poem during this time:

> I sit upright in the Danbury hole.
> Free.
> My jailers are worried, uptight, scared.
> They are the ones in prison.
> My strength and my freedom
> come from within.
> From within
> comes from God.

God comes from
people and faith.
Faith comes from. . .
From the truth.
Again. . .

"Ye shall know the truth
and the truth shall set you free."
I rejoice in my freedom.
The hole has given me new life.
Thank you, Danbury.

We didn't know much about fasting. For the next thirty-three days I drank water, milk, juice, and coffee. I eventually learned, long after this fast ended, that it was definitely not a good idea to drink milk and coffee when fasting, not good for your digestive system. Indeed, I experienced digestive problems on a regular basis for a year after this fast, only healing when I went on a forty-day, much more conscientious, water-only fast against the Vietnam War, in the summer of 1972.

But somehow almost all of us made it to the end of the thirty-three days.

Here's a short letter I wrote to my parents on the second day:

Over half an hour ago a tray of food was sent to my room. It has rested on the spot where it was laid and the spot where I moved it— the toilet—untouched. It is now cold. I am angry that it is still here, angry not at those who want to tempt me and break me, but angry that they cannot understand the depths of what I, we, are doing.

For me to eat that food would be for me to let down my brothers and sisters in prison, in Indochina, in the movement. For me to eat that food would be for me to lose my self-respect, my dignity, my sense of right and wrong. For me to eat that food would be to deny the growth in knowledge that has taken place over the past nine months in prison, over the last 2 ½ years of resistance, over the 21 ¾ years of my life. Such a course would be a denial of the responsibilities I must meet as a free man.

It sits, and gets colder.

I grow stronger.

I told Sarah in a letter who the other four hunger strikers I had leafletted with on August 6 were:

> Two of them I've mentioned before in letters—John and Tom who sleep in the same corner of the dorm as I. Both are draft resisters—John had gotten a September 20 parole date (after 27 months in on a six-year sentence) which he might lose now—a courageous guy. Another one is a guy named David, a resister from NYC who just came in a bit ago on a six-month sentence. The last is Eddie, an amazing guy. He came to prison two years ago on heavy dope charges, cold turkeyed for thirty days in the Charles St. Jail in Boston—he was a heroin addict—and has been coming to the evening discussion groups for about five or six months now. He's gone through some tremendous changes in prison.

On Monday morning six more people passed out leaflets and were taken to the hole. In response seven hundred out of eight hundred inmates stayed away from work for a half hour. The prison "goon squad" threatened the seven hundred strikers with the hole if they did not go to work and forty of them were taken to the hole. Only one hundred prisoners ate lunch.

Off to Missouri

On the evening of August 11, the authorities took action against the eleven remaining hunger strikers. I described it in a letter to Sarah:

> Last night about 5:15 the Danbury scene came alive. Into my room came two very big guards to tell me, "Come downstairs to see the captain." Though I expected a transfer, I cooperated, got dressed and went along. I was led into the receiving and discharge room where I was put in a cage with Phil and Mitch, in time with everyone else who had passed out a leaflet. After signing for our personal property we were loaded into a seven-car caravan and taken for a short ride. Our minds were totally blown as we passed the Danbury airport and then turned onto a road which led to a place where U.S. Marshalls and small private planes were parked. We ended up being piled into two of them rented for the occasion and, handcuffed to a waist-chain and with legs shackled, took off.

The flight was (excuse the expression) quite a trip. It took about six and a half hours, with a stopover in Indianapolis to refuel and to unload (try—imagine—pissing in a urinal while chained to another guy doing the same, being watched by two Marshalls). I enjoyed the motion and the movement, so un-prison-like, as well as the good company I was with.

When we got here—the Springfield, Mo. Medical Center for Federal Prisoners—we were processed—given a shower, a pair of coveralls, bureaucrated (interviewed from our file) and taken to bed. By that time it was 2:30 a.m.

The 11 of us are isolated in one wing of this place, separated from the rest of the population. We each have a single room, unlocked at all times, and a common bathroom and shower. We are able to mingle freely and talk, which is certainly good. We all have our personal property from Danbury so I have books. There's also a working TV in the hall, so we can maintain a bit of news about the outside.

I kept a journal over the course of the forty days that we were kept at Springfield, twenty-nine of them on the fast. Here are some excerpts:

August 12

Quite a bit has gone on today in terms of heavy thinking. Just spent the past three hours talking with the others and trying to come to some agreement on what should be told about how we're not being treated, and why, and how we are being treated, and why, and how we can get out that word. Also, how we can get out the fact that there are three demands which have got to be brought up on the news. Hopefully, friends on the outside will be doing that.

Spent the daytime reading some, writing to my parents and to Sarah, trying to sleep, but I couldn't for some reason, drinking a lot of water, and slowly getting down the routine of this place. Also watching the news on the TV we have here in our isolated wing.

August 13

I am really proud to be part of this group, this community. A very strong, at times seemingly fearless, bunch of individuals. But they're no different from many more people I know but for the fact that they're willing to back up what they believe and think no matter what the consequences. They are willing to risk, a much needed quality, one that seems to be lacking on the part of many otherwise good people today, at the same time that they are willing to sustain their activity—it's not a one-shot deal. Undoubtedly our being together helps our individual strength considerably—at the same time that it occasionally leads to irritability and close quarters' tensions, but we're doing a good job so far of controlling the latter and keeping ourselves together and strong.

I was quite dizzy once or twice this evening. It happened when I jumped out of bed quickly and didn't take some seconds to get used to standing up. One time I was very close to fainting—couldn't see anything, and had to struggle to come back to it. But generally I'm in very good shape, physically fine, though I must be down to around 150 pounds now, a loss of 17 pounds from the beginning.

Life is good, which is why we're doing this—because life should be preserved, enriched and improved.

August 15
Day by day my energy seems to be going, my strength goes down, and I feel tired earlier in the day. Yesterday, after a two-hour visit from Liz [McAlister] and Bill [Cunningham], and after being awoken at 6:00 a.m. to a thermometer being pushed into my mouth, I began feeling a bit weak in the middle of the afternoon. This morning, after being awoken at 6 and drinking milk and juice and then going back to sleep until called for church, I already feel a bit drained.

We talked yesterday among ourselves and with our doctor here at Springfield about the possibility of another transfer—spreading us all over the country after our fast continues for more days and when they realize this transfer didn't stop us. The doctor said we'd have a very good basis for a lawsuit if they did that because since we've been classified as medical patients, this institution has to give the okay before we could be moved out by the Federal Bureau of Prisons. But I wouldn't, and we don't, put anything past [Attorney General John] Mitchell and his friends, so we'll have to wait and see.

August 18

There was a suicide here yesterday—a Mexican kid, that's all I heard. Yes, there is much misery here in prison, as in the world. Leaves one feeling helpless, floating, cut off. Not much to do other than to continue working hard for radical change in all strata, for a lessening of that misery, to try to give hope to those who certainly can't see it coming from the structures of society.

I'm getting more irritable with others—much easier to find fault with their basic personalities (why can't everyone be perfect like me? Hah!) As a result, I keep my mouth shut quite a bit so as not to hurt someone unnecessarily. Another result of the fast.

August 20

The first day of the third week of this thing, and we have yet to hear anything from anyone in authority about the demands we made, the issues we raised. Not surprising but certainly revealing. Revealing, in that it shows they do not wish to have to acknowledge the justice of the points we made. Instead they wish to isolate us, push us off the public stage, intimidate us. I can get very angry thinking of how, by their rigidity and their ignorance, they are destroying people's lives and destroying my country. The mandarins.

But here we have the future—11 resisters who by resisting give hope to the poor, give hope to America, indeed, make the future possible. For there is no future, no human future possible, unless there is resistance. Resistance holds within it both the rejection of the poison of the old and the planting and sprouting of the seeds of the new. Seeds of liberation—yes, not a bad thing to consider oneself, if one is being honest as to commitment and responsible action.

August 21

For the past few days there's been a lot of discussion about food. I suppose it satisfies collective fantasies of sorts. No one's breaking down or losing his will, but we are all quite aware of something missing from our lives, along with other things. I couldn't say whether such discussions are healthy or unhealthy. I suppose as long as they're flights of fantasy and dreams for the future they're basically harmless.

August 23
We were able to go outside on the yard today for half an hour. That was a different way to make the time go by. I ended up sitting by myself, trying to understand why I was feeling somewhat anti-social, I think due to my weakness and thus my increased irritability. I'm wondering if a letter tonight from Sarah will help.

August 24
One of the group began eating today, mainly because of health reasons, it seems, though also some discouragement over the lack of noticeable events which probably added to the physical ailments. The doctor mentioned that he might be developing an ulcer; that's pretty serious stuff.

A few letters to write tonight, to Harold Hughes of Iowa, to Sarah, to the lawyers in New York giving them the names of the lawyers of the others here. It's good to have things to do, to not feel burdened by the time and searching for something to occupy it.

August 26
The word is that there is to be a demonstration outside here this weekend with primarily people from Kansas City and St. Louis. Hopefully there might be some civil disobedience. Also, it seems the plans for a demonstration at Danbury on October 2 is more than just a Danbury happening. There'll also be one in DC, out here, and at as many other prisons as possible. That's certainly good; my major concern is that the war not be forgotten by a concentration on prisons. They're related, yes, but the war has to be constantly emphasized.

Two full weeks here at Springfield. Three full weeks of fasting. Tomorrow begins the fourth week and still no word as to our demands, unsurprisingly. And we continue, persevere and, in certain ways, thrive.

August 29
It was quite noticeable today, on the faces, in the eyes, in the slowness of the motions, in the downward hang of the heads, that we've been without nourishment for quite some time, without

adequate nourishment. People are tired and listless, and there is little wasted effort or discussion in this wing.

August 30
We've just had a visit from Honey Knopp, a prison visitor for the Central Committee for Conscientious Objectors, a great and beautiful woman. She brought lots of good news about coverage on the outside, about support behind our demands, about people doing things, about our statement being widely distributed. It was very heartening.

The visit seems to have given all of us new energy. Her being able to meet with us together down here in our wing was a very good thing. After she left we had some discussion about things she said, as well as about related topics, and it's as if the community has been recharged. Always good to get outside input.

My temperature was down to 94.2[F; 34.5C] this morning. It appears that when you lack food and thus fat, you're much more liable to reflect changes in the weather around you. It's been cooler for a while and the temperature was taken just after we had come back from our time outside in the yard. I'm wearing long pants and a shirt as a result of these developments.

August 31
I talked this morning while walking with Jon Bach about my problem of becoming more easily irritable and less tolerant of others. I find myself becoming more easily able to get upset with other people over very little things—a person's weakness in expressing himself, or his constant attitude of cheerfulness and do-goodness, very basic personality traits that are not mine. On occasion I think I've hurt people by my attitude and comments, either expressed or not, overt or covert. I don't know how well I'll be able to adjust. This might be something I'll just have to live with and hope that it leaves me.

September 6
Today is Labor Day and the institution had a big day of games, hamburgers, hot dogs and cokes out on the yard. There was a

general holiday air with music from loudspeakers competing with the in-person local band. It was also a day that I "celebrated" by drinking a lot more, more than any other day on the fast. I had four cups of milk, two cups of 7 Up, two glasses of orange juice and two cups of coffee. I have much more energy and am less irritable as a result of all this.

Our collective spirit seems to be picking up as we discuss the best ways to end the fast and break the news. It will be good to eat again, knowing that our abstention has been of value.

September 7

There's a noticeable air of anticipation and apprehension as we look forward to tomorrow when we begin to eat once again. We all seem to be in good shape. I was dizzy on occasion today, as was Eddie, but we're all quite in possession of our mental and emotional capacities, and we haven't been damaged in any way by what we've done [this turned out not to be true for my digestive system]. We've been revitalized and given a spiritual lift; we've recommitted ourselves once more (some for the first time) to resistance; and we've contributed something, hopefully, to the lives of others and the "betterment of humankind." Certainly this experience will help us in the future wherever we are—in prison or out, together or separated—in that we've all grown and learned much through this period of a little over a month.

But I am glad today is the last day.

September 9

Some of us ate too much yesterday. I was very stuffed after lunch, after dinner, and after eating some bread saved from dinner, almost to the point of sickness. The stomach had a hard time digesting again after such a long vacation, and I had some fairly strong stomach cramps and pain, as well as a lot of gas. But that now seems to have cleared up pretty well and, beginning with breakfast this morning, I'm exercising a greater degree of discipline over my food intake.

Others had similar reactions. One guy ate too much too quickly and he threw up last night, but he's okay this morning. We should be fine in a few days, though it will take a while to regain our full strength, I'm sure.

Other effects of the eating, other than physical, are these: increased patience, compassion, tolerance, sense of community, willingness to listen, decreased irritability and verbal hostility. There's also more energy and strength evident too, due both to the nourishment and the lessened tension now that it's over.

I prayed tonight before dinner for the first time ever, on my own initiative. I'm reminded of Gandhi's line, "Fasting is the sincerest form of prayer." Perhaps that's one more beneficial result of this life-giving fast, increased spirituality and a new attraction toward the value and power of prayer.

Lots of good spirits in the ward today. And we did see a doctor. Things are moving along well. So much to do, to read, to write, to talk about, to look forward to!!

September 11
The exercising continues. I feel stronger now when doing them and will soon be stepping up the quantity. I'd like to continue these wherever I go from here and also out in the street.

I'm more easily able to discipline myself during meals, not eating so much. I'm confident I won't become fat as an overreaction to eating again, although temporarily I'm a bit on the heavy side.

September 12
A typical day. I finished the two books I was reading and wrote three letters. I watched a bit of TV and was part of a discussion group this evening consisting of all of us. Really a rather slow day and at times boring.

The news today is all about Attica [an upstate New York prison where prisoners took hostages and seized control of a section of the prison. On this day, despite on-going negotiations, the State Police retook it by force, with dozens of deaths]. About murder. About official brutality. About Rockefeller showing his colors, Nixon following suit—the color is red, blood-red, the blood of Attica guards, prisoners, Vietnamese, Indians (the sins of the fathers shall be revisited upon the sons). A day of infamy, tragedy and ultimate folly. Which way America?

September 14

The news from Attica now is that the guards who "had their throats slashed" were instead shot to death. And that even the prison officials admitted that there were no guns in the hands of the inmates. Further, from interviews on the news it seems as if at least some of the guards taken hostage and the families of the slain guards are quite angry at Rockefeller and the higher-ups in prison circles for their decision to invade the prison. Perhaps the consciousness among that portion of America—white, lower-income or working-class people—will grow now that their lives are just as expendable to the powers-that-be as blacks, resisters, Vietnamese, and the poor—perhaps.

September 16

As is so often the case, our condition is one of limbo, of a certain insecurity, of living from hour to hour and day to day not knowing where we'll be shipped to. That state of insecurity comes because we are casting our lives with those of the poor. Risk, prison, poverty, community, insecurity, non-planning (to a degree) for the future—the lot of me and many of my friends and an indication of our practical if not theological Christianity.

September 18

This'll be the next to last day of this journal. We got the word this morning that early Monday morning seven of us will be flying back to Danbury. Unfortunately, two will be staying here for a bit longer and will be coming back later on. The chances of me being one of them are very small due to the Harrisburg case and the need to get back into trial preparation. So I expect to be in the air Monday, on my way back to the East Coast.

September 19

This'll be the last installment. I'm writing now because we've just been told to pack our things and to fill out a personal property form so that they can have all our things ready to go early tomorrow morning when we leave.

It's been a very, very full and worthwhile 40 days, without a doubt the best 40-day period of my imprisonment, if not of my life. There was the fast for 30 of them here in Springfield, and for the past 10 days since the fast ended I've been doing an awful lot of writing, letters and articles.

Thirty-three days of fasting—a long time. Yet many of the world's people daily live on but a little bit more than we did for their whole lives. I won't forget that; I won't forget them. My commitment has grown, and I return to Danbury prepared to continue my hard work, my work of joy and of liberation and peacemaking. What a grand time to be alive!

Returning to Danbury

We made it back to Danbury alive, after wondering if we were going to make it as our plane descended through thick clouds on approaching our landing area. All of a sudden, the pilot gunned the engine and pulled the plane up at a steep angle. An hour or so later we finally landed. We never did find out what had happened.

It was good to be back. Dan and the others seemed a lot better and in good spirits after our return. I guess the eleven of us being taken away as suddenly as we had been had left quite a vacuum. Then, too, we learned that a lot of other Danbury prisoners were getting paroled, a big August response to our action. A new aliveness and spirit were evident.

About a week later I learned that my appeal bond had been granted. I was glad that I would soon be leaving prison, but I also felt sad about leaving a lot of intimate friends I had grown close to over the months I had been there and in Springfield.

As I wrote to my parents a couple of days before my release:

I don't think that getting out of prison is a cause for wild rejoicing. In the first place, I'm only entering a larger prison, with more privileges and temptations that are used to keep me in line and make me be a 'good American.' Secondly, my life has not stopped because I've been put behind the walls. My activity upon release will be only the continuation of work that I carried on before and during this imprisonment. And thirdly, though I am leaving the prison itself, others are still subject to further punishment and oppression of the spirit. For these reasons my feelings are a bit mixed.

But, no question, I was glad to be getting out when I was released on October 1.

As it happened, there was a big rally of several thousand people the very next day in Danbury. Demonstrations were held in more than a dozen places protesting prison conditions in both the U.S. and in South Vietnam, organized by the Harrisburg Defense Committee that had formed to organize support for the Harrisburg 8.

I was a main speaker at the Danbury rally. I concluded my speech with these words:

> I think there are two things we must continue to keep foremost in our consciousness if our movement is to grow and to eventually succeed. The first thing is that we must be strong. We must be willing to resist, to stand up against injustice, oppose oppression and murder, and this has to continue no matter where we are.
>
> The second thing that has to be very much part of our consciousness is that we must continue to maintain a vision of the future, of a new America. It's very easy, especially after being in prison, or just by living in this society, to be so infused with its violence and its insanity and its misuse and maltreatment of people that one can, himself, become violent, become unconcerned with other people, become, in a way, nihilistic.
>
> I think what we have to remember is that, ultimately, what we are trying to create is a society in which men and woman can be human, and men and women can love each other, a society in which people have power over their own lives. And we must continue to believe that even in those times when we are in prison; we must continue to believe that and act out of that belief even in those times when we become tired and when we become despairing, perhaps, of the slowness with which things are moving. We must maintain that vision, and most of all we must remember that that vision is continued, and that vision is there, because we are motivated, primarily, by love.

CHAPTER SEVEN

The Harrisburg 8
(Minus 1) Trial

The Grand Jury Charges that on or about January 1, 1970, the exact date being to the Grand Jury unknown, and continuing thereafter up to on or about January 7, 1971, in the Middle District of Pennsylvania and elsewhere, Eqbal Ahmad, Philip Berrigan, John Theodore Glick, Elizabeth McAlister, Neil McLaughlin, Anthony Scoblick, Mary Cain Scoblick, Joseph Wenderoth, defendants herein did, unlawfully, willfully, and knowingly combine, conspire, confederate and agree together and with each other and with Beverly Bell, William Davidon, Jogues Egan, Marjorie Shuman, named herein as coconspirators but not as defendants, and with divers[e] other persons unknown to the Grand Jury, to commit offenses against the United States.

—beginning of Harrisburg 8 indictment

On April 30, 1971, a grand jury in Harrisburg, Pennsylvania, indicted me and seven others. The indictment said that there were thirty-five "overt acts" undertaken that were alleged to be proof of this conspiracy.

I couldn't believe that I was named as one of the defendants. In the statement I put together in response while in prison in Ashland, I said:

The bombing and kidnapping charges against me are completely false and, putting together my knowledge of the character of the other defendants with their public denials and the things that I have learned from the mass media (such as the latest *Life Magazine* article), I am certain that the charges are also false against them.

The "destruction of draft files" charges have been connected to the bombing and kidnapping charges so as to provide what the government feels is an "out" since they know there is little evidence for their grandiose conspiracy charges.

The manner in which this whole affair has been handled—Hoover's preindictment accusations, the replacing of the original hurried indictment by a second, more vague and broad one, the highly irregular (probably illegal) inclusion of those letters in the superseding indictment, and the inclusion of the draft board charges in the second indictment—all point to a concerted attempt by the government to discredit and intimidate this segment of the anti-war movement and, indeed, the entire anti-war movement.

When I arrived at Danbury after my transfer from Ashland, I took part in weekly defendants' meetings inside a prison room. It was a sparse room up toward the front of the prison, and there were no tables, only chairs, which we put in a circle for our meetings. Each week most of the other defendants, often minus Eqbal, who had other demands on his time, came to discuss details relating to our upcoming ordeal, sometimes with unindicted coconspirators or lawyers.

For most of June and July, there was little real trial preparation, as we were dealing with issues related to a newly formed Harrisburg Defense Committee (HDC) and other matters. However, once Phil and I returned from our forty-day stay in the Springfield, Missouri, Medical Center for Federal Prisoners on September 20, trial preparation began in earnest. The first and most difficult issue was the question of self-defense.

Self-Defense at Trial

At my trial in Rochester, seven of the eight defendants had spoken for ourselves in the courtroom. The result had been an incredibly successful trial, both politically and in terms of the sentences. The tactic of self-defense had loosened up the courtroom process and had allowed us to inject testimony about the war, about the practices of the FBI, and about the motivations for our action that never would been allowed if our defense had been handled by lawyers.

I appreciated that the Harrisburg case was not the same as Rochester. In particular, in addition to the general charge of "conspiracy" against the eight of us, there were nine other charges against Phil, Liz, and Eqbal for sending letters into and out of Lewisburg Prison illegally. Paul O'Dwyer, one of the main lawyers, along with Ramsey Clark and Leonard Boudin, emphasized this in a discussion I had with him when he visited Phil and me during our fast in Springfield, Missouri. He felt that only someone who knew how the legal system worked could prevent them from being convicted on those charges.

I had no problem with this. The problem was that Paul went further, ending up taking a public position, expressed in the Harrisburg courtroom to the judge five months later, that he had concerns about the potential impact on other defendants of my going "pro se."

I wrote to Paul after his visit, saying, in part:

> I fear you may have gotten the wrong impression about how I will conduct myself in the courtroom. I have no intention of disruptions, no intention of pushing things to the point where I am given extra time for contempt. I will ask those questions I consider to be important ones and which highlight the real issues of the trial—the behavior of this government and the need for resistance to that—and will certainly argue to be allowed to ask and receive answers to those questions, but if and when I'm overruled I'll stop—or perhaps come at things from a different angle. In short, my behavior in the courtroom will be very similar to that I used in Rochester, and I think Herman Walz [our lawyer in Rochester] could tell you it was in no way disruptive.

The discussion over this issue went on for weeks among the defendants at our weekly meetings. I wasn't the only one considering this courtroom option. Phil and Eqbal were also. Neil and Liz were strongly against anyone doing it. Their position was that we had been indicted for something we didn't do, and thus our response should not be the same as if we had been indicted for raiding draft boards. In addition, they didn't think there was much hope of being able to say what we might want to say in the courtroom anyway, and, therefore, we should leave the arguing to the lawyers; we should concentrate on activities outside of the courtroom.

After weeks of strenuous debate, we finally agreed that those who wished to go pro se could do so. At the time, I was a definite. Eqbal was a probably, and Phil was wavering, because he was uncertain that he would be able to prepare adequately in jail. He subsequently decided not to begin the trial going pro se but did attempt, unsuccessfully, to dismiss his lawyer Ramsey Clark in order to give his own opening statement on the first day of the trial.

In mid-November, after I had gotten out of prison, we met with the entire legal staff—about six in all—in Leonard Boudin's office in New York City. The major item on the agenda was the decision we had reached. The main concern of the lawyers was that a pro se defendant could "be a source of embarrassment to lawyers," as I wrote in my notes, because of "a wrong statement at the wrong time." To his credit, he did acknowledge a lawyer could do that too.

When Eqbal decided the following month not to go the pro se route, I was left as the only one doing so. I was certainly disappointed, but I had the definite support of four of the other defendants, and I could see no way in which I could do anything else. We continued trial preparation.

On January 10, 1972, we were all in Judge R. Dixon Herman's courtroom for a pretrial hearing. The judge was questioning us individually about our representation. I was standing by myself before Herman in the front of the courtroom, him sitting about four feet above me. I remember telling him I was going to defend myself, enjoying the moment immensely as his eyes darted from side to side, clearly very apprehensive about what was going to transpire in his courtroom with this upstart, assertive, young activist.

I had filled out a form that I thought had firmed up my self-defense position and had listened to him outline the dangers I could pose to other defendants by going the route I was going. From out of nowhere, totally unexpected, Paul O'Dwyer spoke from behind me approaching the bench. He said, "Your Honor, I would like to note for the record my agreement with your concern about the possibility of Mr. Glick saying something which would prejudice the rights of my clients, and I would like to state that if he says something which I feel to be damaging, I reserve the right to move for a mistrial."

Later that day, when in pain and in anger I asked Paul at a meeting of defendants and lawyers why he had done that, he said, to quote from a note I made at the time, "I will continue to do so during the trial if I feel it is necessary." That was bad enough, but when Liz then made a comment to the effect that I was acting like a fifteen-year-old, and no one backed me up, that really did it. I remember leaving that meeting, walking to the nearby Susquehanna River, sitting down totally distraught, and crying for ten or fifteen minutes. I felt isolated and unsupported, almost like I was in a prison, different than Ashland, Danbury, or Springfield but definitely in a box, controlled, stymied in my hope to use this trial to build the movement, similar in a way to how the eight of us in Rochester had used that trial.

I wanted out. I wanted something to change. I wanted to break free. I wanted the truth to come out in the courtroom, the truth of our lives in resistance, not legal maneuvering or technical details that had no relation to my life or the deaths of Indochinese.

I felt powerless, and not the first time, but it was one of the first times in my then twenty-two years that those wielding the power were on my side, on the side of justice, democracy, and peace. I did not know what to do. I continued to cry, eventually leaving the river, temporarily cleansed but not free.

Severed, Thankfully

One week later, a form of liberation occurred: I was severed from the trial of the other seven. What this meant was that, depending upon the outcome of the trial of the others, I might be brought to trial later, alone. Though my feelings were somewhat mixed—I continued to see the trial as a potential gift, a way to speak the truth at a very critical time—the dominant feeling was joy and relief.

I had been working with the HDC ever since I had gotten out of prison in early October. Now, I was able to do so in a much more active way. Within a few days, talking with others in the HDC, we decided that I would now do more traveling and speaking, would work to help bring people to speak in Harrisburg while the trial was going on, and would help pull together a week of action, "Holy Week in Harrisburg," that we were beginning to plan for late March and early April.

As to the trial itself, which began with jury selection on January 24, I had little direct involvement with it or the discussions among the defendants and lawyers, which was fine with me. I had become skeptical about how things were going to be handled given the dominance of the lawyers. I spent no time in the courtroom during the trial, though I did occasionally visit with the defendants over lunch in the U.S. Marshall's room where Phil was kept. Phil was the defendant I felt closest to.

I did make one more effort to have the war be brought into the courtroom. In early March, as part of my HDC work, I attended a conference in Washington, DC, on the most recent developments in the war. I was moved by the horrendous reports and the statistics about the devastation being wreaked upon Vietnam, Cambodia, and Laos because of the continuing, and now escalating, U.S. bombing campaign. I wrote up a long memo to the defendants that concluded, "All I am asking is that the Indochinese be foremost on our minds as this illegitimate escapade goes on and on. All I am asking is that the trial serve the purpose that it has the potential of serving—to re-energize and re-educate and inspire an anti-war movement badly in need of exactly that."

I heard from others who attended parts of the trial that the lawyers made some good statements about the war, though that was in no way the main thing addressed. The main aspect of the trial, without question, was the testimony of Boyd Douglas, the prisoner Phil had befriended and came to trust, and who had carried Phil and Liz's letters out of and into the prison, all the while making copies of them. When those copies were discovered by prison officials, Douglas became an informer and turned over all subsequent clandestine letters to the FBI.

Phil explained his relationship with Douglas in his autobiography:

> I met Boyd Douglas in Lewisburg, trusted him and went to considerable pains to clear him with people at Bucknell University.... Douglas was allowed out of prison to attend Bucknell.... Douglas was the only prisoner in Lewisburg who was allowed outside the walls on a daily basis, and he had been trying to ingratiate himself with me, worming his way into my confidence...
>
> I also knew a lot of the old cons at Lewisburg, guys who were doing double life, thirty years for robbing banks, a dime for bashing in someone's skull. They had a very tight community in prison, played bridge together, and read a lot of heavy books. I liked those people, and used to talk with them all the time. When I asked what they thought about Boyd Douglas, they said, "Don't worry, Phil, he's no stool. He's all right. You can trust him."
>
> After that, I started to confide in Douglas. I told him that we had discussed the possibility of "arresting" Henry Kissinger. I talked about the tunnels under Washington, D.C., and said that I had checked them out to see if our plan might work. And he said, "Look, Phil, I'm a Vietnam veteran. I'm a demolitions expert, and I know all about primer cord." I didn't know anything about primer

cord. "Well," said Douglas, "it's explosive. You can use it for a very limited, concentrated explosion." I told him we had no intentions of hurting anyone. That wasn't our style, and we would never do it, even if it would mean an end to the Vietnam War.

Douglas had agreed to carry my letters outside the prison, and he did deliver them to Elizabeth—after making copies for the FBI. Liz wasn't allowed to write or visit me in Lewisburg. No problem, said Douglas. He would carry her letters inside prison. My conversations with Douglas, and my letters to Liz, provided Hoover with enough "evidence" to launch the Harrisburg trial.[1]

The government's case at the trial took a month to present. Douglas was the primary witness. Here is how the prosecution's case was summed up by Jack Nelson and Ronald J. Ostrow in their book, *The FBI and the Berrigans*:

> March 23rd, [lead prosecutor William] Lynch rested the government's case. In a month's time, sixty-four government witnesses, including twenty-one FBI agents and nine policemen, had testified. But only the testimony of one witness—Boyd Douglas—had been crucial to the kidnap-bombing charge. Without Douglas and the letters, there was not even a hint of a case.
>
> Even the government's evidence on the plot to raid draft board offices had been surprisingly thin. Sister McAlister had been linked through a fingerprint and other evidence, including her own letter. And Fathers Wenderoth and McLaughlin and the Scoblicks had been linked to the Philadelphia draft board raids through the largely uncorroborated testimony of Douglas. There was no evidence, as promised by Lynch in his opening statement, that Father Berrigan was "in on the planning" of the Philadelphia raids.
>
> The government had utterly failed to prove that Fathers Berrigan and Wenderoth had entered the tunnels and Judge Herman was to instruct the jury to dismiss from its mind that crucial part of the bombing allegation.[2]

On the next day, the defendants were given the chance to present their defense, but Ramsey Clark spoke on their behalf on behalf, saying, "Your Honor, the defendants will always seek peace, the defendants continue to proclaim their innocence—and the defense rests."

The evening before, the defendants and lawyers had met, and after an intense discussion, the defendants voted four to three not to present a defense. This was a shocking decision for many of the defendants' supporters, who were expecting to be able to hear from them on the stand, not just the facts of what had and had not happened but, very importantly, the *why* of their involvement in serious nonviolent anti-war activism.

A major reason for this decision was the view on the part of the lawyers that the government had presented a very weak case. It was also felt that this particular courtroom with this particular judge would have been a difficult place to present clearly and fully the "why" of the defendants' resistance activities. And, very importantly, there was concern that the government would use the defense's case and people's time on the witness stand to attempt to learn more about various draft board actions, try to gather more evidence for future indictments and prosecutions.

The case went to the jury at the end of March, during the HDC Holy Week actions. They deliberated for sixty hours over seven consecutive days and ended up hung ten to two in favor of acquittal on the major conspiracy charge. They did convict Phil and Liz on several counts related to the smuggling of letters, later overturned on appeal, with the exception of one count against Phil.

Government Loses—and Not Just in the Courtroom

Without question, the government lost this case and the movement won. And it won not just because of the jury decision, as important as it was, but because of the organizing and activism that took place around the trial.

A network of defense committees grew up in response to the government's indictment. Those defense committees, as well as people and groups from other parts of the movement, pulled together what was called a Pilgrimage for Peace and Freedom, which had two main parts. The first was local activities during the first month of Lent, February 16 through March 17. The newsletter of the national HDC reported that there were about fifty known localities where an action of some kind took place.

The second part was a week of action during Holy Week in Harrisburg itself. There were several car caravan pilgrimages that brought people to Harrisburg to take part in that week of action. And it turned out to be a very powerful week, coming at just the right time, as the closing statements were made in the trial and the case went to the jury.

The national HDC put out eight copies of a newsletter over six months from the fall of 1971 to the spring of 1972. The eighth and final issue, which reported glowingly on all that happened that week, began:

> The week was too rich to be reported in detail, but here are some highpoints worth recording.
>
> Sabotage at York—The American Machine & Foundry plant in York, Pa., just down the highway from H'bg, turns out a heavy share of the bombing tonnage American planes drop in Vietnam. On Palm Sunday evening Ted Glick found press releases in his car inviting reporters to inspect sabotaged bomb casings in a boxcar just outside the plant, awaiting shipment. Two reporters followed the map, found the evidence. While it wasn't part of the planned program, the action fitted quite comfortably into the spirit of things.

After being severed from the trial of the other seven, I helped to organize this action. The late Bill Davidon, an unindicted coconspirator in the Harrisburg case and a leader of the group that successfully removed and released files from the FBI office in Media, Pennsylvania, played an important role in this action, as did a couple of others from the HDC and a couple of nuns, as I remember it.

We spent over a month casing the AMF plant and the railroad siding that ran along behind it. That's where the bomb casings were stored, hundreds of them in box cars, waiting to be shipped to Philadelphia where an electronic "eye" would be screwed into the top of it to make it a "smart bomb," able to be guided to its predetermined destination. Our plan was to use very large bolt cutters to make a gash in the metal threads on the top so that couldn't happen.

I did not go into the boxcars on the night of the action, but I spent a lot of nights leading up to it sitting in the cold and snow on a hill above them, watching to see what happened late at night. We were careful with how we got to this overlook. We would park our cars a couple of miles away and hike through fields and over a couple of wooded hills to get to our location. Once when I and a partner were making this trek we saw a couple of people across a field a couple of hundred yards away. They seemed to be arguing about something. Fortunately, they didn't call out or follow us as we kept going toward our objective.

I was very anxious the night of the action. At the target time we had agreed upon, I went to my parked car a block from my house, which I had made sure to leave unlocked. I looked inside and there, as planned, were several copies of the rubber tops that were screwed onto the bomb casings and several copies of a press release. I spent the next couple of hours distributing them, going to the hotels and homes of the four or five members of the press we had identified as likely to be interested.

This was a definite nonviolent Ultra Resistance–style counterpunch to the Nixon Administration. It was a strong statement that their repressive actions had not succeeded in frightening us into silence or inaction. This was magnified by the actions all throughout the week, as reported in the HDC newsletter:

Holy Week Actions

Panels, Forums, Workshops—With perhaps a few exceptions, the talk sessions scheduled for the Week drew favorable responses and better-than-expected attendance: from 200 to 300 at morning forums and evening workshops; from 50 to 75 at each of the many, many workshops in between. These sessions were, in a sense, the heart of the Week.

Palm Sunday March—A spirited, zestful tone was set for the whole week by its first event. Demonstrators gathered on City Island, donned costumes and dabbed their faces with paint—grey or white for ghastly; yellow, red, blue for gay. The "death" contingent led off, marching to the sober beat of a wooden drum. They were a credible, powerful reminder that real people are really getting killed by our bombs in Indochina. At the end of the death march were a group strewing palm branches in the street and offering them to spectators. Then came the "life" section, colorfully costumed, brightly painted, dancing, singing—suggesting some of the rewards of choosing people over power.

At the State Capitol building, the march turned into a rally, where Tony Scoblick got laughs and long, loud cheers with his review of the defense decision to rest, and where Father James LaCroce of Harrisburg gave the best Palm Sunday sermon delivered anywhere in the U.S. that day. Then came a communal supper and a concert with Peter Yarrow, a wildly happy event.

Women's March—On Tuesday some 40 women, dressed as Vietnamese peasants, marched from Holy Week House to the Federal Building, where they staged a guerrilla theatre die-in.

Wall of Conscience—As many as 300 demonstrators—seminarians, nuns, priests, committee members and sympathizers—surrounded three sides of the Federal Building, grasping a chain and passively blocking entrance to the building. Some 166 were arrested, and 50 chose to spend five days in jail. The action was linked with simultaneous demonstrations in nine other cities, all sponsored by the National Union of Theological Students and Seminarians.

The Bishops' Liturgy—Just as the last seminarians were being arrested, a liturgical procession led by three Episcopal bishops arrived at the steps of the main entrance of the Federal Building. They were Bishops Robert Spears of Rochester, Lyman Ogilby of Philadelphia and Lloyd Gressle of Bethlehem, Pa. Not only the sidewalks but all of Walnut Street in front of the building was packed with people; hundreds received communion. Later the three bishops held a press conference at the YWCA at which they reiterated their own and their church's solidarity with the defendants in the H'bg case.

New Cumberland Army Depot—From 800 to 1000 demonstrators (compared with an expected 250 to 300) mobilized on City Island at noon on Good Friday, motored to a rendezvous near the army depot, then marched to its rear gates. The aim was to plant a "tree of life" on the grounds of the depot in symbolic protest against the use of the base to help spread death in Vietnam by repairing helicopter gunships used there. But the gates were closed and locked, and requests relayed to the base commander to open them were denied.

The demonstrators were about to march to another gate when action stopped discussion: several intrepid types followed the lead of Sue Hertz, climbed the wire mesh fence, stepped over the barbed wire strands on top, leaped or climbed to the ground and planted the first tree. Most of the first contingent got back safely, but before the action was over at least 50 of the crowd had gone over the fence and about 46 had been arrested for it.

A platoon of MPs was marched up to a point 50 yards from the fence—within easy reach of bullhorn appeals by Ted Glick, members of the Vietnam Veterans Against the War and other who asked the GIs with extemporaneous eloquence to "come over to us."

Finally some of the MPs were deployed along the fence. One, caught smiling at the demonstrators, was ordered away from his post and replaced by another. There were no "incidents," no violence, not even verbal. At least four trees were planted before the day was over—but later, word reached the Committee that they had all been pulled up. So it goes.

The Vigil—From the evening of the day the jury got the case—Holy Thursday, March 30—to the day of the verdict, April 5, a 24-hour vigil was maintained at the entrance to the Federal Building. An average of 20 people were there nightly (it was close to a hundred the first two nights). Seven candles, one for each defendant, were kept burning. Each night at midnight there was a worship service, led sometimes by local visiting clergy, sometimes by lay participants. Using sleeping bags and piles of blankets, vigilers slept through the small hours; at other times they talked with each other, with passersby, with defendants who visited them on their way into or out of the courtroom. Daily, during the lunch period, volunteer street speakers talked to people passing the Federal Building about the war and the trial and the Week, getting more listeners and more questions than they had expected. And, of course, leafletting went on semi-continuously.

The Rally—How many people took part in the march and demonstration in Harrisburg on April 1? A local radio station estimated 25,000 while the march was still forming; first guess by the Associated Press was (!) 2,000. The final police estimate was about 8,000, which was only a couple thousand below the HDC estimate. As pictures published in *Life* magazine and elsewhere suggest, it was a beautiful march. One 70-year-old who watched was widely quoted: "This generation is better than mine."

Taking Action at AMF Plant

On April 6, following the announcement of the ten to two for acquittal hung jury verdict, Eqbal Ahmad was quoted in the local Harrisburg newspaper, the *Patriot*:

Addressing a crowd of about 50 outside the Federal Building after court adjourned, Ahmad said: "Be in York tomorrow and Washington on Monday; the war is escalating." All the defendants indicated they planned to be in front of the York [AMF] plant tomorrow, where Bob Hoyt, spokesman for the Harrisburg Defense Committee, said some act of civil disobedience probably would occur.

When the jury verdict came in, I was at the AMF plant leafletting. It had been decided beforehand that when the verdict came in, the defendants and others would come to the plant for some kind of demonstration, and a few of us were maintaining a vigil until that happened.

And this wasn't a pro forma action; at this time the Nixon Administration was in the midst of assembling a huge air and sea armada in and off Vietnam as a prelude to what soon became the mining of North Vietnam's two major ports in Hanoi and Haiphong and the renewed bombing of North Vietnam. A feeling of crisis was taking hold within the anti-war movement. It seemed clear that this was a critical time and a golden opportunity for us—the Harrisburg defendants and the HDC—to make a statement. The AMF plant was chosen as the place to do so.

The action took place the next day, April 6. Joe, Neil, and Eqbal took part, along with about seventy-five other people. We sat-in for a couple of hours on the front steps of the main entrance to the AMF plant, the entrance that management used, but with all of the national TV cameras present, it soon became clear they were not going to arrest us, so we dispersed.

So ended the inside and outside parts of the movement's and the lawyers' response to this act of repression by the government. Four weeks after the verdict, on May 2, J. Edgar Hoover died of a heart attack. It could certainly be seen as a just punishment for all of the fear and human misery he was responsible for over his lifetime that our case, his last major repressive effort, was a failure.

But this hardly registered with me or people I knew in the Catholic Left. Much more urgent was what was happening as far as the escalation of the war, and some of us did our best to respond accordingly.

CHAPTER EIGHT

A "Fast unto Death"

I write on the thirty-third day of a water-only fast begun August 6, Hiroshima Day, as a protest "against any continuation of the war by any method or for any reason." I began it with 13 other sisters and brothers in New York City, as well as eleven brothers in Danbury, Ct. federal prison who also started a fast from behind concrete walls and iron bars on the same day. The prisoners were soon transferred out to a Federal Prison for Medical Prisoners in Springfield, Mo., and two days ago ended their fast after 30 isolated and lonely days of trial. Seven of the original 14 here in New York have for various reasons broken their water fast, though some continue to take only liquids. Seven of us continue, planning at this point a "service of war resistance" on the steps of St. Patrick's Cathedral (having been denied the use of the church for the service) on the 40th day and with no date for termination set beyond that point. Our fast is open-ended, indeterminate in length.
—the author, September 8, 1972

By the beginning of May, a month after the end of the trial, the Nixon Administration had unleashed a massive, unprecedented air bombing campaign against the people of Indochina.

One month later, a group of about ten people met in Dan Berrigan's apartment to discuss a response to that bombing, which continued. One of the members of that group, Rev. Paul Mayer, had just returned from Vietnam and spoke very soberly of the devastation he had seen.

As we discussed how to respond, Dan Berrigan proposed what he called a "fast unto death." The idea was that those taking part in this fast would drink only water and resolve not to come off it until some to be specified action(s) occurred. In this way we would use our wasting bodies to dramatize the suffering the people of Indochina were undergoing every day.

I responded positively to this idea and hit the road to organize for it, traveling to various cities in the northeast to talk about the idea with members and supporters of the Ultra Resistance and anyone else who might be interested. I remember going to a national meeting of the People's Coalition for Peace and Justice in Louisville, Kentucky. When I announced this initiative at the meeting, Dave Dellinger, a national peace movement leader, responded very positively, which was encouraging.

By the beginning of August, there was a group of fourteen people committed to an "open-ended fast" rather than a "fast unto death." We agreed beforehand that it would go a minimum of forty days if at all possible and would continue for an indefinite period thereafter. It would be water-only and could conceivably continue "unto death," but we had received enough feedback and had discussed the action sufficiently among ourselves that we felt we did not want to lock ourselves into something that absolute.

We called our action a Fast for Life, and it began on August 6, 1972, the twenty-seventh anniversary of the bombing of Hiroshima.

Below are excerpts from a journal I wrote during that fast. Though not daily, I tried to make it as much as possible an accurate recording of the events, thoughts, feelings, and changes occurring in my life each day as the fast went on. It was written primarily in New York City, at the New York Theological Seminary where we lived during the fast. We were able to do so because of the support of the seminary president, the late Rev. Bill Webber. Part of it was also written in Miami, Florida, where many of us went to take part in protest actions during the Republican Convention that renominated Richard Nixon for president.

August 6, 1972
I write at the end of a first day on water—distilled for today though our doctor advisor, a good man, raised questions about the value of such a course. I write at the beginning of a long fast undertaken to end the war, and I want to use one sheet of paper for each of those words: TO END THE WAR.

Imagine! 14 people, risking all, TO END THE WAR! Why has it taken so long? The tides of history, our cowardice, our self-contained ruts, our lack of vision? Or the shifting flow of political developments, external of our lives? Whatever the reason for why now and why not earlier, the fact is that WE ARE NOW FASTING TO END THE WAR.

TO END THE WAR.

Simple words. Tonight they have meaning and power and strength. They are backed up with all the force of my own and 13 others' lives. They are real. The time IS now. Time to END THE WAR.

I have lived for 22, almost 23 years. I have been two years in college, one in jail. I have turned in draft cards and burned them. I have torn up draft files and burned them. I have spoken before thousands. I have been on trial. I have written anguished poems speaking of suicide. I have written bitter poems speaking of assassination. I have cried, I have cried out, I have divorced a wife, gained a life, been afraid, been helpless, powerless, nearly hopeless, in pain, in agony, joyless, loveless, alone.

I am no longer alone. I am alive and well with 13 sisters and brothers whom I love and respect. We are saying, the time is now to give it all, live it all, risk it all. TO END THE WAR.

I sense a great power and spirit is working within me. I know the coming days and weeks hold great things in store for me and others. My life is in Your hands, no one else's, and it feels right and good.

My life is in the hands of my countrypeople, men and women, as I lie down to recharge a spiritually high, physically weak body.

I cannot stop writing. I am tired yet I am not.

The action I am taking part in, embarking on, is not "the best thing available" at this time. It is the right action, at the right time, for the right purpose. Period. I have no qualms or hesitations about it. To be true to my life I must not eat, because fasting is the sincerest form of prayer, and I want to pray long and hard right now.

I lie down sure in the rightness of my life, looking toward the present and future to chart my course. I am but a stream feeding into a mighty, life-giving river/I am the river. I am strong. Because our cause is just.

August 7

Last night we had what we billed as a "Celebration of Resistance," which turned out instead to be a freewheeling discussion/argument on the relative pros and cons of the fast. It was most moving at points, like when the 14 of us spontaneously stated why we are doing this. What I briefly said was to quote a statement of Ho Chi Minh to the effect that the nearer you get to the top of a mountain, the harder the climb becomes. He used it in reference to what the Vietnamese could expect as regards an intensified level of the war and the need to redouble efforts at that time. I referred to it in reference to the possibility that the war, now in its worst stage, might be ended if we, as people and as a people, go more deeply into ourselves to find there new resources and strength, if we risk more and suffer more for peace.

There are noticeable physical effects of the fast already. I became dizzy three or four times today when I got up too rapidly. I find a more-or-less permanent condition of heartburn during my waking hours, with a good number of burps. I hope that in addition to that being part of the body's adjustment to this new situation, it is also related to an incipient healing of some of the digestive problems created in prison when I broke our 33-day fast last year too abruptly. Though none of us knows at this point what this fast is going to lead to, for each of us personally and for the movement, it is nice to realize that I may come out of it with a healed-up internal apparatus that has been unhealed for close to a year.

Our press conference—our initial one—was today. Dick Gregory and Paul Mayer, Paul especially, were most moving in their presentations. Paul spoke very simply and honestly of his trip to Vietnam. He spoke of the wholesale destruction of schools, hospitals, churches, pagodas, homes, dikes, the entire structure of the society. And he spoke of the conversation he had with a 70-year-old man who had lost 10 members of his family during a 2:00 a.m. B-52 bombing raid on his village. It was at that point that Paul's voice broke and he shed some tears. I had to fight to hold back my tears also.

It felt good today to hold back the tears though it would have felt better to let them go. It was good to feel that suffering, that pain, and to know that I was sharing in that, acting against that, in the strongest way I knew how. I hope that that feeling can be retained throughout, although I doubt that it can. I expect that as time goes along I will once more, as happened during last year's prison fast, become more self-contained, go deeper into myself, and will have to be conscious of the need to be human and warm with people around me.

August 9

Most of us went to a press conference today for the 11 prisoners in Danbury who are beginning a fast also. It went well. Press seems to be more aware and sensitive, which is good.

We are getting ourselves better organized. There are now two people who will be coordinating press releases and the contacting of press folks about interviews. Another person will be handling volunteer help as well as doing assorted other tasks. We have set two meeting times per day, at 10:15 and 6:30. One is for business details and the other is for a spiritual sharing of some kind.

August 10

Last night I felt incredibly hungry. And today I realized that in many ways, this is not my style, this voluntary sacrifice, this personal deprivation, and the longing and weakness that come with this action. My normal mode of operation is high energy, not the tiredness and listlessness that are becoming more and more my reality during this prolonged action.

I am orienting my hopes toward September as far as more of a response to what we are doing. That is when awareness and support will come, I would expect. Changes could occur before then, or we might feel the need to go longer, even to the end. As is our communal fast, I am open.

I wonder how long I'll be able to keep on writing this. It's beginning to be somewhat of an effort. I remember the days in Springfield during last year's fast when it was literally an effort to push a pen across a piece of paper.

I'm realizing that a great deal of community and a great deal of faith are required for actions of this kind. I feel confident that there is enough of both around.

August 15

Finally, after four days of absence from this writing exercise, I am sitting down to write. I have wished to do this many times in the past few days, but due to either sickness or tiredness or busy-ness I have not gotten down to it. But now, at 11:30 p.m., after a long and full day, I am at last writing again.

Last night we had a good evening rally with Dick Gregory and Dan Berrigan. Three or four hundred people were there. Good spirit and interest. I spoke on behalf of the Danbury inmates (now at Springfield) and was glad to do so. They are certainly undergoing more than we.

I'm still weak but the headache that I've been having is gone and I'm feeling much better. Dr. Fulton from Chicago [a woman Dick Gregory connected us with], who was here Wednesday, was saying that such is the case after the 10th day. We spent much time with her and learned a lot. Among other things, if and when we begin eating, I plan to do it in a much healthier way, maybe becoming a vegetarian. I don't want to wreck my body after learning what I have during this fast and after the fasting does its expected work of cleaning me out.

My attitude towards the death aspect of the fast wavers. At times I see myself going that route. At others, no. I want to live. I see new worlds and new experiences opening up from this action. I want to be around for a long time. Yet I want the war to end even more strongly. This is why I am doing this; that is what will determine our, or at least my, course.

There are times when I consider myself neither a Christian—I do not feel the spirit moving within me—nor a Marxist—I have no ultimate faith in the final victory of the revolution. Yet I am basically hopeful and optimistic, faithful and patient. That is because 1) I know that to do what is "better for God" (not sure if I know what that means or what He is), I must "struggle with all my might against death";[1] and 2) this road that I have taken, with all its pain and suffering, is the best one I can see. The friendships, the fellowship, the communion, the joy; all make this life worthwhile. I am a revolutionary because it is the best way to live and because we all must struggle against the deaths of others, the needless, cruel deaths of others, in order to be true to our own lives and our own responsibilities as human beings. At times that has to mean risking one's own life for the greater good. Such is the nature of things. Such is the reason for this fast.

August 20

I am writing from an air-conditioned hotel room in Miami Beach, Florida, site of the Republican National Convention where Richard Nixon will be nominated for reelection. There are peace and justice demonstrations, including nonviolent civil disobedience, planned for all of the days of the convention; we will take part in many of them.

Five of the 14 of us arrived here by car last night about 11:30 p.m., after a grueling seventeen-and-a-half-hour ride of close to 700 miles in one day. We left Fayetteville, NC, at 6:00 a.m. But I'm glad we did that and I'm glad we're here; it's given us the opportunity both to participate in a demonstration this morning and to catch up on some badly needed sleep. After 7 hours last night I slept for three more this afternoon and feel much better. Not exactly ready to take on the world but at least to face it.

Due to various human and mechanical difficulties, we ended up being either just ahead or just behind the Vietnam Veterans Against the War's "Last Convoy" all the way from NYC. We were very fortunate in that, while in Washington picking up a 1958 Cadillac that someone loaned to us, a driver appeared. His name is Clive Scully. He is visiting this country from Australia, and he has been a great help to us. If he weren't so damned authentic, as a person and as an Australian (accent and all), I'd have severe doubts about his not being a government agent; he came upon us so quickly upon our DC arrival. But he isn't, he's a godsend. Without him, those of us not eating would have had to divide up the driving duties.

There is no question that I'll have to pace myself more than usual down here, the heat being so vicious and overwhelming. I wonder how much weight I've lost by now. The last time I weighed myself it was 20 pounds, but that was three days ago and before this long trip.

For the next few days I participated in various protest activities. I remember being amazed by how much energy I still had two-plus weeks into the fast. Below is a journal I kept while locked up in jail with hundreds of others arrested on one particularly intense night of action. Most of us were arrested after doing a die-in, lying down peacefully in front of the Doral Hotel where Nixon and other top Republicans were staying. It was the night that he was nominated at the Republican Convention for a second term as president.

August 24, Dade County jail, 11:30 a.m.
People sit around quietly talking or lying down. In front of me on these hard metal tables sit some remnants from breakfast. I am glad I am fasting—"enriched" white bread, pasty grits, particles of artificial scrambled eggs. The Sheraton Hotel it is not.

A couple of people are a little panicky. One black guy from here in Miami, a Jesus freak of sorts, is talking around and around, about "all the trashing last night which justified" all the tear gas, his supposed time in Nam, his semi-berating of Father Jim Groppi for arranging a bail deal with a rabbi, etc. Another guy keeps saying that the judge told him we'd be released after two hours; that was about 4:30 a.m. this morning. I wonder if he was one of those who yelled the loudest or threw rocks.

A decent guard has come to the gate and is answering questions. The brothers are much more quiet, less rowdy now. I'm afraid they really want out, and that is the thought going around in their heads. But then, again, the guard has just said that there are 900 of us in here now, and that is not counting the women. That means at least 85% of us are still in—a good percentage.

I just suggested getting together to rap—good reception. The inveterate organizer! With prearranged pen and paper, no less.

August 24, 1:00 p.m.
Lunch is over. White bread bologna sandwiches (two, with one small slice each of spam), lard and sugar cookies, and Kool-Aid. At

most 25 cents per person. At times like this I'm not only in no difficulty by fasting, I think of something Dan Berrigan has referred to, the better treatment of animals in a zoo, the better food they receive. I was just at Prospect Park in Brooklyn three weeks ago, seeing the seals and bears eating meat and fish. Yet we get this stuff.

Lots more people have come up here, I suppose to be put in similar lockups down the way. One was a friend of mine who I'm concerned about. Last night I was with him for a bit after the first teargassing at 34th and Collins Sts., and he spoke of being on probation.

More talking—the word about my fast is getting around and that's good. People are speaking with me about it.

A chant, "All or None," has gone up and subsided in response to people being called up front, for cigarettes it seems and not for a bail call. Good solidarity, hope it holds up.

August 24, 7:10 p.m.
We've been having a continual series of meetings and breaks, among ourselves and with lawyers, over the whole bail situation. What has happened is that, through solidarity among those of us imprisoned here, in various locations across the city where we're located, we seem to have gotten the bail lowered for almost all those arrested. At one point some had bails as high as $500–2,500, so we've won a victory. In addition, we'll all be coming out together, from the various jails, at approximately the same time. The people in the Dade County Stockade, who have the money to bail all 193 of themselves out, are waiting until money is raised for all of us. That is right on and powerful.

There was one meeting today that didn't deal with the bail/legal situation. That was a meeting I helped to pull together, with most of the 40–45 or so here in the block participating, where we talked personally of our backgrounds and some of our politics. Unfortunately, just as it was becoming decent, the meeting was broken up by one of the bail meetings. I think it had its hoped-for result of bringing people more together and establishing a better sense of community. It was good training for me for the next long stretch I do in jail and the organizing I will do there, the organizing which was taught me in many ways by Dan and Phil in Danbury. Who says that jail is a waste? It can be a place for maximum human growth.

There's a young kid in here, about 16 years old, I'd guess, who has the $2,500 bail, or who did. The reason? Because of the name and address he gave to the arraigning judge (who also happened to be the worst judge we collectively experienced, based on what I've heard): Typical Youth, from Anytown, USA. He's young, angry, immature, highly individualistic, yet with great potential, I believe. He brushes off concern for his having to stay in here longer with offhanded remarks that indicate a noticeable lack of communalism and understanding of solidarity.

Is that surprising? As one who's clearly new to the movement, he is full of the cultural values of America which say that a man is one who can stand alone against all hardship and "ride the storm," thus "becoming a man." This is the logic of the military, for example. In the process, much alienation from fellows, bitterness, hardening and destruction take place, leading to an individual who has a hard time genuinely loving or being loved. That is the danger with Typical Youth, and that is why I will go talk with him in a minute.

There are others here who have lives of note. One is a Vietnam vet just returned one month ago from that land of death, one who spent a month in Long Bình Stockade at hard labor for something related to "the wrong attitude." Another is a 17-year-old kid from California who has begun to find a new life in the movement as a result of this action and what is going on in this jail. He was at a seminary in Orange County, is now unsure what he'll be doing. His hair is short and he's straight-looking, something I wouldn't have noted but that he has a white and blue-spotted headband which he made from his own shirt. My hope and trust are that he, a former student body president, will continue to march with us and provide us with the leadership we will continue to need, continue to need to develop.

From all indications, we should be getting out fairly soon. It's been a real good experience, for me and for almost everyone here. I sense that a lot of human growth and political maturation has taken place in the past 24–36 hours of this action. It was well worth the trip down.

August 24, 8:30 p.m.
We just raised up a loud, militant, chant—clapping, pounding, "1, 2, 3, 4, we don't want your fucking war!" As a result the captain of the jail has come up and is threatening us. There's now some negotiation for blankets happening on the other side, in the cellblock next to us. It's been successful, and in addition the main jail guard here, who's been coming up throughout the day, has come up again to tell us he has instructed the night captain to fill our guts tomorrow a.m. (if we're here) with peanut butter and jelly sandwiches and hot coffee. Whoopee. But they have had their effect, both the noisy, spirit-lifting action which turned into a protest demonstration, and the official's efforts to quiet things down with a mixture of hard words and petty bribes.

August 25, 10:00 a.m.
We're still here, and the brothers are singing away, all kinds of old songs from 10 to 15 years back in our collective childhoods. The spirit is high because we were just told that not only are the other prisoners who have bails over $100 getting them reduced, but we are also getting out without any bail at all. Lawyer Mike Sigel just confirmed that; two of us have returned after a bail reduction from $500 to $0.

The power of the people, exhibited in the last 36 hours. An important event, without doubt, for those here and for the movement.

The spirits are high, yet there were a couple signs of wavering this morning when 9:30 came around and we were still here though informed last night that what has happened now would be happening by then. In fact, one of those in the highest spirits now, leading the singing and being generally the loudest throughout the experience here, was the one who this morning was saying he wanted to get out of here, the one with the least patience. The discipline for the long haul is not there, and changes will have to take place if he is to become a true leader.

But there are a small but good number of others here who have the discipline, the patience, the perspective, the self-control and the potential. There are good people, a representative cross section of humanity, here. Herein is our New Society, needing a lot of growth and maturation but here nevertheless. May it grow and grow throughout the next months and years and change this society before it is too late.

August 25 (later, out of jail)
In the failing light, at a table by the window in the card-playing room of the Victor Hotel in Miami Beach, I resume my out-of-jail journal. I'll attempt some kind of a summary of the days just past.

Much of the time leading up to my arrest on Wednesday night at 11:30 p.m. is jumbled in my memory. I know that the Women's Rally on Monday night went off well, and I know that I left when it started to rain and I missed the George Jackson rally. I know that I spent much of Tuesday night running around the outside of Convention Hall during the "Street Without Joy" action, trying to calm those who were pegging rocks at cops or hitting cars as they drove by us or calling the police "pigs." And I know that Wednesday was spent preparing for and involving myself in the eventual sit-down with several hundred others at the Doral Hotel. But rather than go into an account of each of those days, I'll give my overall impression of the people here, the dynamics of the situation, and observations on what this week has meant personally and politically.

Most of the movement veterans were not here this week, those who have been active in one or another phase of the struggle for years. There were exceptions, and a fairly large number of them, but generally most of the people here were fairly new, fairly unsophisticated politically. That was certainly borne out by the jail experience.

Most people with me were in jail for the first time for any movement bust. They were young, wild, freaky, in high spirits generally, and I felt within their company very much like an old hand at this game at the age of 23. That was good in that the 36 hours I spent with them in jail were of real benefit to all of us. I was able to help increase their consciousness and political sophistication, and they were able to teach me more about where that segment of America sometimes called "street people" is at.

At my arraignment at 5:00 a.m. Thursday morning, I noted the occupations given by the other 8–9 people arraigned with me. All responded to the effect that they worked only enough to get money to live on. Their jobs were painter, mate on boats, carpenter, welder, house painter, Copacobana employee, with one other a student and one a more-or-less full-time movement worker from San Francisco. They were from all over the country: New York, Berkeley, Ca., Kennebunk, Me., San Diego, Toledo, Oh., and me from Harrisburg, Pa. They were representative of others also in jail, I'm sure.

They were quite a bunch, these brothers and sisters here this week. Most of them were committed to nonviolence, yes, but with a militance and spirit that verged on violence. I got the sense Wednesday night, after we marched up Collins Avenue, were teargassed and then regrouped on Washington Avenue for the march to the Doral Hotel, that perhaps more than anything else these people needed a clear leadership. They were open to change and growth and they did change and grow, most especially in the 48-hour period from Wednesday afternoon to Friday afternoon, during the most militant street actions and in jail.

The difficulties experienced this week, at the park which was our gathering point and during some of the actions, stemmed mainly from the fact that, for various reasons, leadership was either unclear or diffused among different competitors for it. But the people wanted leadership, that much was clear in jail. Missing were the anti-leadership feelings of past years, and that is healthy and hopeful.

August 28—back in New York City
I left Miami Saturday night after a day during which I slept long into the morning, finished reading *Pedagogy of the Oppressed*, typed up my jail notes and sent them off to *Win* magazine, hopefully for publication, fainted and hit my head on the floor in the Miami Coalition office (from which mishap I had headaches for

the next 24 hours or so), and saw the worst side of Miami on a ride from the downtown section to the airport via public transportation. Yet while riding I felt much at home, there with the poor or near-poor, going through the rundown housing projects.

At the airport I bought several books, one on health foods which I proceeded to read on the way up north on the plane. I also got a small rubber alligator to send to my four-month-old nephew Eric.

Reading the health foods book, I felt like I'm becoming more wise in the ways of good eating. If and when this fast ends, I'm looking forward to following through on this knowledge and actually taking time to learn how to prepare decent foods.

Sunday was a lazy day spent primarily watching TV—the Olympics, a couple of football games and some baseball. I actually disciplined myself to "do" that activity, knowing that I needed some rest after the time in Miami. I think it did help because, whereas yesterday I became dizzy almost every time I got up, today wasn't that way. I believe I'm regaining some needed strength.

Also on Sunday I talked some with the others who are here, and some of the conflicts caused by a number of factors began to appear more openly. Those were dealt with at this evening's meeting.

At the meeting we talked about where we each were individually and collectively at this point in the fast. Not all of us were there—two people have dropped out, others were elsewhere doing different things. To my way of thinking the meeting was good, a re-beginning of a process that has been disrupted.

There were two factors behind the discontent which had some people thinking of going off the fast. One was our not working hard enough at building community, not seeing the necessity for it. The other was our outreach work not proceeding smoothly and clearly. Disputes are by no means fully resolved, and we will have to continue to struggle to define and redefine this action, our tasks and our lives within it, but I think we're pulling through.

Tom Lumpkin, a Catholic priest from Detroit, gave a beautiful rap tonight in which he spoke of how, through meditation and prayer and suffering, he was drawing closer to the Vietnamese and feeling more a part of their lives. He went on to say that through that process he was beginning to feel that he quite possibly could decide to go to the end, as many of them are forced to do. That was good input—to get that seriousness back into our psyches again. We must be willing to go that far, if we think it valid and politically sound. It is from that commitment that much of our power comes. Just as the Vietnamese are strong because they have accepted their deaths and are therefore willing to risk their lives for what is right, so must we be willing to do the same, now and for the rest of our lives.

August 30

I feel—impatient, somewhat intolerant, not open, as if I were someone I would rather not be with right now. It's a certain internal tightness, not so much physically as emotionally. I find myself more prone to become anxiety-stricken to a disturbing degree, where I have to concentrate, breathe hard and deep, in order to relax myself. I feel that anxiety more deeply right now than when I began the paragraph, and I find myself breathing deeply in order to alleviate it.

Dave Dellinger spoke today of Rennie Davis, one of the other Chicago 8 defendants with Dave,[2] at about this point in his fast down in Miami, being extremely uptight and nervous about speaking at one of the evening rallies in front of the Convention Hall. Dave said that he'd never seen him so unconfident and afraid of how he would be received. Dick Gregory cautioned against getting into heated political discussion or arguments, and he himself, at 96 pounds, exhibited a high degree of intolerance and arrogance.

I guess I really am going through a change right now. I'll have to work at staying human and not losing my temper easily, as I'm becoming increasingly prone to do.

We've been spending the past days pulling ourselves together as a community as well as working on outreach, and I feel good about that. Unfortunately, Ann Walsh has come off the fast. She is really a great woman; I hate to see her leave.

I'm very consciously going much more slowly these days. In the way I respond after someone has said something to me, in the way I get up, in most ways—except mentally where I feel very alert—I'm pacing myself much more. This is a necessity during this action.

When I travel in the city I notice a difference in the air quality between certain less traveled side streets and the heavier traveled avenues. That is certainly something new. I clearly notice a difference when in a park or among trees, though I believe I also noted today that the trees in the park at evening seemed much less alive, the leaves less green and vibrant, than when I was last there during the afternoon in the sun.

I've lost about 32–33 pounds now, down to 147. It shows too.

August 31

I've been fairly down most of the day. The two major causes (the first of which has been resolved) were the temporary loss of some clothes brought from Harrisburg for me and learning about the latest Gallup Poll showing Nixon even further ahead, 64–30 percent, over McGovern.

I find myself going deeper and deeper into this fast; that is to say, feeling more and more like it will end up going the whole way. I feel committed at this point to going that route if it seems necessary and if the course of events does not change. Perhaps by our deaths we will be able do what the Germans in the 30s, who knew what was happening, did not bring themselves to do. What would have been the effect if 5, 6, or 7 Germans had allowed themselves to die in protest of the crimes and direction of Hitler before he consolidated his power? No one knows, just as we do not know what would happen here.

Sarah, my ex-wife, once criticized me for always speaking to the whole world. My response was to silently absorb her words. There was not much to say in response unless it's perhaps that, no, I'm not trying to speak to the world as much as I am trying to live up to my conception of my responsibilities as a man and as an historical being. I suppose it's a corollary of that that such individuals are usually much more likely to be "speaking to the whole world," because it, as we all individually do somewhere deep inside, yearns for the right path and the truth. The difficulty is that the way of truth is hard, especially in a country and a century so barbaric and savage—all the more so because of its surface veneer of at-oneness, of achievement, of quality (36 medals for us so far at the Olympics!).

How have we gotten to this state? Is this "God's plan?" What kind of God? What kind of God would be the spiritual overseer of the tragedy being played out down here at this time? Certainly no benevolent God, certainly no Candyman God, certainly no God who sets up and maintains a well-ordered universe.

Well ordered! Things could not be less so! Indochina. Nixon. Brazil. Argentina. Soviet Czechoslovak dissenters in jail or mental hospitals, the recent slaughter of so many people in Bengladesh. And on and on. In such a world, where sits a God of love and justice? For if He is not that, of what use and value is he? None at all!

And yet there are the ones who keep alive the flame of loving freedom, who nourish it, who hide it from the Feds, who make it visible at great risk at times, who spread the sparks. Yet too, there is a peace movement still in this country composed of many dedicated and hardworking individuals, people who by their lives keep hope and faith alive, who embody, if there is such a being, God, who live Him out through their daily lives.

I do not know about God's existence or non-existence, and I would go so far as to say we cannot know, all of us here on this earth. What I know is people, and myself, and the massive evil and oppression around me, the lives that do not give, the hearts that no longer feel, if once they did, the minds that either shut out or never knew. And at times the latter threaten to overwhelm the former, extinguishing my "faith," drowning my "hope," putting to rest once and for all my "dreams." Yet I struggle on and despite all, I do have faith, and hope, and dreams. Indeed, at rock bottom, that is all I have. And, of course, a life, which I am more than willing to give to keep alive in others their faith, hope, dreams, love, joy, communion, friendship, compassion. We all should be willing to do the same. We all should realize that now is the time for just that giving. It is always now.

I wrote and submitted the piece below to various places for publication. The first paragraph, shortened below, is found in full at the beginning of this chapter. In retrospect, I think I wrote it because that day Dave Dellinger told us he was coming off the fast, which was disappointing. He did so because he was invited by the North Vietnamese government to receive and return to the U.S. several American prisoners of war.

> September 8
>
> I write on the thirty-third day of a water-only fast begun August 6, Hiroshima Day, as a protest against any continuation of the war by any method or for any reason. . . . Seven of the original 14 here in New York have broken their water fast, though some continue to take only liquids. Seven of us continue. . . . Our fast is open-ended, indeterminate in length.
>
> Two of the seven are Roman Catholic priests, one a former Jew who was a refugee from Nazi Germany. Two are women in their early 20s under indictment for the destruction of draft files in Camden, NJ. One is a 21-year-old woman whose real desire, were it not for the continuing slaughter of the people of Indochina, is to become the female equivalent of a monk. Another is a 23-year-old graduate of Notre Dame University and the Institute for Nonviolence there, a draft resister. Lastly, there is myself.
>
> I have lost 40 pounds in 33 days and am quite weak physically. Yet spiritually I remain strong, convinced that such an action is not only consistent with the life I have led the past four years, not only much in the religious tradition out of which I came and with which I identify, but also wholly appropriate for the current phase of the war, entirely commensurate with the massive suffering being inflicted upon the people of Indochina as the war rages on and the bombing is continued more heavily than ever.
>
> Believing that my people do not want to be "good Americans," I began and continue this fast to help awaken them to the realities which I perceive and the responsibilities we all have toward one another. My urgent cry: do not give your support or your silent consent to this war and to those who carry it out. Use your vote, your voice, and your life now. We cannot be silent and unwitting accomplices to one of the most horrible and heart-rending agonies of our time—the continuing war upon the people of Indochina.

September 9

We had a quite helpful meeting yesterday. My feeling that the power of the fast was diminishing because people were dropping out (and on that day Dave Dellinger, for very good reasons) was not shared by a number of others, including all those present outside of the fast, yet continually close to it from the beginning. As a result, we decided to go ahead both with the 40-day St. Patrick's event (never really in doubt), as well as a foray down to the DC Nixon reelection headquarters the day before that, the 39th day, armed with empty rice bowls, to see what kind of further press coverage could be gained. After that we would continue on water indefinitely, evaluating on a day-to-day basis according to how we felt, how events were progressing (or not), how our health was deteriorating (or not).

My concern, I suppose, is that not only are we at different levels in terms of a commitment to continue on water—from Tom's willingness to go till death to Cookie and Lianne's not going past the point of irreparable damage to personal health, with me now somewhere in between, leaning more towards Tom—but we are at different levels in terms of physical effects. Tom, for example, is the most weakened and sickly-looking, very hollow and gaunt. He's now down to 99 pounds, from around 140 originally.

Those kinds of differences will have to be kept in mind and worked at in whatever we decide, whenever we decide (as appears will most likely be the course we follow) to go onto juices. But we'll work it out. One of the advantages of our being just seven at present is that we're a more manageable and close community, much more than has been the case in the past.

September 12

Tom Lumpkin is off water, onto juices, and it looks extremely likely that the rest of us will be also by the end of the week, after the 40 days. Tom went off yesterday at the encouragement of the group, because he was doing so badly—having difficulty swallowing and breathing—and at the advice of our doctor out in Chicago, Gregory's friend. He is now drinking grape juice and I think V-8 juice—the main items we will soon be onto—and though he looks as terrible and feeble as ever, he says he feels better. He really does look like a World War II Jew from Dachau or Auschwitz saved from the gas ovens.

We have decided—most of the remaining fasters feel fairly strongly, with Paul and I somewhat more ambivalent—to go onto juices sometime this weekend. It's not quite definite when that will be, though we will be having a break-fast celebration somewhere in NYC for folks who want to be with us for that occasion.

From a physical standpoint that's good for me. Since Sunday, I've not been in the best of shape. I'm now down to about 134 pounds or so, have difficulty drinking water both in terms of not liking the taste and in terms of swallowing. I feel out-of-sorts and by no means healthy, am quite weak and often dizzy, and I find a number of internal digestive problems are reappearing. The swallowing difficulty is related there, I believe. I suppose the health part of the fast is now over and I'm entering the breaking-down-of-the-body stage. Paul Mayer and Cookie Ridolfi, as well as Tom, of course, are also experiencing some difficulties, so it seems not an isolated phenomenon.

I suppose from that angle it's good we're almost through, though politically I feel that if most of the 14 and the Danbury folks were still on it, that even with the effects on our bodies, it'd be best to push on. But, clearly, we see ourselves much differently now than on August 6. Hopefully there is also some difference as far as our action having had some effect. I believe it has, in subtle and hard to pinpoint ways. There are signs—other fasts, letters, statements circulated, people speaking about it, another NBC TV interview this morning, a Collegiate Press Service interview this evening—that it has had and is having effects and will have more as at least some of us continue on liquids.

Tomorrow we're going to DC and the Nixon reelection headquarters with empty rice bowls. Thursday we're in front of St. Patrick's for a service of resistance. Hopefully they'll draw some coverage.

September 13
It's been a long, full and good day. The major event was the action in DC, which went very well. We flew down in the morning and

back in the afternoon. In between was a walk—very, very slowly because Paul Mayer couldn't go any faster—from Lafayette Park to the Nixon headquarters, with the seven of us carrying our empty rice bowls that someone at the last minute, thank heavens, got to us. There were about 25 people in support walking with us, with some well-done signs and a good bit of press coverage.

At the headquarters we read a statement about empty rice bowls and the relation to rice and food in Indochina—possible famine in the north either from dikes breaking or the naval blockade, which is 85% concerned with foodstuffs being kept out. We spoke about the rice riots in Cambodia and the transformation of the Mekong Delta, once the "rice bowl of Southeast Asia," into a rice-importing area, South Vietnam into a rice-importing country. I think it was an effective statement and one touching on an important, new area in many ways.

September 14

Well, here it is, the 40th day. It's almost over, Phase 1 of the 1972 Fast. Tomorrow begins Phase 2, for me, on juices and liquids until the election, at least. It feels good to know that tomorrow I'll be drinking something other than this terrible water that I've come to hate.

The fast ended appropriately; we had a fine service on the steps of St. Patrick's, one which came together well. We were surprised to be able to have it there without being told to move on, but I suppose that even Cardinal Cooke had trouble booting away people who had been on only water, with a bit of lemon and honey, for 40 days.

September 15

"Upon Ending Our Fast for Life," a public statement released by our group:

Today, September 15, 1972, we are ending our 40-day water only fast. Some of us plan to continue fasting, to eat no solid foods, for an indefinite period of time. Others will soon return to a normal eating routine.

In the course of those 40 days on water eight of our original group of 14 have had either to end the fast altogether or switch to a liquid diet. The reasons have been many and varied, ranging from David Dellinger's need to break it because of an invitation to him from North Vietnam to bring back POW's, to Fr. Tom Lumpkin breaking it on the 37th day because of difficulty in breathing and swallowing. All acted, as was true for the fast itself, as free women and men with every intention of continuing serious forms of activity against the war.

We end our fast with a deeper understanding of our lives, of the suffering of the people of Indochina, and of the interconnection between the two. More than ever we feel the urgency of their deaths, their destroyed homes and food, their threatened cultures. More than ever we remember them in this fall election year when their lives and their future hang so precariously in the balance.

As we began our fast in hope and faith so do we end it. We have seen positive signs and results from our action: other public fasts, people devoting more of their time and energy to the issue of the war, positive support and concern from a number of sources, and, we believe, a deepened commitment to the struggle for peace and liberation on the part of greater numbers of Americans. Our action has not ended the war; yet, seen in the context of an increasing variety of activities around the country—traveling anti-war shows, grassroots community education on the war, demonstrations at Nixon reelection offices, peoples' blockades of ships and arms to Indochina, resistance to taxes levied to pay for war—our action has been of value.

At the same time we continue to feel that the level of seriousness of the American people as a whole is not commensurate with the serious crisis the people of Indochina are being subjected to and which led us to begin this action. As we move from one form of struggle and resistance into another we again affirm, in the words of our original August 6 statement: "We believe that the deaths on the battlefield and in the areas under attack by bombing and shelling cannot be tolerated any longer. We believe that the time has come when the American people can and will stop the war." We urge all Americans to join with us in continued work and acts of resistance toward that goal.

    Ted Glick
    Val Hendy
    Fr. Paul Mayer
    Mike McCale
    Lianne Moccia
    Cookie Ridolfi

September 16

It was a week ago that I began to become conscious, for the first time in over a month, of the fact that I was definitely not going to die as a result of this action. Quite honestly, I now realize that I had accepted my death in the midst of this as a real possibility.

I am aware that I must develop some way—psychologically, mentally, and emotionally, much more than financially or physically—to deal with what I have called "the tension inherent in living in a time of death," knowing that I can only consider myself a human being if I am living a life for others, in resistance, not forgetful of the sufferings of my brothers and sisters elsewhere, especially Indochina.

One crucial insight that I believe has been gained, or more fully realized, as a result of the fast is my awareness that other people, a community, loved ones, are essential to my being able to balance that tension. I need others who are struggling with those same questions, first of all and most importantly, but also others who have not yet begun to struggle with them, who are so wrapped up in their own oppressive lives that such questions have never even been posed. I must be willing to help in the posing of questions, the transmission of that sense of transcendence which allows oneself to see his or her position within society and then move from it. In that helping, that teaching, organizing, working, lie the hope and faith which sustain.

Another positive result of the fast is that for the first time I'm dealing with the personal health issue in a very serious way. That is, I'm learning how to cook and eat good foods to make myself feel better emotionally and physically. I'm learning how to breathe more deeply—more deeply around trees than in the subways!—as I discover how important fresh air (water, soil) is to us all. I'm learning how to pace myself and how to combine the hard work that I enjoy with the rest and the play I need. In short, I have been learning how to take care of myself in a decaying and polluting culture. And that is crucial.

It is crucial, and yet I know myself. I know that as I become more responsive to my own real needs and desires, I will not let that become a "selfish" concern. Rather, that concern must be one for the "self," the deepest and truest within me, so that I can then more effectively use and give my life, in whatever risk-taking, organizing, law-breaking, strain-inducing, suffering-bringing ways the months and years will bring.

I will resolve the tension by living with it and cultivating it in myself and in others, by leading myself and by leading others in the same direction, by working with others who want to go the same way. Together we may not achieve the Kingdom of God on earth we strive for, but we will try, and I have no doubt but that Life will win out over Death in the way I live my life and in the life of my country. To that end I dedicate myself.

CHAPTER NINE

Anti-War Burglar Culture

Like William Davidon, the Raineses felt hope was becoming scarce. Like him, they also were looking for more powerful non-violent ways to protest the war. One of John's graduate students introduced them to people in the Catholic peace movement. The Raineses found their optimism renewed, as Davidon did, by the Catholic resisters. John remembers being impressed by the fact that the Catholic peace movement resisters were "angry, but they also were optimistic and hopeful." The Raineses—whose protest and resistance grew originally out of a "deep liking for the country rather than a deep hatred of the country"—came to feel they shared common ground with the Catholic activists.
—Betsy Medsger, *The Burglary*[1]

What was it like on a day-to-day level to be part of the Ultra Resistance? How did its members interact with each other? What were the underlying values? What was the internal culture like?

There were two cultural traditions that influenced our way of interacting. One had deep roots in the best of Catholicism. The other came out of the New Left, specifically the youth-based draft resistance movement that began to emerge in the mid-1960s.

Thomas and Marjorie Melville, a former nun and former priest and members of the Catonsville 9, wrote in a *New York Times* op ed on April 26, 1971, about the role of Pope John the XXIII in "changing things" within Catholicism:

In his famous encyclicals Mater et Magistra and Pacem in Terris he spelled out Catholic responsibility in social matters and launched the process of making the Church relevant to twentieth-century consciousness of war, racism and poverty. When Pope John convoked the Second Vatican Council, he initiated reevaluation in the Church on every level: theological, moral and disciplinary.[2]

As a non-Catholic who, at the time, had had virtually no interaction with priests, nuns, or religious Catholics, I was impressed with the humanity and concern for the individual person evidenced by all of the Catholics I met and worked with. I wasn't surprised by this, on one level. I had grown up in a Protestant church, the Church of the Brethren, and by and large my experiences had been good ones. I had felt support from and a sense of community with other church members. The problems that I developed with the Church of the Brethren as I grew older were due to what I saw as its unwillingness to speak out and take action on major issues of war and injustice.

This wasn't at all a problem with the religious members of the Catholic Left. They combined a willingness to take strong, prophetic action, as advocated by Pope John XXIII, with a "beloved community" way of being together. Both attributes were very attractive to me and to a growing number of others who were neither Catholic nor particularly religious.

Resistance Culture

The other strain that influenced our way of interacting was the culture that emerged as young men who burned or turned in their draft cards and women who supported this tactic actively organized as part of local Resistance groups. The book, *The Resistance*, described it this way:

Meetings were conducted informally, and usually by consensus rather than balloting. Some of the early Resistance organizers, who set the style of their groups, gained their movement experience with SNCC [initially the Student Nonviolent Coordinating Committee; later the Student National Coordinating Committee], which reached most of its decisions by consensus. Other Resistance organizers came from northern student organizations like early Students for a Democratic Society (SDS), Committee for Nonviolent Action or Quaker youth groups, where consensus was the rule. At times Resistance meetings resembled group therapy sessions. Resisters, or those on the verge of resisting, stayed up all night talking, "getting their heads out," probing themselves and each other in a very personal way.[3]

Bruce Nelson, an active member of the Resistance in San Francisco in the 1960s, wrote about it as follows:

Many Resistance members are deeply concerned with the for-mation of community, and in some instances our common com-mitment is leading to the development of strong communal bonds. For at least two reasons this must continue to be a central concern. First, it would be impossible for most of us to face up to the tasks ahead, particularly the prospect of prison, were it not for the strength which derived from the experience of commu-nity. Secondly, the formation of community may bear an essential relationship to the shape of the future. Already, after only a few years of existence, the radical movement of the 1960's stands in danger of being consumed by its alienation from—and, in many cases, its hatred of—the old order. If radicals are to remain faithful to their own values, then they must create mechanisms in which those values can not only be expressed but also experienced in the present.[4]

The Ultra Resistance developed at the same time that Students for a Democratic Society, a major national organization, self-destructed and split into several different groups, the most famous of which was the Weather Underground (WU). WU's first public action was the "Days of Rage" violent actions in downtown Chicago in early October 1969, where several hundred people acted out their anger at the war and racism by vandalizing homes, businesses, and automobiles. There were also battles with the police, leading to dozens of injuries and the arrest of close to three hundred WU members. Soon afterward, the WU went underground and began a campaign of bombings that continued for several years.

In the late 1960s, I was a member of a local SDS group at Grinnell College, in Iowa, but our group was very tame compared to the national SDS scene. I was never attracted to any of the SDS split-off groups, but I agreed with the WU about the need to take stronger action to try to end the war. I agreed with that sense of urgency. But I joined the Catholic Left, because they combined action commensurate to the urgency with a commitment to nonviolence and the building of a beloved community.

The Central Role of Retreats

Most of those who became involved first attended a weekend-long retreat, as I did when I traveled to Baltimore in December 1969. The retreats were for people who were open to the idea of participating in an action. They were run in what Jerry Elmer described as an "encounter group" style:

> The theory was that if you were going to become involved in a high-risk public action together with other people you should first know them very intimately. In the context of possible [long] prison sentences, it was perfectly reasonable to want to know your partners well, to feel comfortable with them.[5]

What this meant in practice was that the discussions at the retreats took place in a circle, which generated more personal connection and built a sense of community. There weren't any long speeches given by those running the retreats, whether Phil Berrigan or other priests, who were most often the leaders. Everyone spoke, and everyone was expected to talk about why they were there, what was motivating them.

The realistic possibility of spending years in prison was a main topic of discussion. "The discussions about prison at these retreats were certainly the best I was ever a part of. There was little superficiality, probably because of the nature of our shared enterprise."[6]

Some who attended these retreats decided that they weren't willing to take part in an action, although my sense of things is that if you were invited to a retreat, the chances were good that you would "sign up." Those from the action community who knew you and had recommended you were usually accurate in their assessment of potential participants. There were also some whose participation at a retreat led leaders of the Ultra Resistance to decide they were not a good match, and who were told that and asked to leave. My sense is that this was rare.

People at the retreats helped to prepare the food for meals and to wash the dishes and clean up afterward. This too was very much part of the process of building community and healthy relationships, participating together in this most essential of life processes.

Those who initiated and led the first years of the Catholic Left understood from life experience that human interconnection was an essential aspect of not just a person's life but the life of a movement. Father Joseph O'Rourke, part of the DC 9 group that disrupted a Dow Chemical office in March 1969, told a story about the funeral in Missouri in late October 1969 for David Darst, the youngest of the Catonsville 9, who died in a car crash:

> [It was] the saddest thing I've ever been to and yet the most celebratory and wonderful. We were in a big trolley barn having a party that night, just holding each other up, more or less. Somebody started to play "Zorba the Greek" on the record player. Everybody started to dance, that old, turgid tune. We must have had 150 people, all with their arms linked, doing the Zorba the Greek dance. We just went on, for half an hour. Funerals and weddings, actions and trials, those were the times for great gatherings of the community.[7]

Barbara Shapiro Dougherty, a participant in the Boston 8 action in November 1969, wrote about her experiences in this way:

> There were many, many wonderful all-night conversations with members of what we called the Resistance community, and for me this was the heart and life source of the movement. That we were capable of extended interest in each other and ideas. That the next day's schedule did not take precedence over the gift of sharing life's ideas and fears with someone else who was as aware as you were that to watch tomorrow come and bring it in by investing yourself in knowing someone else would shape a better tomorrow than sleep.[8]

Ultimately, though, what most mattered within this particular Resistance community was successfully taking action to disrupt draft boards, FBI offices, or war corporation offices or products.

Preparing the Actions

Soon after the Baltimore retreat in late 1969, I left the town of Lancaster, Pennsylvania, where I had been living and doing peace organizing, and moved to Philadelphia to take part in the planning of what became the February 1970 East Coast Conspiracy to Save Lives draft board actions.

John Grady, described in chapter three, was our leader, no question about it. Most of the people doing the preparatory work were young and had no idea of what needed to be done, but John did.

We met often, reviewing plans and determining who would be doing what that day or night. John ran the meetings.

The work of the teams was to observe what was happening inside the building in North Philadelphia that housed a draft board office, i.e., lights that might go on to indicate the movement of a night watchman, as well as to observe the car and pedestrian traffic in the area. We made notes on index cards.

From the house that served as our base camp, we could frequently hear police helicopters flying over the inner city. Once when a couple of people were leaving the house in the middle of the night to go do their casing, a police helicopter was hovering nearby, shining a very bright light onto our block very close to our house. But as far as we could tell they weren't there to surveil us; this was just a part of the way of life for people living in low-income neighborhoods in the inner city, particularly neighborhoods populated by people of color.

I don't remember too many instances of our close communal living quarters causing serious interpersonal conflict. I am sure that both the fact that we were focused on an important task and John's leadership helped a lot in that regard.

The next action I was part of after the East Coast Conspiracy action, three months later in May 1969, was with the group We the People. This group successfully returned to the same North Philadelphia draft board that I helped to case and enter in January and February as part of the East Coast Conspiracy. This time our group was successful, getting into the draft board office and out of the building with thousands of draft files. We did so even though, after the aborted raid in February, the Selective Service officials outfitted the office with alarms on all the doors and windows. We got around that by sawing a hole in an alarmed wooden back door facing onto a stairway where we hid. We didn't have to open the door to get in, crawling in and out through the hole, and, therefore, the alarm didn't go off.

In preparation for this action a number of us lived for about a month in the Germantown section of Philadelphia in a house owned by a university professor and his wife. They had three wonderful small kids, all less than five years old at the time. The attic was our office, where we kept our maps, charts, and everything else we needed. It was a special situation to be interacting with young children and having meals sometimes with the family, as we did our preparatory work.

The third action I was part of took place in Delaware. There were two groups that prepared for actions in Wilmington, Dover, and Georgetown, all of the draft board offices for the entire state. One group worked out of a rented apartment in Wilmington; the other group, which I was part of, about six or seven of us, camped out for several weeks in the middle of the state. Every night, we would leave the public campsite to go do our casing of the Dover and Georgetown draft boards. The proprietor of the campsite, who was friendly, never questioned us about our almost daily late evening trips. All three of these nighttime draft board raids were successful.

My fourth action was the one in Rochester. This one was not organized by the Ultra Resistance but primarily by Suzi Williams and DeCourcy Squire. However, they reached out to our network for additional people and expertise. I arrived in town several days before the planned action to take part in the final preparations.

My fifth and last action took place after I was indicted in the Harrisburg 8 (Minus 1) case and after I had gotten out of prison for the Rochester action. While living in Harrisburg helping to prepare for the trial, a group of us came together to organize the action in March 1972 at the AMF plant in York, where bomb casings for use in Vietnam were produced. Most of us who did the preparatory casing work for the action lived in Harrisburg or central Pennsylvania; one, Bill Davidon, lived in Philadelphia. (This action was described in more detail in chapter seven).

Joy, Fear, Relief

Participation in these actions engendered a range of emotions, among them: nervousness, fear, excitement, joy, and a deep feeling of peace after they were over.

I was not raised to engage in illegal burglaries. I had no family members who had done so. I didn't particularly like TV shows or movies that portrayed burglars in a positive light. Growing up, a "burglar" wasn't something that I was planning to become. But the Vietnam War changed everything. So when I took the step of joining the action community and participating in the preparation of the Philadelphia action, the dominant emotion was a great feeling of joy, almost a joyful relief, that I had found and become part of this community.

But there certainly were a lot of nerve-racking moments, as we prepared for and carried out the actions.

There was the overwhelming wave of fear I felt as I walked into the Rochester Federal Building that first Friday afternoon in September 1970 to hide in the dusty tower for thirty-two hours before letting my seven co-burglars in at midnight on Saturday.

There was the fear our We the People group felt as we were riding in a van heading out of town with lots of duffel bags full of draft files, and we heard a police siren and then saw a police car coming up fast behind us. Fortunately, it passed us and kept going.

There was the time a co-burglar and I had driven through snowy fields and into the woods not far from the AMF plant in York, Pennsylvania, where we planned to do some late-night casing. All of a sudden, the car engine died, and we couldn't get it started. Fortunately, after trying everything else, we were able to jump start it by rolling it down a hill, and we were able to do our work and get back to Harrisburg okay.

There was the time I was arrested by the Camden, New Jersey, police for stupidly jumping a turnstile at 2:00 in the morning after I had spent several hours checking out the Camden Federal Building with a co-burglar, writing information down on note cards, to see if we might include it in the action plan of the East Coast Conspiracy. We spent the night in jail, were questioned by a detective about the note cards, and were relieved the next day when, at arraignment, the judge let us go with a warning to not jump the turnstiles again (I never have) and a small fine. I felt very ashamed as I returned to the house we were working out of.

There was another time I was questioned by the police after I and a co-burglar had parked our car on a loading ramp about four feet off the ground with a great view of the North Philadelphia building we were casing. When a police cruiser came upon us, we were fortunate to be let off with a warning not to park on private property again.

Then there was the excitement of successful actions, of getting away without being arrested.

It felt tremendous to be burning those thousands of draft files in May 1970 on the farm west of Philadelphia after we had successfully burglarized the North Philadelphia draft board office.

There was the excitement of the Rochester trial, our successful presentations of "why we did it" evidence in the courtroom, the hundreds of people turning out nightly for our evening events in the Central Presbyterian Church across the street from the federal building.

There was the quiet excitement of developing close personal ties to new people who had similar feelings of despair about the war and racism but new hope from involvement in the Ultra Resistance.

After the East Coast Conspiracy actions in Philadelphia and DC, I participated in my first group press conference taking responsibility for these actions. It was new and exciting for me to speak publicly before the press in this way, something I've done many times since in my life of activism and organizing.

And there were many more such positive experiences.

Harrisburg Indictment Brought Changes

However, it is beyond doubt that the actions of the government in bringing the Harrisburg indictments led to changes for the worse within the action community. Being in prison in Ashland, Kentucky, when the first indictment came down on January 12, 1971, insulated me for a while from those changes, but once I was charged in the second, superseding Harrisburg indictment on April 30 that year and was moved to the Danbury, Connecticut, prison, I began to learn about them.

To be an active member of the action community meant that prison was something you had considered and determined you were willing to risk. Even after the actions were no longer standby actions and were being undertaken with the intention of getting away from the "scene of the crime" afterward, there was still the very real risk of getting caught, Rochester being Exhibit A. So being indicted by the federal government wasn't necessarily something that would have dramatically impacted our culture or how we interacted with each other.

The Harrisburg indictment was different, beginning with the severity of the original charges. Under the indictment, people convicted would have been subject to life in prison.

But probably more significant were the things revealed by the indictment and, most particularly, the smuggled letters between Phil and Liz:

- Though the idea of a nonviolent kidnapping of Henry Kissinger was dropped at the meeting where it was floated,

Liz had written to an imprisoned Phil as if it had not been, and Phil had responded with his input on the best way to do it.

- There was a willingness on at least Phil's part to consider whether explosives might be used to blow up heating tunnels under DC government buildings.
- Phil and Liz considered themselves to be married despite no ceremony of any kind.
- Phil had written about his brother and Eqbal Ahmad as too intellectual and not sufficiently committed to anti-war action.
- Phil had trusted Boyd Douglas, whom he did not know well, to transport the letters in and out of prison.

These revelations did not engender confidence and trust; they did engender fear and hesitation, which, without question, was one of the government's main objectives.

The high-powered lawyers—Ramsey Clark, Paul O'Dwyer, and Leonard Boudin—brought in to defend those indicted also created divisions in the action community. I wrote about this in chapter seven, the fact that their approach, supported by a majority of the defendants, was to deprioritize using the courtroom to go after the government for its crimes and to focus on prioritizing getting an acquittal for the defendants, no matter how it was done.

For those who had been part of actions over the previous three-plus years, the practical effect of all of this was to discourage, though not stop, the organization of new draft board raids or similar actions and to shift people's energies either to something else altogether or to working in one of the many Harrisburg defense committees that sprang up in 1971.

Even prior to the Harrisburg indictments, there was internal discussion about whether it made sense to keep doing actions at draft boards. I remember talking about this with others prior to the action at Rochester in 1970. Part of it was that a number of us were feeling like it was getting "old" as a tactic; something more creative was needed. In addition, the role of U.S. troops in Vietnam and Indochina more broadly was shifting.

In 1970–1971, there was a decided U.S. government policy shift from direct, boots on the ground military action by draftees and other soldiers to more of a U.S. support role as a government policy of "Vietnamization" of the war was implemented. The number of U.S. troops was reduced pretty dramatically, the air war was ratcheted up, and South Vietnamese troops were overwhelmingly the ones going out on combat missions or major campaigns against National Liberation Front or North Vietnamese troops.

These realities impacted to some extent the nature of the actions undertaken by the Ultra Resistance. One example is the March 1971, Media, Pennsylvania, FBI office action, as well as the action in March 1972 at the York AMF bomb making plant during the Harrisburg trial itself. But, in between, there were at least eight other draft board actions, all on the East Coast, with the exception of one in Evanston, Illinois. A draft board raid was still a blow against the war and the government prosecuting it.

Because of the Harrisburg indictments, there was a decided shift in what you could call the "power relations" within the action community: the eight people indicted at Harrisburg became the public face of our movement and the cause—our freedom—around which everyone was expected to rally. From what I observed, many in the action community by and large accepted that. But we had not been chosen by that larger community to play that role.

Given the tensions and disappointments due to what was in Phil and Liz's letters, as well as the prominent role of the lawyers, our assumption of this role was not helpful to the process of building a healthy community.

Tony Scoblick, one of the Harrisburg defendants, was so upset by these changes that he undertook a fast outside the Harrisburg Federal Building for a number of days prior to the trial, ostensibly protesting actions of the government but really as a kind of prayer for the re-coming together of the action community.

Tony's fast might have had some impact. The action community and many beyond it, particularly Catholics and religious people but also the broader peace and justice movement, did come together under the leadership of the Harrisburg Defense Committee, manifested most visibly during the successful Holy Week week of action described in chapter seven.

There was also the post-trial Fast for Life (chapter eight) involving fourteen people, at least ten of them participants in at least one Ultra Resistance action. That group consciously worked to build a beloved community, with some success, at the same time that we engaged in serious action for peace, some of us going on a forty-day water-only fast.

And there were at least three Ultra Resistance–type actions between the end of the Harrisburg trial in April 1972 and the signing of the Paris Peace Agreement on January 27, 1973. That accord did not end the war—it continued until April 30, 1975—but it did represent an acknowledgement by the U.S. that it could not impose its will militarily on Vietnam, ultimately leading to the 1975 withdrawal of all U.S. troops.

There is no question but that the Harrisburg trial marked a change in the nature of the Catholic Left. But it didn't mean the withdrawal of those who identified with it from the movement for peace and justice.

CHAPTER TEN

After Harrisburg

And so the Harrisburg Eight conspiracy case with all of its courage as well as its shadow sides seemed to offer a natural line of demarcation for something new to begin. Some tried to hold onto this style of peacemaking through the Plowshare actions, which were nonviolent attempts to "beat nuclear warheads into plowshares" at major nuclear missile sites.

These were courageous and generous actions that generated some public support including my own, but I sometimes guiltily wondered whether the time had come to create new imaginative modes of resistance. Others also saw the need to leave this noble tradition behind with deep gratitude and to move on to address the challenge of building the larger mass movement for peace and social and economic justice.

—Father Paul Mayer, *Wrestling with Angels*[1]

When the Fast for Life ended in 1972, I moved back to Harrisburg for a while, then to Washington, DC, where I began working with a newly formed group made up of ex-prisoners and allies, Prisoners Strike for Peace (PSP), on a campaign to get Phil Berrigan, who was still serving time for the Baltimore 4 and Catonsville 9 actions, out of prison. That campaign was successful; on December 20, 1972, Phil was paroled from Danbury. The head of the parole board told Jack Nelson, a reporter from the *Los Angeles Times*, that only Jimmy Hoffa had had more letters sent on his behalf.

In early 1973, in the aftermath if this campaign, I moved to East Harlem, in New York City, to work out of the PSP office. We had organized an ongoing vigil in front of St. Patrick's Cathedral during the massive and prolonged 1972 U.S. Christmas bombing of North Vietnam. I worked for weeks in Washington, DC, with Peg Averill, a PSP member from Akron, Ohio, who eventually became my second wife, to help organize a massive demonstration on January 20, 1973, the day of Richard Nixon's inauguration.

In March, I flew out to South Dakota to work for several weeks in support of the American Indian Movement occupation of the town of Wounded Knee, with Kevin Jones, another PSP member who I had gotten to know in Danbury prison, and who had also participated in the thirty-three-day hunger strike. We responded to a call issued by the leaders of the occupation for people to come out to support that action.

While living in Washington, DC, in the fall of 1972, working on the campaign to free Phil Berrigan from prison, I participated a number of times in a vigil outside of the Department of Interior Affairs building, which housed the Bureau of Indian Affairs. The agency was being occupied by hundreds of Native people who had participated in a Trail of Broken Treaties caravan that had traveled across the country, calling attention to the widespread and continuing violations of treaties and the basic human rights of Native Americans. I was conscious of these realities and the importance of their demands, so when the call came from Wounded Knee, I was glad to be in a position to respond.

It was around this same time that the Camden 28 went to trial. This was the last big trial of the Catholic Left. Twenty-eight people had been arrested on the night of August 21, 1971, as they were breaking into the Camden Federal Building and the draft board offices housed there. It turned out that there had been a government provocateur, Bob Hardy, in their midst. They were all arrested before any significant damage was done, and a year and a half later their trial began.

The Camden 28 defendants were acquitted by a jury in what was widely seen as a repudiation of both the war and the government's repressive activities. Bob Hardy's decision to change sides and testify for the defense rather than the prosecution was a major reason for the verdict.

In an amazing about-face, Hardy filed an affidavit for the defense. He had done so after long talks with Father "Mick" Doyle, one of the defendants, the priest who had also converted him to the

Catholic faith. Hardy had also been deeply touched by the concern shown for him by several of the defendants when his young son was killed in an accident.[2]

Hardy's affidavit included this testimonial and critique of the group:

I never doubted [the group's] moral conviction, sincerity and honesty. They are the finest group of Christian people I have ever been associated with. They are not even capable of hurting anyone. They were willing to give up everything they had for what they believed, and at no time did they show any un-Christian behavior. For me, it was the best cooperative effort I've ever experienced; it was a community bound together by love and dedication. I will never forget them. But as far as mechanical skills and abilities, they were totally inept. . . . It definitely wouldn't have happened without me.[3]

The judge at Camden, as was the case at Catonsville in 1968 and Rochester in 1970, allowed a fair amount of testimony about the war and the "intent" of the defendants, some of which was very moving. "Speaking for themselves in language devoid of legal jargon, the defendants testified at length about who they were and what they stood for."[4]

It was a great victory for the Resistance and a real setback for the government.

Traveling and Learning

In the summer of 1973, with PSP having serious internal problems, primarily personal tensions between key members, I decided to take some time to travel around the East Coast to see and spend time with old friends from the Ultra Resistance. I traveled to Buffalo, Boston, Providence, New York City, Philadelphia, Baltimore, and Washington, meeting with upwards of a hundred people in the course of the trip.

I wrote about what I learned in a piece titled "12 Points on the Anti-War Movement." Here are excerpts:

Over the past few years, with the notable exception of crisis situations, the frequency of war-related resistance actions—either in small group form or in large numbers—has decreased. Many people, most of them outside of the movement, have pointed to that fact as evidence that the movement is dead. It is not. Some of the forms through which that movement manifested itself have changed, but a basic commitment to work and action on behalf of peace, justice and liberation remains.

People around the east whom I spoke with either spoke of or exemplified several important differences in their attitude toward movement work. One was the need and desire people felt to plant some roots, to find a location and a lifestyle which was connected much more deeply and regularly to the lives of people around them. Instead of living by responding to crises, there is an attempt being made to develop ongoing, day-to-day ways of living which are consistent with one's personal and political beliefs. People are struggling to define their lives and direction for themselves, not have it done by the same government we are attempting to overcome.

The war in Vietnam, the issue which was the first to bring a process of radicalization for most of those I met with, is no longer the end-all or be-all of existence. Speeded up by the recent signing of the "cease-fire agreements," the last few years have seen a broadening awareness of many other important issues. People have come to see the issues as interconnected, flowing from a totalized system which is exploitative, imperialistic, racist and sexist. Though anti-war work continues to be done and seen as important, it is with a different perspective and a greatly decreased intensity.

People who once acted more out of a sense of guilt and desperation than anything else now reject that position. In numerous discussions this point came up. There is a widespread recognition that more than these must be present if we are to be successful in reaching out to our fellow Americans, in relating to their lives in effective ways, in transforming this society into something human. Guilt is seen primarily as a middle-class phenomenon. The values of middle-class society—individualism, materialism, "keeping up with the neighbors"—are being rejected as we struggle for something new in *our* lives, not just in those of the Vietnamese.

There is a felt need for an analysis, strategy and theory out of which to operate, as well as the need for a rediscovery of traditions with which to identify. As the movement has shifted from anti-war to anti-capitalist, from reform-minded to revolutionary, the "how" and "towards what end" of making a revolution are being studied and seriously considered. Marxist and anarchist literature, histories of other countries' revolutionary struggles, and literature on radical struggles in U.S. history are common staples of movement peoples' reading diet.

Just as there is a rejection of a "politics of guilt" motivation there is a rejection of those "leaders" who have used and who continue to exhibit sexism, authoritarianism, manipulation and elitism in their work. Honesty and openness are much more expected and seen as essential to a positive process of work; skepticism and a healthy dose of distrust meet attempts to impose one way, one direction or one analysis upon others. We have seen that it is no longer a case of the good guys versus the bad guys. The good guys, i.e., us, can be just as egotistical, just as chauvinistic, just as power hungry as those whom we are supposedly opposing.

With the recognition of our fallibility has come a sense that we must inspect our lives more deeply, struggle with our weaknesses more openly, deal with faulty practices on a more continuous basis. This is not meant to imply that such is occurring with the kind of regularity that might be expected or hoped for, but in different and oftentimes sporadic and halting ways this process is at work.

There is a growing recognition that we must become nothing less than a full-scale alternative to the culture and society out of which we come. There can be little strength or meaning gained from the institutions which are responsible for mass murder in Indochina and oppression at home, little sustenance from a racist, sexist and violent culture in which competition is the cornerstone of success. Conscious attempts to understand the extent to which race, sex and class have determined our consciousness and lifestyle must be and are taking place. The result is a growing sense of what we must become, how we must develop, and why we need to transform ourselves so that what we bring into being is true to the best and the deepest within us.

People are looking to themselves and the institutions we have created—food co-ops, free health clinics, communes, alternative newspapers, etc.—for the strength to press on. A revolutionary culture is developing, painfully and in starts and stops, which serves as both the new society within the shell of the old and the base from which to move out into the old society to organize.

There is a concern not just to develop internally—as individuals and as a people—but to reach out to, serve, learn from and get together with people with whom meaningful contact has been almost nonexistent in the past. Building a mass base among wide sectors of the American people, particularly the working class, is seen as crucial to our survival and our ultimate success.

The development of an historically significant national movement, in whatever form it takes, can only come about as a result of the success of local/regional developments. We should be about our development where we are, building connections locally and regionally with others, growing in a variety of personal and political ways, and becoming a truly revolutionary people—honest, loving, strong and committed to a constant struggle to know and act upon the truth.

The circulation of this document and the feedback I received led me to take the initiative with others to pull together a meeting of former Catholic Left activists. The letter of invitation sent out said, "Though our paths may appear to be divergent we feel we are all headed in the same direction. The specific roads and means of travel are what we have to keep searching for, together."

The Last Ultra Resistance Gathering

In late September, 1973, we gathered at a camp in Harriman State Park, in New York. There were somewhere in the neighborhood of fifty people present, a pretty good representation of the action community.

The meeting covered a lot of ground. There was a spirit of open back-and-forth about how people saw things, grounded in a sense of our community as one that had done important work, whatever our weaknesses since Catonsville.

The meeting was very different from any Catholic Left meeting I had previously attended. I remember only bits and pieces of what happened:

- Ann Walsh, from Boston, who had been part of the Boston 8 action in 1969 and the Fast for Life in 1972, and who was a stalwart of the action community, spoke early to say that the goal of the meeting could not be to create a group ready to plan some kind of action. It had to be, she said, a meeting reflective of where the overall (former) action community was at, and that wasn't where it was.

- Suzi Williams, my codefendant at Rochester, spoke about how we should defend the right of women to be part of the U.S. military on an equal basis as men. For someone who had been so militantly nonviolent and anti-military, it was a surprising change of position.

- I am sure that there was discussion at the meeting of the issue of sexism both within the Catholic Left and society at large. As was true for other parts of the peace and justice movement, the rise of a new women's movement in the late 1960s had a definite impact and reverberations within the action community. The dominant role of Catholic priests within the Catholic Left did not go unchallenged as it evolved in the early 1970s.

- Paul Couming, from Boston, talked about the community organizing work he was doing in the working-class community of Dorchester, where he had grown up.

- Jon Bach, whom I had served time with in Danbury, and who was about to move to Baltimore to join with the Jonah House community, was still into small-group actions and was disappointed that not too many others were.

About Jonah House, formed in 1973 by Phil Berrigan and Liz McAlister, it has been written:

> They supported themselves by house painting and lectures. They lived in voluntary poverty, managing on the food supermarkets could no longer sell, sharing with their black neighbors when they could. "We embraced a Judeo-Christian ethic," explained one member. "Life in Jonah House," said Esther Cassidy, who gave birth in the house, was "monastic, with lots of prayer. We were all up by 7:30 and four nights a week we would have meetings, reading Scripture, praying, planning actions."[5]

Phil described it this way in *Fighting the Lamb's War*:

We wanted a place where people could share meals and ideas, study Scripture together, and support one another through the long haul. When friends went to prison, we would care for their children. We tried to be a loving family, committed to the spirit and reality of nonviolent resistance.[6]

As it evolved, Jonah House became a center for the organization of Plowshares actions, small groups taking symbolic action at nuclear and military sites to protest the dangers of nuclear war and militarism.

There was criticism of this approach among more than a few people who had been part of the Catholic Left. I was one of them. I remember being disturbed following a personal conversation with Phil in Baltimore in the spring of 1973, after he had gotten out of prison. I remember talking with Peg Averill afterward about how Phil seemed to be at a different place than we were when it came to strategy and tactics. I felt he was pretty much at the same place he was when he went into prison.

James Harney, a member of the Milwaukee 14, put it this way:

I personally would not participate [in Plowshares actions] because I think it's simply prophetic and nothing more. It says nothing in terms of moving people to the point of any critical consciousness as to what's happening. It's very isolated. I have my doubts about risking a jail term under these terms, simply for prophetic reasons—crying out in the darkness and not engendering any kind of response. . . . How is it that one can maintain that the same type and form of actions that were done in '67 up to this point are the things to be done, in terms of really talking about change in this society?[7]

There were no notes of the meeting at Harriman State Park, at least none that I can remember or find. It's too bad there weren't, because it was the last broadly representative meeting held by the Catholic Left, at least the Vietnam War era Catholic Left.

Living in DC

I returned to Washington, DC, where I had moved in late summer. I lived in one of the houses of the Community for Creative Nonviolence (CCNV), a group that engaged in peace and justice actions and ran a soup kitchen, a house for people awaiting trial who needed a place to stay, and a medical clinic.

While living at CCNV, I took part in one of the more creative actions I've ever been involved with. We learned that Henry Kissinger was to receive a Pacem en Terris (peace on earth) award from the Center for the Study of Democratic Institutions. Five of us got tickets to the event at a big hotel in downtown DC. There were at least a couple thousand people in the room when Kissinger started speaking.

Our crew of five had divided into two groups. At a point early in his speech, three of us sitting on the side a few rows back from the stage hit the buttons on the laugh boxes we had all brought for the occasion. As a high-pitched, eerie laugh wafted throughout the hall, Kissinger stopped speaking. As he did, Father Ed Guinan, founder of CCNV, stood up and said something like, "Henry Kissinger, it is an outrage that you are getting this award after the millions of deaths you are responsible for in Indochina." The acoustics were good in the room, and his words were clearly heard.

After a couple minutes of commotion, Ed and the other two people with him sat down, and Kissinger started in again. A couple minutes into it, I and my co-actionist, sitting about a dozen rows back directly in front of the stage, hit our laugh box buttons. We were immediately jumped by people behind us. Kissinger stopped again. There was some scuffling, and we were soon being escorted out of the hotel.

A couple months later I was visiting my parents over Christmas. At one point, they asked me about this action; they said they were watching it on TV and had seen someone who looked like me interrupting Kissinger. They weren't sure, because the person was wearing a suit (which I rarely did then). It was great to learn that our action had been seen by a national TV audience.

Over the two years after getting out of prison in the fall of 1971, I survived economically by keeping my living expenses down, living with others, and taking various short-term manual labor jobs. In Harrisburg I was a taxi driver for a while. I did day work, mainly construction, through the temp agency Manpower. And I had gotten some money from the Harrisburg Defense Committee for my work there prior to the trial.

In DC, I decided that I wanted to join the industrial working class, with the expectation that once I did so I would become a workplace organizer. I remember traveling to the Midwest and, while there, successfully connecting with historian and author Staughton Lynd. I had first had contact with Staughton at a national draft resistance conference I had attended in 1969. By 1973, he was living in northeast Ohio and working with a group that was organizing rank-and-file workers. It was inspiring for me to get a chance to talk with him at his house for a few hours.

Since there was very little heavy industry in DC, I traveled up the road to Baltimore and applied for a job at the Sparrows Point steel mill, where thousands of people worked. Unfortunately, after being interviewed and given a physical, I was turned down because of the glasses I wore for to my pretty serious nearsightedness. I had not yet gotten contact lenses, which, had I, might have led to a different result.

After some more job searching, I ended up finding employment in the DC area after all but not in heavy industry. For many months I earned my pay as a groundskeeper at a cemetery in Landover, Maryland, the only white person on a groundskeeper crew of seven or eight, the rest being African American. I got along just fine with my coworkers, who I think wondered why I was working there. I was open about my political views, which they related to supportively.

In late October 1973, something happened that had a big impact on me, leading me to take on a wholly different kind of social change work.

On October 20, President Richard Nixon moved to stop the work of an independent counsel, Archibald Cox, who was looking into the Watergate burglary of the Democratic National Committee office during the 1972 presidential campaign, when Cox subpoenaed him to provide copies of taped conversations recorded in the Oval Office on his authorization.

What happened that night became known as the Saturday Night Massacre, because Nixon's Attorney General Elliot Richardson and Deputy Attorney General William Ruckelshaus both resigned rather than carry out Nixon's order that they fire Cox. Next in line, Solicitor General Robert Bork, was sworn in as acting attorney general and did the deed.

Organizing for Nixon's Impeachment

Like many people, I was shocked at the brazenness of the act and soon found myself getting deeply involved in a local impeachment group, the Washington Area Impeachment Coalition, which then initiated organizing to form a National Campaign to Impeach Nixon (NCIN), founded several months later at a conference in Chicago. I became one of its national coordinators, and for the next half year or so, until Nixon resigned on August 9, 1974, this was my life: working from 7:00 a.m. to 3:00 p.m. at the Landover cemetery, then working in the NCIN office in the evening and on weekends.

I explained why I got so deeply into this work in an article I wrote after the Saturday Night Massacre, "12 Points on Watergate and Impeachment." Here are a couple of the key paragraphs:

> The impeachment issue presents a major opportunity for the left. At no other time has there been an issue so potentially vital to the building of a mass-based popular movement in such a relatively short period of time. Nixon has been exposed and even those who support him no longer can feel totally happy with his continuation in office. Just as the war led to splits within the ruling circles, so has impeachment. Watergate has penetrated even the highest levels of power, which shows the extent to which there is space for the left to move.
>
> The left has an absolute responsibility to "sieze the time" and involve itself as deeply as is individually and collectively possible in the impeachment movement. We must help get Nixon out, for our sake, for the sake of the American people, for the sake of the Indochinese (who are, I believe, now more likely to see a major reescalation as a result of the way Nixon has moved), for the sake of the world's people; and two, to make connections between administration despotism and corporate plunder, government repression and financial gain, illegal war and frozen wages and high prices. We must use that issue as a means toward our development over the coming months into a deeply rooted movement intelligent and mature enough to resist repression and develop itself into a revolutionary force.

As it turned out, though some on the left became active in the grass-roots impeachment movement, most did not. My arguments and those of others fell on a lot of deaf ears. But, very importantly, Nixon was eventually forced to resign, in August 1974.

At just about the same time as his action, I also resigned, not from any job or office but in an "Open Letter of Resignation from the Catholic Left." What moved me to do this?

CHAPTER ELEVEN

Resigning from the Catholic Left

Make me wise so that I may understand the things
you have taught my people.
Let me learn the lessons you have hidden
in every leaf and rock.
I seek strength not to be greater than my brother or sister
but to fight my greatest enemy, myself.
Make me always ready
to come to you with clean hands and straight eyes
So when life fades as the fading sunset
my spirit may come to you without shame.
—Chief Yellow Lark, "Let Me Walk in Beauty"[1]

In May 1974, while employed at the Landover cemetery and working for the impeachment of Richard Nixon, I reached out to Phil Berrigan by letter. The month before I had seen Liz McAlister, his wife, at Georgetown University, where she had spoken, which motivated me to do so.

I explained that I was writing because I had seen a long interview with him in the *Washington Post* a month and a half previously. I had written but never sent a letter to him afterward, because:

> I was concerned that you wouldn't understand what I was trying
> to say. In the letter I spoke quite strongly about some of the state-
> ments you were quoted as having made, and though I don't trust
> the press to be accurate, my sense, from knowing you and knowing
> of the work you're doing, was that the quotes were correct.

I was especially upset with this quote:

The very idea of building a mass movement again to protest war is absurd. It's only your most dedicated, most purified [by arrests and suffering] people who keep going. The movement was a question of stamina. There are only pockets of resistance now where that survives.

I wrote to Phil that I rejected that line of thinking. For one thing, there *was* still mass anti-war action. I referenced two current examples, a demonstration of five thousand people at Kent State, in Ohio, against the bombing of Cambodia and the work of the Indochina Peace Campaign, a national anti-war group led by Tom Hayden and Jane Fonda that was getting a good response.

I also wrote that I felt Phil's approach was elitist. "When it is only those who have been 'purified by arrests and suffering' who can provide leadership," the conclusion must be that the leadership would necessarily primarily come from him and those gathered around him.

I wrote that I was upset about the interview and his current work because of its disconnect from the realities of life for most people in this country.

For the past two years I have been struggling to live in a way which responds to the lives and suffering of *my* people, the American people, to understand the confusion and fear and pain with which they live their lives. I am convinced that the key to revolutionary change is the kind of rootedness the movement has in the lives of such people. They are the motive force of history, not small groups of "purified" cadres. Only the people, their consciousness and willingness to act raised in part because of our work among them, can force the kind of change necessary.

Political organizing—that is what is needed. Moral witness, "purified" actions—these lead, in the long run, to demoralization and little growth. Only political organizing combined with a commitment to live moral and upstanding lives can lead us to where we want to be going.

Phil wrote right back, but he didn't substantively respond to what I raised. He did invite me to connect with him to talk in person, but that never happened, largely because I didn't reach out to set something up.

I wrote back and acknowledged his offer but said that I first felt the need to be clearer about a "mutually agreed on basis of unity and/or disagreement" before we spoke in person. I expressed my anger at his letter. I said, "Could it be that you don't want to deeply ponder the points which I raised and seriously deal with them?"

Phil's letter in response was substantive. He was critical of the tone and some of the language I used, wondering why I was being so judgmental and insulting, which I was (see below). He asked if I thought the suffering I had experienced was of no significance and referred to how, leading up to India's independence, Gandhi and several hundred thousand others had spent time in jail. He said he accepted my decision to work on the impeachment and said that I should accept what he and those with him at Jonah House had accepted as their work for peace and justice.

In my response back, I semi-apologized for the tone of my letters, but I also said this:

> On the other hand, I couldn't help but feel "good" that what I was saying was clearly being dealt with in some way. That is a function of the difficulty in "getting through" to you that more people than myself have had when we have tried to raise these questions.

Shared Concerns

I knew from my connections to and discussions with a number of the activists formerly part of the Catholic Left movement that a number of them shared my sentiments. I had heard them at the weekend meeting that I had helped to organize the preceding September in Harriman Park, in New York.

I also knew about several people who had moved into Jonah House in Baltimore to be part of that community with Phil and Liz and had left within a year, having been turned off by the internal dynamics.

Phil wrote about this, in general terms, in his autobiography, *The Lamb's War*:

> In retrospect, I realize that I could be rather hard on people who were new to the faith and resistance movement. I was impatient, even intolerant at times. I granted no doubts or uncertainties, wanted everyone to be absolutely dedicated to the Kingdom of God.
>
> I did feel confused and uncertain, at times, about community life. The best account of community life in scripture is from the

Acts of the Apostles. Every now and then, the early Christians would go through a crisis, struggling over the meaning of nonviolence, over persecution from the state, and their own superficial, essentially violent interpersonal relations.

Our community too was destined to go through a series of crises; we lost members, and people left in difficult circumstances.[2]

At the end of my letter to Phil, I gave him my phone numbers, so we could get together if he was in DC, and I said that if I went to Baltimore I'd reach out. "It would be valuable to get together, and I'd like to see you," I said.

But it didn't happen, not until eighteen years later, in 1992, because soon after I sent my letter to Phil, a peace movement magazine, *WIN*, published excerpts of a commencement address Phil gave on June 23 at Antioch College, in Columbia, Maryland.

The title of his address was "On Kingmaking." This was in reference to a story from the Bible about the prophet Samuel and his criticism of the Hebrew people for their corruption, support of slavery, and desire for a warlike king to rule over them. Phil analogized that situation to the reality of the American people in 1974.

Phil made the case that people in the U.S. were just like the Hebrews in Samuel's day.

> An impressive case can be made for the suspicion that Americans want what the Jews wanted. We want prosperity. Therefore, we want, however unhappily, ruling [by a kinglike president], war and slavery. . . . If our kings, from Washington to Nixon, have any crowning fault, it is their fidelity to the people's wishes. . . . If Americans want prosperity at such a price, they want a king, they want war, and they want their own slavery.

I couldn't believe what he was saying. Richard Nixon was on the verge of being driven from office. He had been forced to sign a peace agreement in 1973 with the Vietnamese in large part because of the massive opposition of the American people, including GIs in Vietnam, to the war. For me, there was the memory of the jury in our Rochester trial, who had been so moved by our defense case that none of them wanted us to spend long years in prison, while three of them wanted to acquit us. And there were a proliferating number of issues—women's rights, gay rights, small farmer survival, democratic trade unionism, FBI and CIA repression, Native American sovereignty, housing rights, and more—being taken up, acted upon, and organized around.

It was exactly the main issue of our correspondence, my critique of an approach to social change that essentially wrote off the American people as incapable of change, a very hopeless and, in my opinion, inaccurate view of the reality at the time and the future possibilities.

My "Resignation"

My response was to write what I called "An Open Letter of Resignation from the Catholic Left." I began it with excerpts from a poem of African American poet Langston Hughes, "Let America Be America Again":

> O, let America be America again—
> The land that never has been yet—
> And yet must be—the land where every man is free.
> The land that's mine—the poor man's, Indian's, Negro's, ME—
> Who made America,
> Whose sweat and blood, whose faith and pain,
> Whose hand at the foundry, whose plow in the rain,
> Must bring back our mighty dream again.
>
> ***
>
> Oh yes, I say it plain,
> America never was America to me,
> And yet I swear this oath,
> America will be!![3]

I went on to describe the correspondence between Phil and me. I explained how my worldview and my views on peace and justice activism had changed. I said:

> I have moved very far away from the "moral, Catholic, witness action" kind of life that I once was part of due to my involvement in the draft board raiding community. My political development in these ways came directly out of the 11 months in prison I spent for raiding draft boards and an FBI office in Rochester, NY, in September of 1970. There I saw at first hand and close up the dynamics of class and race as they affected the prison population. There I took note of the privileges given to those who were

white, well-connected or boot-licking to the prison administration (the ruling class). And there I developed a deep and abiding trust in the ability of those who are oppressed to resist that oppression and create a more just and decent way of living if those who consciously saw themselves as organizers were among them to learn from them, to organize them (not dominate but make more coherent) and to resist with them. I became convinced that that way lay the future.

I am "resigning" from the Catholic Left (or what is publicly identified as it, because there are many, many former "members" who have moved in similar ways as I) because I no longer want there to be any confusion on the part of my movement sisters and brothers and people I come into contact with as to the present direction of my life. It is away from simplistic views on violence and war and toward an understanding of class, sex and race—sexist, racist capitalism and its mirror image, state capitalism in the Soviet Union—as the root of such evils. It is toward some kind of socialist/feminist, revolutionary, personal/political theory and practice. It is towards the digging in of roots, authentic, honest and ongoing, with poor Third World and working-class people. And it is toward the kind of politics and vision expressed in Langston Hughes' beginning poem. Our freedom will only come through a struggle *with* the American people for change. That is our direction for the future.

Looking in the Mirror

However, and it is a big however, I was far from being the kind of person I intellectually knew I and others in the social change movement needed to become. Phil picked up on this in my letters to him, and looking back these many years later, I am not proud of that aspect of the younger Ted Glick.

I began to get some glimmering of this problem about a month after I got out of prison. In November of that year, 1971, I wrote a letter to my wife Sarah in which I reflected on behavior on Phil's part related to my own behavior:

[At a] meeting we had up at Danbury a few days ago, Phil was very disruptive of the whole process of growth and cohesiveness that was (and now is again) developing among we, at least seven, maybe eight [Harrisburg defendants]. He was very confrontational of people and seemed unwilling at points to accept people's differences of style and approach; he wanted them to be more his style. That seemed to me very distasteful, almost obnoxious, and maybe through that I came to see myself a bit more clearly, maybe sometimes, in the past, and perhaps in the present, in relation to how I've approached you and us.

In Phil's last letter to me a few years later, several things he said about some of the tone and language I had used in my letters to him were accurate:

> In your second letter, the charges continue. I took the liberty of sharing your letters with others in the house, all of whom are your friends. One said with some wonderment, "Why does Ted have to be so damned insulting?" I wouldn't mention it except that all here saw it, and most know you as well as me. So at the risk of leveling a countercharge—why be so contemptuous of your friends? I know it isn't intended, but it creeps through—all under the heading of ideological and/or tactical controversy.

I didn't really take this constructive criticism on Phil's part to heart, at least not back then. That is clear to me now as I reread what I wrote and how I responded. I essentially justified my insulting tone:

> I am trying to raise in as honest and direct a way as I can major criticisms and problems I have had with the work you are doing for a long time. I think that it's to be expected that the initial raising of those long repressed feelings is not going to be done [by me] in a manner and with an understanding on the part of the one on the receiving end (you) as would (hopefully) develop in the future, as exchange continues.

Unfortunately, that exchange didn't continue. I "resigned from the Catholic Left," kept moving on along a new path, and made no effort to reach out to former prison buddy and codefendant Phil to try to build upon the issues raised by our exchange of letters.

I did, however, initiate correspondence with Jon Bach, another prison buddy and a member of the Jonah House community, a couple of months later, and my tone in that letter was even worse than in the initial one to Phil. At the time, I was really into "struggle over differences honestly and openly," as I put it in my last letter to Jon.

Thinking back to that time, I remember that the mid-1970s were a time of much "ideological struggle," organizational rivalries, and internal debates among people on the political left. I can't think of another period in the over fifty years that I have been a progressive political activist that was as intense in this regard. Part of it, a large part, was that many young people who had been active in the civil rights/Black Freedom and peace movements discovered the writings of Marx, Lenin, Mao Zedong, and other Marxist leaders as they struggled to figure out how to fundamentally transform the USA. Within that political tradition there was a great deal of polemical writing, strong attacks on other Marxists for not having the correct points of view, as well as actual repressive action, particularly by Stalin, after Lenin died, against those who opposed him. This had an impact beyond the Marxist groups, none of which I ever joined but whose members I did interact with, and I am sure it had some impact on me.

For many years after my open letter of resignation, I had virtually no contact with Phil, Liz, or the Jonah House community.

This began to change eighteen years later. I was sitting on the steps of the U.S. Capitol building in Washington, DC, with about a dozen others. We were in the third week of a forty-two-day hunger strike, from September 1 to October 12—water-only for most of us. It was 1992, the five hundredth anniversary of Christopher Columbus and his men being found in the Caribbean by one of the many Indigenous nations that had lived for thousands of years in what is now the Americas. In the U.S., of course, the government and the powerful had made plans for big celebrations of this five hundredth anniversary of Columbus's "discovery of America."

A very broad and active movement was taking action against those planned celebrations, calling for an open acknowledgement of the devastation to Native and African peoples and the environment that began with Columbus's arrival in the Americas. Three people who were part of that movement, anti-war Vietnam veteran Brian Willson, Detroit teacher Karen Fogliotti, and former federal government employee Scott Rutherford, had called for and organized this forty-two-day fast. The purpose was to underline how critical it was that the U.S. as a nation acknowledge and act upon those historic realities, so that the next five hundred years would be very, very different than the last five hundred.

It had been twenty years since I had fasted, but I was moved by this initiative and ended up joining it.

On this particular day in September on those Capitol steps, I met a young woman, Michelle Naar, who had just joined the fast. We started talking, and it turned out that she was living at Jonah House with Phil and Liz. She told me that they had three children, one of whom, Frida, was now eighteen. I remember vividly how this affected me. I thought back to my youth and how I had turned in my draft card at the age of nineteen and met Phil when I was twenty.

I was very impacted by this news. I think I was particularly struck because I was on this long fast, and on long fasts you have the time and the inclination to reflect upon things you might not reflect upon otherwise. And coming face to face with the reality that Phil and Liz now had a child who was almost as old as I was when I first met them really hit home.

Reconciliation

I knew that I had to take the initiative to correct this situation. When the fast ended, I began communication with Phil and Liz. Within a fairly short time this led to a reestablishment of our friendship, a highlight of which was an overnight stay with them at a time when all three of their children were present. Although they were continuing to organize Plowshares nonviolent direct actions, and I was then working to try to form a progressive third party, there was no tenseness, no sense that we were anything other than brothers and sisters working together along parallel tracks towards a common objective of a world free of war, sexism, racism, and exploitation.

I continued to have occasional friendly interactions with Phil and Liz afterward, and that has continued with Liz since Phil died in December 2002.

Phil and those of his generation who were like him were heroes to me as a young person. They were models, examples, people I looked up to and followed. They helped to get me onto the road of struggle for justice and for this I will always be grateful.

But through my interactions with Phil, and eventually coming to grips with my youthful arrogance, I learned another important lesson:

the need to respect differences on this road of struggle, to resist thinking that my way is *the* way, to develop the humanity and humility that Phil's God, the God he believed in, would want us to develop.

This is not just a spiritual or a personal lesson; it is also a political lesson.

It is not easy to stay positive and hopeful in the world we are living in. And if we are not positive and hopeful models, there is little chance we will be able to help others find the courage to stand up for their rights, for justice and peace, and for a deep connection with and love for all life-forms on earth.

The movement for justice and human liberation is full to overflowing with examples of political, tactical, and personal differences that keep us separated, if not at each other's throats. However, I am glad to be able to write that I see changes for the better in the movement today, in 2020. I see among many activist young people, in particular, a less rigid and more flexible style of human and political interaction. This is generally (but not always) true, from my experience and understanding, when it comes to the climate and climate justice movements, the Black Lives Matter movement, the immigrant rights movement, the Indigenous rights movement, the massive movement grounded among youth that almost succeeded in winning the Democratic presidential nomination for Bernie Sanders in 2016, and the massive people's resistance movement since Trump won the Electoral College vote—but not the popular vote.

What are other lessons learned and personal reflections on the Ultra Resistance that are relevant as we begin the third decade of the twenty-first century?

CHAPTER TWELVE

Lessons Learned

> And what does God ask of you but to do justice, love kindness, and
> walk humbly with your God.
> —Micah 6:8

Looking back to my Catholic Left years of activism a half century ago, I can see a number of things that I learned back then that have stayed with me over all these years. One of them is the importance of continually being open to shifting what I do and where I put my activist energies, to not get stuck in a rut.

From 1969 to 1972, I believed that organizing small group actions at draft boards, FBI offices, and corporate war office and production sites was the right thing to do. But I didn't believe that by 1973, so I began to move in another direction.

The same thing happened with me in 2003. After twenty-eight years of active involvement with groups working to build a progressive alternative to the Republican and Democratic parties, I decided to shift my main focus of work to the issue of global warming. I did so because of a major heat wave in the summer of 2003 in Western Europe that led to tens of thousands of deaths.

This was my wakeup call on the climate issue. I spent several months reading books on the subject. I learned that the earth was heating up more rapidly than I had thought, and worldwide climate catastrophe was a very real possibility in my lifetime. I decided to change my life and become a full-time organizer on this issue, which is what I'm still doing today in 2020, seventeen years later.

I understand that there are other very important issues, and that there are often interconnections among them, but the fact is that there is a definitive time urgency to the climate issue. There are climate tipping points after which it will be extremely difficult for humanity to recover from the devastation we have caused. If human society does not rapidly shift from fossil fuels to renewable energy and serious energy efficiency, in addition to other actions to protect and sustain our natural environment, we face a disastrous future.

There are similarities and differences between the social impact of the Vietnam War back then and the deepening climate crisis today. Both were/are issues with massive, world-changing, negative impacts if not positively resolved. Both led/are leading to growing numbers of people stepping outside of the normal parameters of their daily lives and taking risks to stop the war/prevent climate catastrophe. Both had/will have big impacts on young people, leading to political activism on a broad scale.

But there haven't been multiple political suicides (thankfully) by self-immolation in the fight to stabilize the climate, though there has been one, David Buckel, in Brooklyn, New York, in early 2018. And though there are a continuing series of risk-taking, nonviolent direct actions around the country to try to prevent the building of oil and gas pipelines and fossil fuel infrastructure, there is nothing resembling the Ultra Resistance. I think a major reason for that is that there is nothing comparable to a forced military draft today.

A draft affects millions of young people. It's a direct threat. It makes a faraway war much more personally real. It provided a focus for organizing masses of people, and many draft boards were relatively accessible targets.

Climate disruption is also very real, and those who experience extreme weather events fueled by global warming, years-long droughts, massive flooding, hugely destructive superstorms, supercharged wildfires, sea level rise, etc. are definitely victims of climate disruption. But in the United States the connections are not as widely understood or perceived due to the political and economic power of the oil and gas industry, the impact of continued climate denialism, the shameful, minimal at best, mass media coverage of the connections, and the fact that extreme weather events, while more intense and more frequent today, have been experienced by humankind for millennia.

To my mind, this argues for stronger, more edgy actions, because, without question, those extreme weather events are going to become much more frequent and much more destructive. As they do, it is essential, imperative even, that the world as a whole makes a conscious and deliberate shift away from the destructive power arrangements and practices that have brought us to this crisis point.

Nonviolent Direct Action

In late August and early September 2011, over a two-week period, 1253 people calling upon then President Obama to reject the Keystone XL tar sands pipeline were arrested in front of the White House. This was literally the moment that the climate movement burst onto the scene for the country as a whole. There had been civil disobedience actions where people had been arrested prior to this; I had taken part in five of them. But none came close to the size or the two-week duration of this one.

The positive effect of that two weeks of nonviolent civil disobedience in front of the White House is an illustration of the tactic's power, when it is used strategically and intelligently. I had learned this during my Catholic Left days. I had seen how the willingness of people to risk time in jail or prison by taking disruptive action, while refusing to put anyone else in danger of injury or worse, could have a powerful political impact.

This power was described in an important book, *This Is an Uprising: How Nonviolent Revolt is Shaping the Twenty-First Century*. In it, the authors, Mark and Paul Engler, write about how, to be ultimately successful, social change movements need to be willing to be "dividers," willing to temporarily polarize things.

Without any idea of this theory, that is what I definitely did by turning in my draft card, then burning its replacement, and then burning the subsequent army induction notice. I had a lot of support, but I also created rifts with some in my large extended family. I remember a cousin at a family reunion many decades after I had broken with the Selective Service System making a comment to me about how "extreme" my actions had been. And then there was what happened in Louisville in 1969, when I burned my 1-A draft card on the stage in front of two thousand people, minus as many as two hundred who walked out when I announced I was going to do so.

Here is some of what the Englers say about the necessity of this polarization and division:

Practitioners of nonviolent conflict have regularly shown themselves willing to be intentionally divisive, making use of a complex
yet critical phenomenon known as "polarization." In doing this,
they grapple with an undeniable tension: broad-based support is
vital if campaigns of civil resistance are to prevail. And yet many of
the tactics of nonviolent disruption tend to be unpopular.

Notwithstanding these dangers, the experience of social movements shows that polarization can also be a powerful friend. By
taking an issue that is hidden from common view and putting it
at the center of public debate, disruptive protest forces observ-
ers to decide which side they are on. This has three effects: First,
it builds the base of a movement by creating an opportunity for
large numbers of latent sympathizers to become dedicated activists. Second, even as it turns passive supporters into active ones, it
engages members of the public who were previously uninformed,
creating greater awareness even among those who do not care for
activists' confrontational approach. And third, it agitates the most
extreme elements of the opposition, fueling a short-term backlash
but isolating reactionaries from the public in the long run.

Polarization . . . makes the battle lines clear. And in a climate
where silence and indifference had become fatal, this was a deci-
sive advance.[1]

The actions of the Ultra Resistance were definitely polarizing, but, at
the same time, they were of critical importance to keeping up the morale
of, and bringing more people into, the broader resistance movement to
the Vietnam War.

I've experienced this dynamic in recent years through the actions
of the group Beyond Extreme Energy (BXE).

BXE was formed to draw attention to and try to affect the decisions of the Federal Energy Regulatory Commission (FERC). Among
FERC's responsibilities is deciding if and how the natural gas industry
can expand pipelines, import or export terminals, storage terminals,
compressor stations, and other gas infrastructure. For thirty years, it has
been a rubber-stamp agency for the gas industry, approving just about
every one of their proposals for gas infrastructure expansion.

With the rise over the last decade of the toxic and unhealthy practice of hydraulic fracturing, or fracking, for shale gas, as well as the

emergence of low-priced, clean and renewable energy alternatives to all fossil fuels, a growing movement has arisen to fight fracking and the infrastructure needed to transport fracked shale gas. In July 2014, that led to the first ever mass demonstration of more than one thousand people at FERC headquarters in Washington, DC. On the next morning, twenty-five people were arrested for blockading the entrances to the FERC building.

Four months later, in early November, a dynamic, weeklong blockade of FERC took place. Every morning at 7:00 a.m., scores of people began blockading all the entrances. Over the course of the week seventy-five people were arrested, one person had her arm broken, and Federal Protective Services police used pepper spray, but by the last day we had figured out a way to keep the employees out of the building for several hours. We conducted a teach-in on the sidewalk for the hundreds of FERC employees unable to get inside.

Since then, BXE has continued to undertake similar actions and to work closely with the local groups all over the country fighting the expansion of fracking and other fossil fuel infrastructure. One result is that, thanks to mass media and social media press coverage, FERC is now widely known as a problematic rubber-stamp agency by many people. While at the outset BXE's tactics were somewhat controversial within the climate movement, that has become much less the case as the movement to stop fracking has grown into a majoritarian movement, according to the latest polls.

Fasting and Hunger Strikes

One of BXE's more effective actions was an eighteen-day, water-only hunger strike conducted on the sidewalk in front of the FERC building in September 2015, just before the arrival of Pope Francis in DC.

Twelve of us took part in this action.

This fast actually felt harder than any of much longer ones I had done in 1971, 1972, and 1992. Part of the reason, I'm sure, is because I was much older. Another reason was that we camped out on the sidewalk in front of the FERC building from 7:00 a.m. to 6:00 p.m. every day that FERC was open during the strike, and many of those days were very hot and humid. We had to walk a mile or more to get from the church where we were staying to the FERC building. All in all, it was very hard for me and others from the second day on.

But like the other fasts, it was effective. We talked to thousands of people, FERC employees and people living and working in the area or just passing by. We got decent press coverage. And it definitely strengthened local activists around the country fighting their battles. Their morale was raised, knowing that we were stepping it up and refusing to let up on our FERC-focused campaign.

Fasting and hunger strikes are similar to nonviolent direct action where people are arrested. They are a way to increase the likelihood of the general public noticing an issue. They also raise the question of why people would be risking time in jail or damage to their body for an issue. These tactics underline the urgency.

Fasting and actions with the risk of arrest are the nonviolent equivalents of armed attacks where people can get injured or killed. The nonviolent actions, however, cannot be used so easily by our enemies or antagonistic media outlets to isolate or undercut support. Such actions also ensure that the only people who suffer or are hurt, or even risk suffering and being hurt, are on the justice-seeking side. And our voluntary willingness to take those risks has a positive political impact.

Although fasting is part of the traditions of Indigenous peoples and some religions in the Americas, most people in the United States have never been on a fast of any duration. Probably the most extensive use of fasting as a method to educate and raise consciousness has been in the prison system, with prisoners hunger striking for basic human rights. Since the early 1990s, however, there have been a growing number of people who have fasted around a variety of different causes, including the movement that opposes celebrating "Columbus Day."

Fasting is a simple yet profound way of combining the spiritual and the political. Mahatma Gandhi, the most famous nonviolent revolutionary of the twentieth century, called it "the sincerest form of prayer."

Cesar Chavez, leader of the farmworkers' movement, explained why he fasted in these words:

> This fast is first and foremost personal. It is something that I feel compelled to do. It is directed at myself. It is a fast for the purification of my own body, mind and soul. The fast is also the heartfelt prayer for purification and strengthening for all of us, for myself, and for all those who work beside me in the farmworkers' movement. It is a fervent prayer that together we will confront and

resist, with all our strength, the scourge of poisons that threatens our people, our land and our food.[2]

Fasting is a way of connecting, of remembering, of feeling the pain of those who "fast" involuntarily. Pax Christi leader Marie Dennis, who fasted for forty-two days in 1992, spoke in a statement during that fast of those who

> cannot choose to stop when it gets overwhelming; rather, theirs is the daily, grinding hunger of simply being too poor to find enough food; it is a hunger that is ever-present and gnawing, that consumes their children slowly or quickly; it is a hunger for a more than minimal existence—for education and health care and housing.

Fasting brings you face to face with yourself and what is really important to you, what you believe and how deeply you believe it. You cannot help but think about the *why* of your not eating, *what* it is that is most important to you, and *how* you can be more consistent so that your beliefs and your actions are one on a daily basis. It is a way to stay centered and focused and clearer, which in turn makes the cause about which one is fasting more understandable and of greater significance to others.

Using the Courts

My experiences during the Rochester and Harrisburg trials, two very different experiences, taught me about the positive potential and the limitations of using the courtroom to advance a cause.

Down through history courtrooms have provided a forum for the airing and arguing of important issues: Socrates in 399 BCE, Thomas More in 1535, John Peter Zenger in 1735, John Brown in 1859, John Scopes in 1925, Fidel Castro in 1956, the Catonsville 9 in 1968, and the Chicago 8/7 in 1969. It is a dramatic thing when a person's life or freedom is on the line, with the final result up in the air, dependent upon the decision of either a judge or a jury. Like a long hunger strike or a well-organized nonviolent direct action, a trial can clearly focus the attention of the public on the cause or principles at stake.

Key to that happening is the ability of defendants to call witnesses to testify about the "why" of the action they are on trial for, what is often called a "necessity defense." Defendants and their witnesses need to be able to argue credibly that their intent was not criminal, just the opposite, that their breaking of the law was justified, was a necessity, because a much greater crime was being committed. If they are able to do so, then there are grounds for hope that a jury, or some on it, will refuse to convict.

In our Rochester trial in 1970, we were able to call witnesses and argue that our intent was not criminal, in part because of the decision of seven of the eight of us to defend ourselves. That tactic usually opens up the courtroom, because the judge is more likely to give some leeway to someone not trained as a lawyer when it comes to how the case is presented.

Our efforts to open up the courtroom were also helped significantly by the way that we and our supporters followed up our arrest with widespread community organizing in Rochester. We spoke publicly about why we had taken action and were interviewed by the media. Local groups came out with statements of support. We put out and widely distributed literature that explained our case. We mobilized people to attend the trial and to take part in daily rallies in the evenings. By the time the trial began, the local newspapers, which had editorialized against us in no uncertain terms after our arrest, had softened their positions. They weren't supporters, but they did a good job of presenting an objective, at times semi-sympathetic, account of what took place during the two-week trial.

In the case of the Harrisburg 8/7 trial, the mobilizing outside the courthouse was the primary way in which the peace movement attempted to use the trial to draw attention to the ongoing brutal war in Indochina, with success.

The trial process, however, did little toward that end, in part because of the judge handling the case. The common assessment of both the defendants and the lawyers was that it was going to be difficult to do what we had done in Rochester or anything close to it in his courtroom. Without question, when determining what kind of defense to offer and assessing the likelihood of being able to present a "necessity" defense, who the judge is going to be needs to be taken into account.

The other difference at Harrisburg was the dominance of lawyers in determining the day-to-day defense tactics. I have worked with many lawyers in my more than fifty years of social activism and organizing. What I have experienced in too many of my interactions with them, though not all, is essentially an attitude of "I'm the expert on the law, let me handle all the courtroom stuff." In some cases, it's even worse—it's fundamentally elitist: "You don't know how things work, I do, and I'll run your defense." I know where this comes from; it's how they are trained in law school.

There is no question but that lawyers are a very important part of the work of social movements challenging injustice, oppression, and wrong. They can play and often have played absolutely essential roles. They have kept people from being railroaded by unjust prosecutors or judges. They have won victories that have helped grassroots people dealing with bureaucratic, even hostile, agencies or branches of government.

But the best lawyers will not get uptight and nervous when defendants decide after careful consideration that they want to defend themselves in court. They will, instead, offer to help train them so they are as prepared as possible when the fateful day arrives.

Dealing with Government Repression

My first years of progressive activism and organizing took place during the presidency of Richard Nixon, who, without a doubt, led one of the most, if not the most, repressive presidential administrations we have experienced in the U.S. in the modern era. It was under Nixon that the Republican Party, with its "southern strategy," began to move toward becoming the kind of regressive entity that allowed pathological liar, racist, and sexual predator Donald Trump to be elected president in November 2016.

During Nixon's first term, from 1969 to 1973, he oversaw the use of government agencies to attempt to destroy groups like the Black Panther Party and the Young Lords, including murderous attacks by cops. Newly enacted conspiracy laws were used to indict leaders of the peace movement and other movements. An entirely illegal and clandestine apparatus was created to sabotage the campaigns of his political opponents in the Democratic Party, leading to the midnight break-in at the Watergate Hotel that eventually led to the exposure of this apparatus and Nixon's forced resignation from office in 1974.

I personally experienced this repressive apparatus primarily as a defendant in the Harrisburg 8/7 case.

I learned several things during those Nixon years about how to deal with government repression. Unfortunately, given the reality of a Trump/Pence administration, those are very relevant lessons today.

One critical lesson is that there is a disparity in the government treatment of people of color—Black, Latino, First Nation, and

Asian—compared with the treatment of people of European descent—white people. The historical realities of military aggression, broken treaties, slavery, Jim Crow segregation, assumed white dominance, and institutionalized racism continue to have their negative, discriminatory impacts.

Among these impacts is a willingness by some police to carelessly shoot and brutalize young black men and other men of color for no justifiable reason, which has given rise to the deeply important Movement for Black Lives.

Another impact is the unequal treatment meted out within the legal system, from police to prosecutors to prison personnel, when it comes to people of color compared to white people. For example, people of color arrested as part of a nonviolent civil disobedience action may be subject to heavier charges or additional hardship while in police custody or behind bars compared to whites.

Those of us of European descent must be conscious of these realities and act accordingly, ready to speak up and challenge unequal, discriminatory, or explicitly white supremacist words and actions wherever they happen. This is also our responsibility when it comes to discriminatory words and actions toward immigrants, LGBTQ people, women, or any other group.

Another lesson about dealing with government repression is that it can't be allowed to paralyze or divide organizations or movements. This is one of the objectives of an unjust government trying to repress those who challenge its policies and practices. It is a known fact that government infiltrators are trained to look for differences within a group or movement and make efforts to deepen and harden them. That is one of the reasons why we need to be about the development of a movement culture that is respectful and healthy. Such a cultural environment makes it much harder to create divisions.

Much the same is true with regards to agent provocateurs, people who try to get others to engage in violent speech or action targeting police or other government representatives.

Anger against injustice and oppression is not just legitimate; it is necessary to successfully build a movement for real change. But anger needs to be used in a disciplined way. Those who are quick to call cops "pigs" or throw bricks or otherwise display anger negatively are either government agents attempting to discredit the movement or people who need an intervention. They need to be taken aside and spoken with in a direct, to the point, and loving way about the counterproductiveness of what they are doing. Some will keep doing it, but others will change, maybe not right away but over time.

We need to accept that government surveillance, including informants like Boyd Douglas attempting to worm their way in as far and as deep as they can go, is a given if we are serious about challenging the oppressive system and fundamentally changing it, if we are about revolutionary change. We should be on the alert for such people. When legitimate suspicions are aroused, we should carry out the required research and, if it seems necessary, directly confront the person or persons in question.

I did some confronting a couple of years ago during one of the BXE weeks of action at the FERC. On the second or third day, a new person who, as far as I knew then, none of us organizing the action knew in any way showed up at one of our semi-public meetings. There was something about him, an individualistic, very assertive way of speaking, that raised my antenna. Over lunch I took him aside and asked him in as nice but as direct a way as I could how he had heard about our action and if he knew of or had worked with any of the groups that were part of it. It turned out that he had worked with a couple of us, and when I spoke to them afterward they confirmed that he was okay, even though they understood, given the way he spoke, why I might have been suspicious.

This person took some offense to my questioning him, and he left the meeting, but, to his credit, he did return later that week. I apologized to him when I saw him, and he said it was okay, he understood why I had done it.

There are other affirmative steps we can take to prevent government disruption of our actions. For example, if we are organizing a nonviolent direct action that includes the element of surprise, we need to take whatever steps are necessary, like using encrypted email and other secure forms of communication and consciously limiting what is said or written beforehand to what is absolutely necessary.

Ultimately, what I have learned is that government repression can have a disruptive impact on our work, but we can turn a negative into a positive. The extent to which we can creatively, intelligently, and fearlessly demonstrate the truth of what we are about when responding to what they are doing to us is the extent to which will we strengthen and build our movement.

Unlearning White Supremacy

Without any doubt, it was my eleven months in prison that got me firmly onto the road to consciously attempting on a daily basis to be anti-racist and a strong ally of people of color, because of the many black and brown people I met, befriended, and interacted with every day. I already believed intellectually that all people should be treated equally and fairly. In prison I came to see that all people *are*, in essence, the same, with similar feelings, ideas, hopes, and dreams.

Prison was also where I very clearly saw the way in which class and race are interconnected. I saw the class system of the prison: at the top, the warden, then the other administrators, followed by the prison guards (with their own hierarchy), the prisoner "trusties," and the white-collar prisoners, all of whom are very predominantly white. Trusties and white-collar prisoners tend to be the ones who get extra privileges, including work release and single-cell dorm rooms. Finally, there's the general prison population, a majority of which are black and brown. Seeing this in prison left me much better equipped to understand the class/race structure in society at large. It's not as stark and clear-cut, but it's definitely there.

Ever since, I've tried to put these understandings into practice, taking action and speaking out in support of genuine equality, true justice, and human rights for all people. This has meant participation in more demonstrations than I can remember against police killings or beatings of people of color. In 1999, after Amadou Diallo was shot forty-one times, I was arrested in front of the New York City police headquarters, joining with others to call for a swift indictment of the police officers responsible. From 1993 to 2001, it meant fasting for the first twelve days of every October for freedom for Leonard Peltier and for Columbus Day to be renamed Indigenous Peoples Day. It has meant speaking up at meetings when something has been said that is overtly or subtly racist. Sometimes I don't do so, truth be told. It's not always easy, and my fear sometimes wins out over my best intentions.

It has meant joining organizations that are predominantly African American and following, and sometimes taking part in, those groups' leadership. And it has meant continuing to wrestle with whether I am doing enough, whether I should be doing something more or something else, whether I really am being a good anti-racist ally.

There's a particular responsibility that those of us who are white have in this work—the responsibility to interact with and organize among white people, particularly low-income and working-class white people, those who should be more open than they sometimes are to the message that to improve their living conditions, they need to join with working people of all races and cultures. We need to help them realize that white supremacist ideology in particular, as well as other divisive and oppressive ideologies and practices, are not in their best interest.

To sharpen the point: white progressives need to be willing to intelligently risk being uncomfortable, unpopular, or even victims of psychological or physical abuse for speaking up among a predominantly white group of regular folks. I don't mean so much a predominantly white group of progressives, though there are often subtler, less overt issues there too. I am talking about average working-class or middle-class white people.

Usually, in that kind of setting, sooner or later, there's going to be white supremacist ideas expressed. That's not necessarily because the group as a whole or the person(s) expressing them are hard-core KKK members. It's because, as the mass response to the racist (and everything else) Trump campaign and presidency has shown us, white supremacy is very much alive and well among a huge portion of the U.S. white population.

It is critical that more and more people of European ancestry in the U.S. appreciate that a hopeful future for them and their families lies in joining together with, not being hostile to, Blacks, Latinos, Indigenous people, and Asian/Pacific Island people. It was put this way in a 2016 statement by the group Showing Up for Racial Justice:

> While people of color bear the brunt of racism, large numbers of white people have also been failed by the system—facing job loss, inadequate housing and cutbacks in core services. Instead of addressing real fears and insecurity, racist elites actively target white working class white people into blaming people of color for the problems their families and vulnerable communities face.[3]

How Whites Organize Whites

This is also critical.

Guilt-tripping isn't the way to do it. People who act primarily because they are feeling or have been made to feel guilty about their whiteness are people who are going to have a hard time interacting with whites who are suffering economic hardship or the white masses in general. Instead, while acknowledging the legitimacy of guilt felt over the historically brutal violence, oppression, and discrimination by huge numbers of white people, generally, against Indigenous, African, Mexican, other Latinx, and Asian peoples, we, as whites, must move past guilt. We need to be clear that white supremacy also hurts white people, engenders guilt and fear, for example, and makes united action on common issues like housing, healthcare, or the right to organize more difficult.

It's also critical that whites organizing whites take up the economic, health care, education, or other issues impacting predominantly white communities, to show that they are concerned about all forms of inequality and want a just society for everyone. This is key. A good organizer knows that you need to start with people where they are, make connections on the basis of issues, experiences, or other things held in common. As those connections are made, as people get to know and respect the organizer, they are more willing to listen and think about constructive criticism from her/him or ideas other than those they are ordinarily exposed to.

Finally, white organizers who are serious about anti-racism need to have ongoing connections to people of color, by participating in a multicultural organization of some kind, at a minimum. It is better if that happens at the same time that healthy friendships are developed with individual people of color. We, as whites, need ways to be continually reminded about how white supremacy works. We need friends of color whom we support and who will support us, who criticize us for things we say or do that reflect our upbringing in a white supremacist culture and help us to develop into better and more conscious people, better organizers, better and stronger human beings.

Unlearning Sexism

My first contact with the second wave women's movement began at college in Iowa, in 1968. It was a pretty shocking introduction. My girlfriend at the time, whom I really liked, started attending a women's consciousness-raising group, and my response when she told me about it at dinner one evening was ridicule. She walked out on me and, despite my efforts, we didn't talk again for months. I felt both terrible and guilty, and reading and discussions with others led me to take the issue of sexism seriously.

By the time I joined the Catholic Left in late 1969, I was much better educated on the issue and certainly less sexist. But it hardly registered with me that almost all of the people leading this wing of the peace movement were priests. The person who ran the first retreat I went to in Baltimore was a Catholic priest, Neil McLaughlin. The person who ran the "casing" operation in Philadelphia as we prepared to enter Selective Service offices in Philadelphia in February 1970 was John Grady. Phil and Dan Berrigan, both priests, whom I saw little of until I was sent to Danbury prison, were the intellectual and emotional leaders of the movement and, in Phil's case, behind-the-scenes, overall practical leader.

There were certainly strong and vocal women in our midst, nuns, former nuns, and others. And the process of organizing for illegal night-time raids on draft boards, FBI offices, and war corporate offices and production sites did tend to break down gender roles as we all pitched in to do what needed to be done. So as far as I was concerned, there wasn't a big problem.

I remember reading and thinking about this issue in prison. One of the books I read in the "great books" course organized by Dan and Phil at Danbury was *Sisterhood Is Powerful*.[4] But with nothing but men everywhere I looked inside the walls at Ashland, Danbury, and Springfield, there were limits to what I could do about the issue, with the exception of speaking up when somebody made a sexist or misogynist remark. I don't remember doing so very often, but I also don't remember a lot of those types of remarks, which seems strange, in retrospect, and is probably a sign that at the time I still had a lot to learn.

In the two years of my active participation in and close to the Catholic Left after I got out of prison, I saw that women, especially the younger women, were playing a more assertive role. I know from my research for this book that the women I worked with and respected had criticisms of the ways in which some of the Catholic Left men, including leading men, interacted with women—essentially, the way in which the women were not listened to or respected in the same way that other men were.

Sexism/patriarchy is different than racism/white supremacy in one very major respect: women and men interact daily in U.S. society, whereas historic and continuing segregation mean that many whites, particularly in rural areas, have little real interaction or personal connection with people of color. I think that in general this has made it possible for the issues of women to be taken more seriously by society as a whole than the issues of people of color.

Over my years as an organizer for social change I have come to believe that, as in the words of the song "Bread and Roses," "the rising of the women means the rising of us all." In part, that's because women are half of the world, and virtually all are oppressed by sexism and patriarchal structures and ideas that are intertwined with the structures and ideas of greed, power-seeking, and white domination that continue to have such a huge impact within many cultures.

This is not just an issue of numbers, though that is part of it. And it's not just an issue of justice and equality, though that's definitely part of it. It's also that the culture of women is different than the culture of men, for the better, generally.

Male dominated, patriarchal culture is actually a relatively new social construct for Homo sapiens as a species. The book by Riane Eisler, *The Chalice and the Blade*,[5] does a superb job analyzing how, up until five or six thousand years ago, human beings in most of the world lived in a relatively egalitarian and cooperative way, with both women and men playing leadership roles on a day-to-day basis. Given that Homo sapiens emerged at least two hundred thousand years ago, this puts the several millennia of male dominance in correct perspective. It also provides hope that the process of female empowerment and the decline of patriarchy will continue and play an absolutely central role in the process of positive social change.

For millennia, under patriarchy, men have been the hunters, the warriors, the breadwinners, the leaders. With the rise of capitalism emerged the dominance of an ethic of competition for the purposes of individual gain and of individualism generally. That ethic has led us to the precipice of a possible unraveling of human societies and the web of life on earth due to global heating and other environmental destruction.

Women's culture, the ways they talk and relate and think and feel, in general, is not like this. It is much more cooperative and group-centered rather than individualistic and hierarchical. It is more attuned to the common good than just the individual good.

These are values and a way of viewing oneself and the world that are desperately needed today.

A Positive Movement Culture

I joined the Catholic Left primarily because I felt a personal need to take the strongest action I could to stop the Vietnam War. I also joined because of my religious upbringing, a positive one for me, and the leadership of priests and nuns within the Catholic Left.

Within this resistance community I found the emotional and spiritual support I needed to be able to play an active role over a period of years, including close to a year in prison. At Danbury, I had the great fortune of spending my prison time with Phil and Dan Berrigan, from whom I learned a great deal. They were not perfect people; Phil, in particular, as he publicly acknowledged in *Fighting the Lamb's War*, had some rough edges. But they both made conscious efforts to be not just stalwart activists against the war but loving human beings toward others, as did just about everyone else in this wing of the Vietnam peace movement.

I have tried to be such a person. I have tried to help social change organizations I have been a part of ever since the Vietnam War era be organizations whose internal culture functions like this. In general, I have found that just about all organized efforts to challenge injustice or work for peace or solve the crisis of climate disruption, any efforts to improve the world, claim to function this way or, at least, hope to. But I have also found that a desire to create a "beloved community" does not, by itself, ensure consistent success. Indeed, the experiences of the Catholic Left are a case in point.

There is a great deal of destructive cultural conditioning that we cannot avoid experiencing within a capitalist economic system built upon greed, power-seeking, individualism, racism, sexism, heterosexism, and other negative ideas and social practices. I have learned that unless these issues are explicitly identified and worked on, they will ultimately undermine, corrupt, or destroy organized efforts for positive social change.

Fortunately, there are societal counterbalances to all of this: positive family interactions (in many cases), healthy spiritual and religious traditions and practices (not all of them are), and organizations that transmit more cooperative and personally supportive values (unions, community groups, groups based on identity).

The emergence of the anti-racist civil rights movement of the 1950s and 1960s, particularly the leadership and growth of the youth-based and youth-led Student Nonviolent Coordinating Committee (SNCC), led, in the ensuing years, to literally thousands of progressive groups being created and widespread, progressive mass consciousness. These groups and this consciousness are about challenging the many different forms of oppression within both the world at large and, for many of them, within each of us as human beings. Without all of these alternatives to the dominant institutions, the world would be a very hopeless place indeed. Because of them, there is hope for a new world.

How can organizations or movements structure themselves so that they stay true to their best instincts and model the new world that must be brought into being? One example can be found in the group Beyond Extreme Energy (BXE), in what we call our "Organizational Principles and Practices," bylaws of a sort. The first section is very specific about how we can create a positive, non-oppressive, and liberating culture. These are the headings of this overall section and the sub-sections:

1. BXE is committed to the liberation of all people of the world, and therefore embraces anti-oppression action and opportunities for restorative justice.
   A. Power and privilege are omnipresent in our group dynamics and we must continually struggle with how we challenge them in our collaborative work.
   B. We strive to acknowledge privilege and domination when they appear and work to actively counter them as they manifest in our work in everything we do, in and outside of organizing spaces.
   C. The privileged need to keep other privileged people accountable and not rely on the oppressed to raise the issue.
   D. Listening happens first in our anti-oppression practices.[6]

Another example is the culture of the community of thousands of First Nation and other activists at Standing Rock, North Dakota, in 2016, which for months held off Energy Transfer Partners in their efforts to build an oil pipeline across the Missouri River just upriver from the Standing Rock Sioux reservation. Those who undertook nonviolent direct action to stop this pipeline called themselves "water protectors" not "protestors." They maintained an encampment for almost a year.

Despite heavy repression by police forces, including the use of mace, teargas, rubber and plastic bullets, sound grenades, high-pressure water hoses, and twenty-four-hour-a-day surveillance of their camp by drones, planes, and helicopters, in the main the water protectors maintained their nonviolent discipline. Key to that happening was the leadership given by elders who integrated prayer into the day-to-day functioning of the camp and into the actions themselves. I have seen videos of leaders speaking about the importance of humility to what they are all about.

Micah 6:8, my favorite Bible verse, says it all for me: "And what does God ask of you but to do justice, love kindness and walk humbly with your God."

If more and more of us take these sentiments seriously, pray on them, meditate about them, act on them, and if we take action commensurate with the urgency of the climate crisis and the state of our struggling human race, I believe that we can change the world. I really do.

Notes

Introduction

1   Jessica Corbett, "Thankful to Avoid Prison, Acquitted Valve Turners Lament Lost Chance to Defend Planet-Saving Necessity of Pipeline Shutdown," Common Dreams, October 10, 2018, accessed February 17, 2020, https://www.commondreams. org/news/2018/10/10/thankful-avoid-prison-acquitted-valve-turners-lament-lost-chance-defend-planet.

2   Bulletin Staff, "It's Now 2 Minutes to Midnight," *Bulletin of the Atomic Scientists*, January 25, 2018, accessed February 17, 2020, https://thebulletin.org/2018/01/it-is-now-2-minutes-to-midnight/. The updated Doomsday Clock for 2020, places us at 100 seconds to midnight: see John Mecklin, ed., "Closer Than Ever: It Is 100 Seconds to Midnight, " *Bulletin of the Atomic Scientists*, January 23, 2020, accessed March 11, 2020, https://thebulletin.org/doomsday-clock/current-time/#full-statement.

3   Martin Luther King Jr., "The Three Evils of Society," August 31, 1967, accessed February 17, 2020, https://buyblackpodcast.com/podcast/martin-luther-king-three-evils-society/.

The Draft Resistance Movement, 1965–1968

1   Daniel Berrigan, *The Trial of the Catonsville Nine* (New York: Fordham University Press, 2009), 91–92.

2   Betty Medsger, *The Burglary: The Discovery of J. Edgar Hoover's Secret FBI* (New York: Alfred A. Knopf, 2014), 15.

3   Michael Ferber and Staughton Lynd, *The Resistance* (Boston: Beacon Press, 1971), 31.

4   Phil Berrigan, with Fred A. Wilcox, *Fighting the Lamb's War: Skirmishes with the American Empire* (Monroe, ME: Common Courage Press, 1996), 85.

5   David Miller, *I Didn't Know God Made Honky Tonk Communists* (Berkeley, CA: Regent Press, 2002), 13.

6   Bruce Dancis, *Resister: A Story of Protest and Prison during the Vietnam War* (Ithaca: Cornell University Press, 2014), 75–76.

7   "Muhammad Ali's Inspirational Speech on Why He Wouldn't Fight in Vietnam," *New York Daily News*, June 4, 2016, accessed February 18, 2020, https://www.nydailynews. com/sports/more-sports/muhammad-ali-statement-wouldn-fight-vietnam-article-1.2661120.

8   Ferber and Lynd, *The Resistance*, 60.

9   David Harris, "I Picked Prison Over Fighting in Vietnam," *New York Times*, June 23, 2017, accessed February 18, 2020, https://www.nytimes.com/2017/06/23/opinion/vietnam-war-draft-protests.html.
10 Dancis, *Resister*, 130–33.
11 Berrigan, *Fighting the Lamb's War*, 87–88.
12 Ibid., 89.
13 Charles A. Maconis, *With Clumsy Grace: The American Catholic Left 1961–1975* (New York: Seabury Press, 1979), 21–22.

My Personal Transformation

1   Margaret Hofmann, *Vietnam Viewpoints: A Handbook for Concerned Citizens* (Austin, TX: self-published, 1968).
2   Malcolm X, with Alex Haley, *The Autobiography of Malcolm X* (New York: Grove Press, 1965).

From Catonsville Onward

1   Quoted in Daniel Berrigan, *The Trial of the Catonsville Nine* (New York: Fordham University Press, 2004), 56.
2   Charles A. Meconis, *With Clumsy Grace: The American Catholic Left 1961–1975* (New York: Seabury Press, 1979), 24.
3   Philip Berrigan, with Fred A. Wilcox, *Fighting the Lamb's War* (Monroe, ME: Common Courage Press, 1996) 93–94.
4   Daniel Berrigan, *Essential Writings* (Maryknoll, NY: Orbis Books, 2009), 116.
5   Shawn Francis Peters, *The Catonsville Nine: A Story of Faith and Resistance in the Vietnam Era* (New York: Oxford University Press, 2012), 176.
6   Berrigan, *Fighting the Lamb's War*, 100.
7   Ibid, 101.
8   Daniel Berrigan, "Our Apologies, Good Friends," in *Essential Writings* (Maryknoll, NY: Orbis Books, 2009), 106–7.
9   Michael Ferber and Staughton Lynd, *The Resistance* (Boston: Beacon Press, 1971), 201–3.
10 Meconis, *With Clumsy Grace*.
11 Peters, *The Catonsville Nine*, 251.

Taking on the FBI Too

1   Ronald L. Goldfarb, "Politics at the Justice Department," in John C. Raines, *Conspiracy: The Implications of the Harrisburg Trial for the Democratic Tradition* (New York: Harper & Row, 1974) 113.
2   Ibid.
3   Ibid., 111.
4   Jerry Elmer, *Felon for Peace: The Memoir of a Vietnam-Era Draft Resister* (Nashville: Vanderbilt University Press, 2005), 114.
5   Excerpt from a mimeographed transcript of the speech among Ted Glick's personal papers.
6   Betty Medsger, *The Burglary: The Discovery of J. Edgar Hoover's Secret FBI* (New York: Alfred A. Knopf, 2014), 28.
7   Charles A. Meconis, *With Clumsy Grace: The American Catholic Left 1961–1975* (New York: Seabury Press, 1979).
8   "8 Held in Raid on 3 Federal Buildings," *Democrat and Chronicle*, September 7, 1970.
9   *Journal* supplement, early 1971.
10 Ibid.

Changing Hearts and Minds in the Courtroom

1   The Jesuit priest Father Joe Daoust was a personal friend of the defendant Frank Callahan.

Prison

1   Bruce Dancis, *Resister: A Story of Protest and Prison during the Vietnam War* (Ithaca: Cornell University Press, 2014), 277.
2   Robin Morgan, ed., *Sisterhood Is Powerful: An Anthology of Writings from the Women's Liberation Movement* (New York: Random House, 1970).
3   Sylvan Fox, "4 South Vietnamese Describe Torture in Prison 'Tiger Cage,'" *New York Times*, March 3, 1973, accessed March 1, 2020, nytimes.com/1973/03/03/archives/4-south-vietnamese-describe-torture-in-prison-tiger-cage-center-of.html.

The Harrisburg 8 (Minus 1)

1   Phil Berrigan, with Fred A. Wilcox, *Fighting the Lamb's War: Skirmishes with the American Empire* (Monroe, ME: Common Courage Press, 1996), 130–31.
2   Jack Nelson and Ronald J. Ostrow, *The FBI and the Berrigans: The Making of a Conspiracy* (New York: Coward, McCann & Geoghegan, 1972), 286.

A "Fast unto Death"

1   This is a quote from Albert Camus, *The Plague* (New York: Modern Library, 1991 [1947]).
2   The Chicago 8 (Abbie Hoffman, Rennie Davis, Dave Dellinger, Jerry Rubin, Tom Hayden, John Froines, Lee Weiner, and Bobby Seale) were eight people prosecuted by the government following police riots against peaceful demonstrators at the 1968 Democratic Convention. Black Panther Bobby Seale would eventually have his case severed, and the remaining seven would be known as the Chicago 7.

Anti-War Burglar Culture

1   Betty Medsger, *The Burglary: The Discovery of J. Edgar Hoover's Secret FBI* (New York: Alfred A. Knopf, 2014), 478.
2   Thomas and Marjorie Melville, "The Catholic Resistance," *New York Times*, April 26, 1971, accessed March 8, 2020, https://www.nytimes.com/1971/04/26/archives/the-catholic-resistance-i.html; also see Pope John XXIII, Mater et Magistra, May 15, 1962, accessed March 3, 2020, http://www.vatican.va/content/john-xxiii/en/encyclicals/documents/hf_j-xxiii_enc_15051961_mater.html; Pope John XXIII, Pacem in Terris, April 11, 1963, accessed March 3, 2020, http://www.vatican.va/content/john-xxiii/en/encyclicals/documents/hf_j-xxiii_enc_11041963_pacem.html.
3   Michael Ferber and Staughton Lynd, *The Resistance* (Boston: Beacon Press, 1971), 158.
4   Ibid., 162.
5   Jerry Elmer, *Felon for Peace: The Memoir of a Vietnam-Era Draft Resister* (Nashville: Vanderbilt University Press, 2005), 75.
6   Ibid.
7   Charles A. Meconis, *With Clumsy Grace: The American Catholic Left 1961–1975* (New York: Seabury Press, 1979), 58.
8   Barbara Shapiro, unpublished manuscript.

After Harrisburg

1   Father Paul Mayer, *Wrestling with Angels*, unpublished manuscript.

2   Charles A. Meconis, *With Clumsy Grace: The American Catholic Left 1961–1975* (New York: Seabury Press, 1979), 120.
3   Ibid., 121.
4   Ibid., 124.
5   Murray Polner and Jim O'Grady, *Disarmed and Dangerous: The Radical Lives and Times of Daniel and Philip Berrigan* (New York: Basic Books, 1997), 326.
6   Philip Berrigan, with Fred A. Wilcox, *Fighting the Lamb's War: Skirmishes with the American Empire* (Monroe, ME: Common Courage Press, 1996), 167.
7   Meconis, *With Clumsy Grace*, 134.

Resigning from the Catholic Left

1   Excerpt from Chief Yellow Lark, "Let Me Walk in Beauty," in Eknath Easwaran, ed., *God Makes the Rivers to Flow, Sacred Literature of the World* (Tomales, CA: Nilgiri Press, 2003), 188.
2   Philip Berrigan, with Fred A. Wilcox, *Fighting the Lamb's War: Skirmishes with the American Empire* (Monroe, ME: Common Courage Press, 1996), 159.
3   Langston Hughes, "Let America Be America Again" (1935), Poetry Foundation, accessed March 8, 2020, https://www.poetryfoundation.org/poems/147907/let-america-be-america-again.

Lessons Learned

1   Mark Engler and Paul Engler, *This Is an Uprising: How Nonviolent Revolt Is Shaping the Twenty-First Century* (New York: Nation Books, 2016), 199–200.
2   Quoted in "The Story of Cesar Chavez," United Farm Workers, accessed March 5, 2020, https://ufw.org/research/history/story-cesar-chavez.
3   "Poor and Working Class Commitment: Statement from SURJ National Leadership Team," Showing Up for Racial Justice, April 26, 2016, accessed March 4, 2020, https://www.showingupforracialjustice.org/poor-and-working-class-commitment.html.
4   Robin Morgan, ed., *Sisterhood Is Powerful: An Anthology of Writings from the Women's Liberation Movement* (New York: Random House, 1970).
5   Riane Eisler, *The Chalice and the Blade: Our History, Our Future* (San Francisco: Harper& Row, 1988).
6   Beyond Extreme Energy (BXE), accessed March 4, 2020, https://beyondextremeenergy.org/.

Bibliography

Books

Berrigan, Daniel. *Essential Writings*. Maryknoll, NY: Orbis Books, 2009.

Berrigan, Daniel. *The Trial of the Catonsville Nine*. New York: Fordham University Press, 2004.

Berrigan, Philip, with Fred A. Wilcox. *Fighting the Lamb's War: Skirmishes with the American Empire*. Monroe, ME: Common Courage Press, 1996.

Dancis, Bruce. *Resister: A Story of Protest and Prison during the Vietnam War*. Ithaca: Cornell University Press, 2014.

Dougherty, Barbara Shapiro. Unpublished manuscript.

Eisler, Riane. *The Chalice and the Blade: Our History, Our Future*. San Francisco: Harper & Row, 1988.

Eknath, Easwaran, ed. *God Makes the Rivers to Flow: Sacred Literature of the World*. Tomales, CA: Nilgiri Press, 2003.

Elmer, Jerry. *Felon for Peace: The Memoir of a Vietnam-Era Draft Resister*. Nashville: Vanderbilt University Press, 2005.

Engler, Mark and Paul. *This Is an Uprising: How Nonviolent Revolt Is Shaping the Twenty-First Century*. New York: Nation Books, 2016.

Ferber, Michael, and Staughton Lynd. *The Resistance*. Boston: Beacon Press, 1971.

Freire, Paulo. *Pedagogy of the Oppressed*. New York: Seabury Press, 1970 [1968].

Hoffman, Margaret. *Vietnam Viewpoints: A Handbook for Concerned Citizens*. Self-published, 1968.

Malcolm X, with Alex Haley. *The Autobiography of Malcolm X*. New York: Grove Press, 1965.

Meconis, Charles A. *With Clumsy Grace: The American Catholic Left 1961–1975*. New York: Seabury Press, 1979.

Medsger, Betty. *The Burglary: The Discovery of J. Edgar Hoover's Secret FBI*. New York: Alfred A. Knopf, 2014.

Nelson, Jack, and Ronald J. Ostrow. *The FBI and the Berrigans: The Making of a Conspiracy*. New York: Coward, McCann & Geoghegan, 1972.

O'Rourke, William. *The Harrisburg 7 and the New Catholic Left*. Notre Dame, IN: University of Notre Dame Press, 2012.

Peters, Shawn Francis. *The Catonsville Nine: A Story of Faith and Resistance in the Vietnam Era*. New York: Oxford University Press, 2012.

Polner, Murray, and Jim O'Grady. *Disarmed and Dangerous: The Radical Lives and Times of Daniel and Philip Berrigan.* New York: Basic Books, 1997.

Raines, John C., ed. *Conspiracy: The Implications of the Harrisburg Trial for the Democratic Tradition.* New York: Harper & Row, 1974.

Films

Hamilton, Johanna, dir. *1971.* New York: First Run Features, 2014.

Tropea, Joe, and Skizz Cyzyk. *Hit and Stay.* Baltimore: Haricot Vert Films, 2013.

About the Authors

Ted Glick has been a progressive activist, organizer, and writer since 1968. He was imprisoned for eleven months for his draft resistance activities during the Vietnam War. He has been active in the independent progressive politics movement since 1975 and since 2003 has been a national leader in the climate justice movement. Since 2000, Ted has been writing a twice-monthly "Future Hope" column of political and social commentary, available at tedglick.com.

Frida Berrigan is a contributor to TomDispatch.Com and writes the Little Insurrections blog for WagingNonviolence.Org. She helped to found the group Witness Against Torture and long served on the National Committee of the War Resisters League. She grew up at Jonah House, the Christian resistance community founded by Phil Berrigan and Elizabeth McAlister in Baltimore. She lives in New London, Connecticut, with her husband and three children, where she works in community gardens and a community land trust.

ABOUT PM PRESS

PM Press is an independent, radical publisher of books and media to educate, entertain, and inspire. Founded in 2007 by a small group of people with decades of publishing, media, and organizing experience, PM Press amplifies the voices of radical authors, artists, and activists. Our aim is to deliver bold political ideas and vital stories to all walks of life and arm the dreamers to demand the impossible. We have sold millions of copies of our books, most often one at a time, face to face. We're old enough to know what we're doing and young enough to know what's at stake. Join us to create a better world.

PM Press
PO Box 23912
Oakland, CA 94623
www.pmpress.org

PM Press in Europe
europe@pmpress.org
www.pmpress.org.uk

FRIENDS OF PM PRESS

These are indisputably momentous times—the financial system is melting down globally and the Empire is stumbling. Now more than ever there is a vital need for radical ideas.

In the years since its founding—and on a mere shoestring—PM Press has risen to the formidable challenge of publishing and distributing knowledge and entertainment for the struggles ahead. With over 450 releases to date, we have published an impressive and stimulating array of literature, art, music, politics, and culture. Using every available medium, we've succeeded in connecting those hungry for ideas and information to those putting them into practice.

Friends of PM allows you to directly help impact, amplify, and revitalize the discourse and actions of radical writers, filmmakers, and artists. It provides us with a stable foundation from which we can build upon our early successes and provides a much-needed subsidy for the materials that can't necessarily pay their own way. You can help make that happen—and receive every new title automatically delivered to your door once a month—by joining as a Friend of PM Press. And, we'll throw in a free T-shirt when you sign up.

Here are your options:

- **$30 a month** Get all books and pamphlets plus 50% discount on all webstore purchases

- **$40 a month** Get all PM Press releases (including CDs and DVDs) plus 50% discount on all webstore purchases

- **$100 a month** Superstar—Everything plus PM merchandise, free downloads, and 50% discount on all webstore purchases

For those who can't afford $30 or more a month, we have **Sustainer Rates** at $15, $10 and $5. Sustainers get a free PM Press T-shirt and a 50% discount on all purchases from our website.

Your Visa or Mastercard will be billed once a month, until you tell us to stop. Or until our efforts succeed in bringing the revolution around. Or the financial meltdown of Capital makes plastic redundant. Whichever comes first.

Towards Collective Liberation: Anti-Racist Organizing, Feminist Praxis, and Movement Building Strategy

Chris Crass
with an Introduction by Chris Dixon and
Foreword by Roxanne Dunbar-Ortiz

ISBN: 978-1-60486-654-4
$20.00   320 pages

Towards Collective Liberation: Anti-Racist Organizing, Feminist Praxis, and Movement Building Strategy is for activists engaging with dynamic questions of how to create and support effective movements for visionary systemic change. Chris Crass's collection of essays and interviews presents us with powerful lessons for transformative organizing through offering a firsthand look at the challenges and the opportunities of anti-racist work in white communities, feminist work with men, and bringing women of color feminism into the heart of social movements. Drawing on two decades of personal activist experience and case studies of anti-racist social justice organizations, Crass insightfully explores ways of transforming divisions of race, class, and gender into catalysts for powerful vision, strategy, and movement building in the United States today.

"In his writing and organizing, Chris Crass has been at the forefront of building the grassroots, multi-racial, feminist movements for justice we need. Towards Collective Liberation takes on questions of leadership, building democratic organizations, and movement strategy, on a very personal level that invites us all to experiment and practice the way we live our values while struggling for systemic change."
—Elizabeth 'Betita' Martinez, founder of the Institute for Multiracial Justice and author of *De Colores Means All of Us: Latina Views for a Multi-Colored Century*

"Chris Crass goes into the grassroots to produce a political vision that will catalyze political change. These are words from the heart, overflowing onto the streets."
—Vijay Prashad, author of *Darker Nations: A People's History of the Third World*

"A deeply important, engaged, and learned defense of anarchism, class politics, and anti-racism. Grounded in study, organizing, and struggle, Towards Collective Liberation is a significant contribution to the recent history of the U.S. left."
—David Roediger, author of *Wages of Whiteness*

Save the Humans?
Common Preservation in Action

Jeremy Brecher

ISBN: 978-1-62963-798-3
$20.00   272 pages

We the people of the world are creating the conditions for our own self-extermination, whether through the bang of a nuclear holocaust or the whimper of an expiring ecosphere. Today our individual self-preservation depends on common preservation—cooperation to provide for our mutual survival and well-being.

For half a century Jeremy Brecher has been studying and participating in social movements that have created new forms of common preservation. Through entertaining storytelling and personal narrative, *Save the Humans?* provides a unique and revealing interpretation of how social movements arise and how they change the world. Brecher traces a path that leads from the sitdown strikes on the pyramids of ancient Egypt through America's mass strikes and labor revolts to the struggle against economic globalization to today's battles against climate change.

Weaving together personal experience, scholarly research, and historical interpretation, Jeremy Brecher shows how we can construct a "human survival movement" that could "save the humans." He sums up the theme of this book: "I have seen common preservation—and it works." For those seeking an understanding of social movements and an alternative to denial and despair, there is simply no better place to look than *Save the Humans?*

"*This is a remarkable book: part personal story, part intellectual history told in the first person by a skilled writer and assiduous historian, part passionate but clearly and logically argued plea for pushing the potential of collective action to preserve the human race. Easy reading and full of useful and unforgettable stories. . . . A medicine against apathy and political despair much needed in the U.S. and the world today.*"
—Peter Marcuse, author of *Cities for People, Not for Profit: Critical Urban Theory*

"*Over the last decades, Jeremy Brecher has known how to detect the critical issues of a period, to sort the many realities of suffering and injustice, and to emerge with a clear, short, powerful description. He does it again in this important book-it is about people: how our system devalues people and what needs to be done.*"
—Saskia Sassen, author of *Territory, Authority, Rights*

"*One of America's most admired activist-scholars shines his light on the path forward, reminding us that social change is both possible and urgent.*"
—Mike Davis, author of *City of Quartz: Excavating the Future in Los Angeles*